YEARS OF
IMPATIENCE

To Kate Williams

hommage de l'auteur

Gérard Pelletier

9.V.87

YEARS OF
IMPATIENCE
1950~1960

GÉRARD PELLETIER
Translated by Alan Brown

ⓝ METHUEN
Toronto   New York   London   Sydney   Auckland

Years of Impatience 1950–1960
First published in French under the title *Les Années d'impatience, 1950–1960*
Copyright ©Les Editions internationales Alain Stanké Ltée, 1983

English translation copyright ©1984 by Methuen Publications

Canadian Cataloguing in Publication Data

Pelletier, Gérard, 1919–
    Years of Impatience 1950–1960

Translation of: Les années d'impatience.
Includes index.
ISBN 0-458-98270-9

1. Pelletier, Gérard, 1919– 2. Politicians—
Quebec (Province)—Biography. 3. Journalists—
Quebec (Province)—Biography. 4. Quebec (Province)
—History—1936–1960.* I. Title.

PN4913.P393A313 1984   971.4′04′0924
C84-099333-1

Design: Fortunato Aglialoro

Printed and bound in the United States of America
1 2 3 4 5   84   89 88 87 86 85

To Alec
who was in the midst of all
the events described in these
pages

and without whom the book
would still not even have
a title

AUTHOR'S NOTE

The errors contained in these pages are due to
lapses of memory on my part; the accuracy of
dates and other figures is attributable to the
expert verification of Professor Yvan Lamonde.
The author also claims for himself alone the
paternity of any errors of syntax and
punctuation. If by chance these should be few
in number it is thanks to Jacques Hébert, who
pressed friendship to the last comma.

CONTENTS

FOREWORD

What is it that impels a man to write his memoirs or, more modestly, his recollections?

For some, no doubt, it is nostalgia, the pleasure of remembering happy times, the "melancholy delight" of which the ancient moralists spoke. Others perhaps yield to the ambition of belonging to posterity. Suspecting, with some cause, that no one else will write their biography, they undertake it themselves. Still others have scores to settle. Pensioned off, they can no longer act. They attempt by writing to rectify their accounts, whose unfavourable balance leaves them no peace.

And there are others, like myself, neither nostalgic nor retired, fundamentally predisposed to let lie a past that is not yet cold, and not in the least inclined to look backward when the future with all its demands still calls to them insistently, who simply give in to irritation. It is Instant History, an invention of these last decades of our century, that exasperates them. How can they read without impatience the flights of fancy already being published about their recent past, touching events they lived through only yesterday and in which they still feel partially embroiled because their commitment at the time was so whole-hearted—events they find totally distorted in books now sold on every street-corner?

The principal virtue of Instant History (in the sense of "instant coffee") is no doubt that it entangles in its net a

thousand details which otherwise would have disappeared
without a trace by the time the real History came to be
written. But if the authors in question, professionals of the
preterite tense, those-who-recount-the-recollections-of-
others, invent or spread abroad false details or sanction
legends, then . . .

That is what impelled me to write these pages: the desire to
put on record my own testimony, partially inaccurate, no
doubt, like all the others, but also likely to throw a less
indirect light upon certain situations in which I was involved.

CHAPTER 1

The Rendezvous

*I am always punctual at appointments,
because I have noticed that early arrivals
talk of nothing but the failings of those
who keep them waiting.*
BOILEAU

There are three of us sitting at the table in a small private room of the restaurant *Chez Stien* in Mackay Street: Pierre Trudeau, Jean Marchand and I. The place is quiet. Spring has arrived—or is this the fall of 1961 with its Indian summer? In any case, my memory is sure that the sunlight is strong. And, even if we've been waiting more than an hour for René Lévesque, I still don't feel impatient.

My two companions do.

Marchand never could stand waiting for people unless there was good reason for it, and Lévesque never has good reasons for keeping people waiting: it comes naturally to him, like breathing. Trudeau, for his part, considers lateness a mark of contempt for those who are kept waiting. But he is resigned to it and has imperturbably ordered his lunch. We do the same, and here we are, all three of us, busy with dessert.

Lévesque still has not shown up.

"Do you know what he wants to talk about?" Trudeau asks.

I reply that René phoned me a few days ago and asked to see us here to discuss "certain problems of an economic nature facing the Quebec government," with no further details. My secretary at *La Presse* made the necessary phone calls. And here we are, waiting for René.

As long as he was busy eating, Marchand managed to contain his irritation. Now that he has finished his strawberry tart his indignation gets the better of him.

"Look, he's doing this on purpose. It's unbelievable. He sets the meeting up for twelve-thirty. It's now after two and there's not a sign of him. This is really intolerable."

Silence. Trudeau smiles at Jean's vexation. "Come on, you know him. All these years... If you didn't want to wait for him we should have arrived here at two. It's very simple."

"What do you mean?" replies Marchand, glad to be able to turn his wrath on someone present instead of a phantom. "That wouldn't have helped. Let me tell you what happened last week in Quebec City. We were submitting a paper to the Cabinet from the CSN. Because we know René we went to his office first for a chat. By some miracle he was there. When it was time to go in, he guided us to the Cabinet room down a maze of corridors. There we continued our chat with him while the ministers strayed in. But when everybody was seated, ready for the hearing, our Lévesque ups and leaves. 'Where is he off to?' asked Jean Lesage, astonished by this departure. And some comedian pipes up, 'You know René can't bear to be on time. He'll be back an hour from now, good and late as usual.'"

Marchand's throaty laugh punctuates all his stories. Trudeau and I laugh with him. Then there's a silence, during which the waitress brings our coffee.

"You didn't see Mr. Lévesque downstairs?" Trudeau asks.

"The one on television?" she says. "No, we were looking for him just now. Somebody phoned but he wasn't there."

"Well," grunts Marchand, "that does it. If he ever does

come he'll be an hour on the phone before he sees us here. I've a good mind to leave."

Trudeau is laughing. At Marchand's ill-humour? At the funny side of the situation? Perhaps at the waitress's reaction, because he says: "'The one on television.' Did you hear that, Marchand? That's how you get famous in this country. Lévesque's been in the government sixteen months, a full-fledged minister and star of his party, but for that girl he's still 'the one on television.'"

"The one on my..."

Marchand doesn't finish his phrase. Trudeau is still amused. He turns to me.

"Pelletier, you've known him for a long time. Is he really always late like this? Is it a malady or a mania? Funny thing..."

"There's a reason," I tell him. "Or at least I have an explanation. For what it's worth."

I talk about working on television, and the few programs I've done with Lévesque, the time limits he had to respect, his fury when he was obliged at the last moment to cut a few paragraphs he felt were indispensable, so as not to run over the twenty-eight minutes thirty seconds of broadcast time. He would swear like a trooper: "Son of a bloody son of a b——, they get two hours and a half Saturday nights for their damned hockey games, and we get twenty-eight minutes thirty seconds to explain the whole world." He swore, but he kept within his time.

"Yes," notes Trudeau, in a sidelight, "but he invited guest *experts* on his show who'd get stuck there listening until forty-five seconds from the end, while René wound up saying, 'Mr. So-and-so, I was hoping I could ask you what you think of the economic effects of the crisis in the Middle East, but...,'and the program would end without the guest's ever opening his mouth. That happened one night to Claude Ryan, and he's never forgotten it."

"I'll tell you this," Marchand grumbles, "he'd never do that twice to me."

"Oh," Trudeau teases, "you'd do just like the rest of them, like what you're doing today, cooling your heels in a restaurant with Pelletier and me when it's such a fine day outside. We should have gone for a walk in the woods, the three of us."

Trudeau always had a spare plan up his sleeve, whatever his occupation of the moment.

I forge ahead with my explanation. In fact René's radio and television training, with the need in both for strict punctuality, might have made him into a clock-watcher. I know others whom I suspect of making love on the hour, so conditioned are they by the precise second when they must say, "This is the Canadian Broadcasting Corporation."

But for René the opposite happened. When he became a free man after fifteen years of Radio-Canada's constraints, he wanted total freedom. Not only could he express his personal opinions without impediment, he set about sabotaging every time-table.

I remember an evening in the spring of 1959. We had both been invited to the convention of the French-language Medical Association. There was a symposium on "Medicine as Seen by the Citizen," with a moderator, four participants, and several hundred in the audience. It was in the Mount Royal Hotel, and the weather was hot and humid. Each panelist had twenty minutes in which to expound his views, after which there was to be a dialogue between the audience and the rostrum. I was the first to speak: ten minutes. The second participant: fifteen. Then René: two hours by the clock for his premises, twenty minutes more for his conclusion. We never did find out what the fourth participant thought. No doubt we missed something profound.

"And the doctors stayed and listened to him?" asks Marchand aggressively.

"Well, it was interesting. But I remember it was very hot there."

"He'd have lost me pretty fast, I tell you."

"Never, Jean," says Trudeau, mocking. "You'd have

stayed to the bitter end, like today."

"Yeah? Then watch me leave."

Marchand stands up, dabs at his mouth with his serviette, picks up his pipe from the table and . . . the door opens. René bursts in, his long forelock flying, an enormous briefcase under his arm, his tie crooked, a cigarette hanging from his lips, full of energy.

"Hello, guys! Eaten already? Never mind. I'm having a steak. Miss? Yes, a steak. Rare. Blue. And some strong mustard. Good." He sits down. "What a hell of a life! Just got in from Quebec City. Couldn't leave last night. In fact, it's urgent that I see you all." He takes out two files. "You have to do three things at once in this bloody job. Trudeau, you've worked on public appropriations, haven't you? God, we're short of competent people in Quebec. I don't only mean the ministers. There's no public service in our dear province. None. Only last week, for example . . ."

Marchand has his pipe going again, but his expression holds a grudge. Trudeau has shoved his chair back a little from the table and is balancing on the back legs. He smiles, looking at Lévesque as at an oddity. And indeed he is one. The flood of words continues without a pause. You wonder how he has time to breathe or manages to light another cigarette without leaving the slightest gap in his discourse where you could get a word in.

"It's the damn problem of available funds! It's great to want to do things, and God knows there are things to be done, but the money, where do you get the money? To nationalize electricity, for example. If you ask me, there's no way around it. We'll have to nationalize. Fifty years ago, Ontario . . ."

The door opens again. The waitress has brought René an enormous steak. But the talking continues in a torrent, while our table-companion goes about seasoning his meal. First, a layer of mustard so thick that the colour of the meat is obscured.

"If Ontario could nationalize in 1907 or 1912, whenever

it was, Quebec can surely do it in 1962 or '63. Look, I have the preliminary figures here, I had them drawn up by..."

I realize that neither Marchand nor Trudeau nor myself is listening. All three of us are spellbound by the culinary operation that is under way. Lévesque has snatched up the salt-shaker and is strewing on the already mustard-camouflaged steak a flurry of salt that again covers it entirely. Does he have a steel-lined stomach?

"Of course these aren't final figures, they indicate an order of magnitude, that's all. If I had time I'd go over them with you in detail. I'd like to know what Trudeau thinks of them." A glance at his watch. "But I have an appointment at three." He shrugs. "Too bad."

Trudeau looks at me, a twinkle in his eye. Marchand says drily: "Oh, we have lots of time, René. You must have known that, by the way."

Lévesque gets the point and answers with a guilty grimace, followed by the smile—half-charming, half mischievous—that he calls upon so often. He is back in his files again, and his steak is getting cold. Jean's expression is beginning to relax, as if he were soothed by the thought that at this moment someone, somewhere, is also cooling his heels as we have done for the last two hours.

Waiting for Godot, alias René Lévesque, minister of National Resources in the cabinet of Jean Lesage.

CHAPTER 2

Protagonists

Ah, Trebutien! Trebutien! Let us try to become something and not die obscure.
BARBEY D'AUREVILLY

W here did they come from, these three men meeting around a table, who were about to play such prominent roles in our country's life? Before going farther, I would like to tell something of the circumstances in which I met them, what I knew about them at that crucial moment in their lives, and how I came to act as a link among them.

*   *   *

It was autumn, 1939. Quebec City, and its old Latin Quarter. The time, mid-evening. The *carabins*, as students were called in those days, had invaded the street for their annual rag: happy, noisy, loud-mouthed, firmly resolved to live it up until the small hours of the morning. I happened to be passing through Quebec, fresh from my country origins (Victoriaville, Nicolet, and Mont-Laurier where I had just completed my B.A.), and I decided to join the celebrations.

In the middle of the street, four ribald stalwarts had just

formed a circle around a pretty passer-by. Gazing at her with appreciative lust, they sang a refrain that belongs to student folklore, to the Russian tune of "Dark Eyes":

> Lovely feet, she has!
> Lovely ankles, she has!
> Lovely legs, she has!
> Lovely knees, she has!
> Lovely thighs, she has!
> A lovely mmm..., she has!

It was sung with the lips closed for words that are a trifle bawdy. The girl blushed to the roots of her hair, then went off holding the arm of one of her tormentors, while the remaining three began the process with renewed enthusiasm on the next pretty pedestrian they found, provided she was young and shapely.

That was a time when the level of political awareness was very low on the campuses. In those days, a demonstration meant a big party with plenty of pranks like the above, ending up in some tavern. That was exactly what happened to me that evening. Was it in the tavern near the Capitol movie theatre (the one they called the Chapel because of its white-walled interior) that I got to know Jean Marchand? I'm not sure. It was either there or in a friend's room in the rue Saint-Louis. In any case, it was an encounter I will never forget.

To meet Marchand was to receive a shock. Already at the age of twenty he had the presence, the high voltage, the natural impatience and the aggressivity that made him one of the most remarkable men of action I have had the privilege of knowing. He made such a strong impression on me that I'm certain I would still remember him even if I had never seen him again. Who else was in that room (or around the tavern table)? I have not the slightest idea. But I can still see Marchand, his small stature, the dark mass of his hair, his lively eyes, and something that suggested a runner waiting for the starting pistol.

I can hear his brassy voice, and the way he pronounced his r's (he was born in Champlain in the Trois Rivières region). His gift for a phrase also sticks in my memory—the inflections of his voice and the ever-present emotive charge that were to make him a public orator of unusual power.

But these were only superficial impressions. The shock I received came from something else.

We were both twenty. As everyone knows, that is the age for asking agonizing questions. We wonder anxiously what we are going to do with our lives. We firmly intend to change the world, but we are not too sure how to go about it, nor where to start. Well, Marchand seemed sure. That was what made him different from the rest of us. He had emerged from the dreaming stage and was already living in reality. He talked about combats to be fought and struggles to be undertaken. He had chosen his ground: the union movement—a choice that in those days, in student circles, was so advanced as to be almost prophetic.

Was it that evening, or the following year when we met for the second time, that Marchand told me, with the cruel irony he employs so well, about his first disappointment with nationalism?

He had been recruited into one of the innumerable leagues that existed at the time (each one with twelve or fifteen members), all of which wanted to overthrow the government and put an end to democracy. That was the spirit of the age. Of course, the half-baked leaders of these little groups had no precise notion of what political action meant. They dreamed, they grew intoxicated with words, and in the basements of middle-class houses they cooked up heady plots which no one ever dreamt of acting on. Marchand, however, failed to understand why, for example, they might want to steal weapons from the COTC (Canadian Officers' Training Corps) if they had no intention of using them. He demanded to know what the plan of action was—and discovered that there was none.

Or was there? The leader, a noted nationalist at the time, decided one day to organize a great demonstration to cool the impatience of his troops. The plan was drawn up; each member received precise instructions. Jean imagined himself already on the barricades (the idea delighted him), but he wanted to know what the leader's role was to be, and what his own place would be in the initial parade. He was sadly let down: "You'll be leading the parade," replied the leader. "I'll be following along by car. I can't possibly compromise my authority in a demonstration. Just imagine, if I got arrested! The future of the movement..."

Marchand could imagine that very well. Above all, he realized that he was in with a gang of dreamers led by a poltroon. But as every experience has some value, this one delivered him forever from all lyrical illusions. Later, involved heart and soul in the struggle of the union movement, he always put himself on the firing-line and squarely faced the consequences of his decisions.

It was not to be too much later for Marchand. At the age of twenty-four he was running his first strike, in the Saguenay, in the pulp and paper industry. Shortly after, he became head organizer, then Secretary-General of the CTCC[1] as it then was, now the CSN.[2] I know only by hearsay this period in his life, in which he received his baptism of fire in the union movement. During the ten years that followed our first meeting I saw Jean only at long intervals and always by chance. Our respective jobs kept us apart.

In tandem with Gérard Picard, stone by stone he built up a group of affiliated trade unions, using the spongy material available in the Catholic unions, a spineless movement more or less dominated by the clergy. Those unions were a refuge for a handful of authentic militants, but also for a flock of blind and amenable followers full of good will. Some day Jean Marchand himself or another militant from those early days should tell the story of the rebirth of that confederation

---

[1] [*Confédération des travailleurs catholiques du Canada*. Tr.]
[2] [*Confédération des syndicats nationaux*. Tr.]

of Catholic workers of Canada.

Until the war years the movement had lived under the tutelage of the clergy. A company union? Not always. In certain situations of extreme injustice (I'm thinking of the textile strikes and the violent conflict at Sorel in the '30s), there was the occasional conjunction of authentic workers' leaders and courageous chaplain-priests. In those cases struggles did take place, but they were local and episodic. They were quickly snuffed out, and the movement as a whole returned to its half-hearted, drowsy existence, to its fears and the lack of any authentic social thought that had characterized it until that time.

When Marchand tries to explain the state of mind that prevailed in the Catholic unions on his arrival, he tells this story: during a study session organized by the CTCC, a group of militants proposed establishing a strike fund. The meeting rejected the project. The minutes record that several speakers pointed out the fact that, as there were so many chaplains in the movement, there was no call for such a fund!

With the arrival of the Picard–Marchand team and a whole crew of new militants they attracted in their wake, the situation changed rapidly. By the end of the war, the CTCC had become an authentic federation, ready to take up the challenges the working class was obliged to meet in Quebec. This was the movement that entered the great post-war struggles: for the miners, the metalworkers, and those in the textile and petrochemical industries.

Ten years, then, after our first meeting, I came together with Marchand again. At Asbestos. To get there I myself had made a rather long detour via youth movements, South America, the blood-stained Europe of the immediate post-war days, international relief work and journalism. But it was not chance that brought us together in the little mining town on the evening of February 14, 1949. What Jean Marchand had learned in the Saguenay among the pulp and paper workers had also been revealed to me, first in Chile and Argentina, then in the ruins of Europe, in the sprawling workers' suburbs where conqueror and vanquished alike knew a poverty that the war had never changed, except for the worse. I had come back to Canada in 1947 with what in those days was called a "social conscience" and a predilection for working-class action. I had become a journalist out of a deep conviction: I believed in the primordial role of information in any undertaking for social change. This conviction had led me to *Le Devoir*, where, among other things, I covered the union beat.

Then, on February 13, 1949, the asbestos strike began. No one guessed at the time that it would last for months, or that it would become the symbol of the workers' struggle for the period that followed. We were so unaware of these facts that no one was prepared for a long struggle. I remember sitting in Gérard Picard's tiny office in the rue de Montigny (now Maisonneuve), the afternoon of the 14th. The strike had broken out in the middle of the preceding night, and I had had no trouble convincing Gérard Filion, the paper's publisher, and Pierre Laporte, the news editor (as we called the position then), that the place where I belonged for the next while was Asbestos, if my title as labour reporter had any meaning.

"I quite agree," Filion had said. "But you know we haven't a penny for travel. You're on your own."

I managed on my own. Gérard Picard had given me a very cordial reception.

"Of course we can get you there. And it won't cost us anything, which makes it all easier. You'll go up there with René Rocque. Here he is, by the way. He's leaving in half an hour."

Into the cramped office came a gentle, myopic giant.

"Not in half an hour," the giant warned. "More like five minutes. Jean Marchand just phoned. We must get there tonight for a meeting."

"Fine," said Picard. "You're on your way, then. I won't keep you."

It was my turn to protest. "But I'm not ready. I've got to go home and get my bags."

"What bags?" Picard asked, lighting a cigarette. "Buy yourself a toothbrush in the drugstore across the street. You'll only be there a few hours. You can be sure the Johns Manville Company won't hold out long. They have more orders than they can fill. You'll be lucky if the strike isn't over before you get there!"

Gérard Picard's estimate (like that of the rest of us) was out by a mere five months. If his optimism had been well-founded I might never have seen Jean Marchand again. But there was little chance of that. We had all just stuck our fingers into a mechanism that was firmly in gear, driven by powerful forces whose existence we barely suspected, but which were to convulse Quebec society and change our personal destinies more profoundly than any of us could yet imagine.

*   *   *

Where was Pierre Trudeau on February 14, 1949? Somewhere in the world, in Europe or Asia. In any case, very far away. He would not be back before spring. At that time he would visit the picket lines of the asbestos strike and make a speech to the miners. He would also meet Jean Marchand. And both Trudeau and myself would be arrested by the Quebec Provincial Police, leading to farcical scenes at the police station where we were taken together under heavy guard. But I'm getting ahead of my story.

Where did I see Trudeau for the first time? In the rue Cherrier, early in 1941, when he had just finished his first year of law school. He was not alone: three or four of his former schoolmates at Brébeuf[3] were with him. I seem to see around him (I may be wrong) Guy Viau, Pierre Vadeboncoeur and maybe Gaby Filion, the painter. They were all wearing sporty clothes which made me very self-conscious

---

[3]Jean de Brébeuf College, run by the Jesuits, which then was favoured by the sons of Outremont's upper middle class. Trudeau took his classical courses there from 1932 to 1940.

about my shirt and tie on such a hot and sunny day. But the "guys from Brébeuf" were like that: they always made you feel that you didn't know how to dress or walk or speak or live properly. They had a style that commanded attention, creating around them the reign of a minor orthodoxy. If you didn't know their slang, if you weren't in on their jokes, if you hadn't read the same books, you felt inferior. They loved to perplex newcomers to their circle. The previous week, in fact, I had met a "guy from Brébeuf" who threw up his hands because I had never read Panaït Istrati. And as I had some pretensions to literary erudition...

But on this occasion they weren't talking literature. I asked them: "Where are you going in that getup?"

"To Abitibi."

"To do what? Are you going fishing?"

"No."

"What then?"

"Nothing. We'll paddle and portage there, through the forest, following d'Iberville's itinerary. It's not the destination that counts, it's the means of locomotion."

By now I didn't know if they were talking about a real project or just making fun of me. And it was not the first time I'd come up against them. I had never seen Pierre Trudeau before, but he had already had an opportunity to poke fun at me, and didn't miss his chance. In an article published by his college newspaper a few months earlier he had pulled my leg, gently and without malice, but with a kind of wit that made me realize the excesses of my militancy at the time. And here I was face to face with the man.

Stung to the quick (of my vanity) by his article in *Le Brébeuf*, I at once tried to find out more about this fellow, called Piotr or Pierre Elliott by his friends, about whom some spoke admiringly, others aggressively, but none with indifference. What I discovered placed him very far from me. He was the son of a millionaire, lived in Outremont, was a first-class athlete, and did all his classical studies with the Jesuits. My father was a station-master, I lived in a minuscule, bedbug-infested room on the rue Saint-Hubert, came from the country, was small and unathletic, and had a horror of that Jesuit education which had the pretension of turning out the *élite* of society. If Trudeau was really a product of his surroundings, we had no chance of getting along, because I was the product of mine and had not the slightest desire to disown them.

But there he was before my eyes, and everything changed. (Thank God, neither of us was a slave to social categories.) He made no show either of his money or his muscles. Nor of his intelligence. But despite a strange shyness that will never leave him, and which made him less than talkative on first acquaintance, he aroused one's curiosity.

Oh, if I only had had enough money to invite the group to a nearby café! We could have chatted and gotten to know each other. But at that moment I was earning five dollars a week. My room-rent was three, leaving only two dollars for seven days' meals. The opportunity was lost.

During the years that followed I met Trudeau in the street or going into movie theatres, or at occasional political demonstrations against conscription. I read a few articles by him in the *Quartier latin*, the student paper at the Université de Montréal; I was present at a debate in Plateau Hall where he was the star. This academic exercise ended with a colossal practical joke when Trudeau suddenly brandished a revolver he had kept hidden under his gown and fired a few blanks in the air, to the consternation of a federal cabinet minister of the time who was chairing the occasion. I don't even remember the subject of the debate, but I remember that my militancy (or my deficient sense of humour) failed to find much fun in these pranks worthy of spoiled children.

Finally it was François Hertel, a most uncommon Jesuit, who brought us together around a table to discuss . . . philosophy! I really don't remember how the discussion came about. Neither Trudeau nor I had any philosophical pretensions. But I can see us grouped around a table in an Outremont basement. André Dagenais, with marvellous glibness, set forth his theory of composites (neither pure form nor pure matter) which in the final analysis would justify certain premarital sexual contacts, particularly the "contemplation of beautiful bodies." I can hear Hertel accusing Dagenais, "But you are a Platonist, my dear fellow!"

At the end of the evening I walked for a while with Hertel on my way home.

"Tell me, do you take Dagenais's theories seriously? Calling him a Platonist... I'd be flattered if I were in his place."

"You didn't understand," replied Hertel. "If I call someone a Platonist, it's a roundabout way of telling him that he's talking rubbish."

Those were strange evenings. Trudeau talked very little. We had our first real conversations in Paris, in 1946. If I were less afraid of digressions and anything else that might distract me from my first purpose, I would explain here the importance for our generation of our first visit to Paris. How can one say in a few words what an obsessive desire we had, almost all of us, from our very childhood onward: to leave Quebec, to leave Canada, to leave America itself. To leave! For us, there was not the slightest hesitation as to where to go. We knew New York, some of us had pressed on as far as South America or at least to Mexico, but our intellectual pole was located across the Atlantic, in France.

I have often wondered about the reason for the strange power of this attraction. Were we giving in to a kind of sentimental nostalgia, or a blind atavistic instinct? Was it the real France that fascinated us, or merely a dream country secreted during the confinement of the thirties within the barbed wire of the depression or the war?

It must be said that the material and spiritual poverty of the times gnawed at us from the time we were old enough to think. One must also remember the means of communication available to us then. Aboard the freighters that took us to Europe, it took eight or ten, sometimes fifteen days to cross the sea. How distant Paris was! It is hard to imagine it today. Even to remember it. Jean-Paul Riopelle told me once about his first crossing. He had cattle to keep him company. I found myself lucky by comparison, having sailed with oranges and fresh eggs. But all of us, beyond a doubt, were in search of our origins. We were on the pilgrimage to the source, of which we had always dreamed.

Later, in an article in *Cité libre*, Jean Le Moyne explained that we in America, like the American Henry James, were "provincials without a capital." We dreamed of a culture whose epicentre was not in Quebec or Montreal but on another continent. Our reading, whether in literature, politics, sociology or history (except that of Canada), transported us inevitably to Europe. The masters who taught us to think, see and feel were called Claudel, Péguy, Tocqueville, Mounier, Maritain, Michelet, Malraux, Braque or Picasso. Dead or alive, they were all *elsewhere*. And it was toward that "elsewhere" that we ardently wished to go.

I was foolish enough to try to explain this state of mind to a young college teacher from Quebec whom I met in Strasbourg. He replied, with the most superb contempt: "Well, nowadays we don't give a damn what happens in France. We don't want any part of it. Quebec's good enough for us." I wished I could feel sorry for him. He obviously believed that from now on our people could fashion its own culture quite alone. He didn't know that in the thirties, in the very trough of our intellectual poverty, some young people, nationalists like himself, had thought the same thing. And they were fools. Above all, he seemed not to realize that no people on this earth, even the greatest, can afford to fence itself inside its own culture: it would risk slow but certain suffocation.

Back to Pierre Trudeau.

It was 1946. He was in Paris, studying political science. I was in Geneva, or rather Switzerland was my home base. But as Field Secretary to the World Student Relief Fund I gadded about Europe, from Dublin to Vienna, from Naples to Brussels to Prague, via Paris as often as I could arrange it. And I ran into Pierre Trudeau. What I recall from our encounters in those days—four or five, no more—is, of course, the fun (Trudeau straddling an enormous motorbike that backfired through the echoing streets of an almost empty Paris), the good humour, a few good meals, but above all some very serious conversations about the choices open to us.

If I were to say that we talked politics, it would be a statement that was true and false at the same time.

To clear up this paradox, I have to talk a little about what was for us the intense atmosphere of post-war Europe. We had the feeling that around us the world in which we would live our lives was taking shape. And we were right. In those days politics in our eyes was a "world plan." Stalinist communism was surging across Europe, as had Christianity two thousand years earlier. In an environment of extreme poverty, of near-famine, there arose a great hope which told of a changed world and announced the end of injustice and inequality. The old revolutionary dream, revived by young people who had been in the Resistance, took on a new vitality. This time, however, it was not *The Declaration of the Rights of Man* that underlay it, but Marxism. The question was no longer one of choosing between two parties or even two economic doctrines. The choice was between two conceptions of life, two explanations of the world, two modes of thought that called for total commitment of the individual and the whole of human activity.

Jean Duvignaud, in *Le Ça perché*,[4] writes about the state of mind of a young communist of that era:

> We were fools, no doubt, but with a single folly, the one which must be measured against the absolute we thought we represented. To take part in a revolutionary movement without constructing a general ethical, aesthetic and philosophical vision of what we should do, seemed absurd or merely trivial. One does not walk into the "great system" as if it were a Five and Ten store.

---

[4]Paris: Editions Stock, 1976, p. 138.

The "great system," the Marxism that claimed to solve all problems, was, I admit, a tempting abyss for me at the time. It conflicted with my religious beliefs, but that conflict had been resolved by the "progressive Christians." For them, not only was it possible to reconcile Marxism with Christianity (the traditional conservatism of the Churches had led us to think this could not be done), but for my friend Jean Chesneaux, today a professor at the Sorbonne, any Christian who did not belong to the Communist party was being untrue to the logic of his Christian faith.

At this distance in time it may seem inconceivable that this question of a choice held me in distressing indecision for many long months. If one forgets the extreme poverty of those times, the hunger, the cold, whole neighbourhoods flattened by bombs, the pile of rubble Europe had become and the bankruptcy of pre-war conservatism that was everywhere apparent; if one ignores the fact that we then knew nothing of the horrors of the Soviet *gulag* or the monstrosities of the "great system;" if one neglects to say that we had just discovered Auschwitz, Dachau and Bergen-Belsen, then, no doubt, our indecision may seem ridiculous. In 1946 it did not. It justified our vehement discussions which lasted far into the night, and was for me the occasion of getting to know Pierre Trudeau.

Need I say that in those days I was a political illiterate?

A B.A. acquired in the 1930s by no means prepared us for the confrontations of the 1940s, to say the least. As for my personal reading, chance and my own tastes led me almost exclusively to literature, history and religious writings. Canadian politics had never interested me, except briefly in the conscription episode, and that was because of my admiration for André Laurendeau.

Now, through Pierre Trudeau, I discovered a political culture whose existence I had never suspected. He knew about books, events, schools of thought, historical trends, facts and statistics that gave our conversations a direction and style that for me were entirely new. I would be quite here to reproduce any of those long discussions, but I ...il have a vivid double impression of them: Trudeau talked about politics in a tone that was more rational than emotional, in contrast to all his interlocutors at the time; and his remarks showed a knowledge of the problems that none of us possessed. I finally began to perceive in what he said (his remarks were rather rare and always brief; he was never garrulous) a highly personal search for a political line of thought appropriate to the Canadian situation. Everyone around him was speculating about the future of the world— and he too, at times. But he was the only one to have already begun reflecting on the evolution of politics in Quebec and in Canada. His ideas had begun to take form, nourished by the greatest writings and steeped in the highest sources. I was to watch their development with fascination.

At the time I never wondered about the reasons that might have brought me close to men like Marchand and Trudeau. Friendship, like love, is always slightly miraculous. The one who is its object finds it inexplicable. Yet circumstances always play a part in the creation of these bonds.

I think I have indicated what drew me to these two men. Only they could say why they gave me their friendship, but I might mention two favourable circumstances.

To Jean Marchand, especially when he was in the thick of his militant activity, a blank sheet of paper appeared more threatening than an over-excited crowd of five thousand workers. My facility in writing, my ability to compose a text rapidly and put on paper the essence of an improvised speech he had just made, the practice in summarizing given by journalism—all this fascinated him. Yet he was a rare master of the magic word. His trenchant oratory made him a legend in the union movement. But he needed a helper who could produce in a few minutes (he was always in a rush) the few paragraphs he needed for the press. I became for him, from the very start of our long association, that "poor man's intellectual" called a journalist.

Trudeau, on the other hand, insisted on writing the slightest text he required. Even petitions, collective declarations and other manifestos that he was called upon to sign always had to undergo a long process of improvement and revision, including a meticulous final polish. The ease with which I wrote impressed him not at all. Only the quality of the final product interested him, even if attaining it meant long delays. What interested him in me as a journalist was not the "poor man's intellectual" aspect, but the man of action. When he came back from his world tour (with rucksack) in the spring of 1949, he was very much aware that his long years of study and his stays abroad had made him into an academic who was a little remote from Canadian reality. He hated being seen as a pure intellectual. My experience with youth movements and later with international labour gave me in his eyes some of the qualities of the man with a commitment that he himself wanted to be—not only on the level of ideas (he was that already), but in the field of concrete, immediate action.

"It's terrific," he said to me as we were driving to Asbestos that fine morning in May 1949. "It's barely two years since we saw each other in Paris, and here you are up to your neck in adventure, right in the middle of the most important things that are happening here."

I was flattered and reassured by his enthusiasm. But honesty obliged me to say: "Wait till you meet Jean Marchand."

* * *

I made Trudeau's acquaintance via a student newspaper; it was radio journalism that revealed to me, and the public, the third of the exceptional characters this book is about.

In fact, his name was not totally unknown to me. Jean Marchand had talked about a certain Lévesque, a student from the Gaspé, with whom he had often played cards rather than suffering the unbearable lectures of Father Papin Archambault or Father Jean-Baptiste Desrosiers at the Social Science School. I knew vaguely that this René Lévesque had crossed the border in 1940 to join up as a war correspondent with the American armed forces.

I remembered all that when his reports started coming in from Korea, in the fall of 1951. Those reports were a revelation, in the strictest sense of the word. They revealed to us an *electronic* journalist who was like no other. And if the discovery came so suddenly and unexpectedly for most listeners, it was because René Lévesque had up to that time worked for the International Service of the CBC. He could be heard on short wave at the ends of the earth before he became known in his own country. To describe my enthusiasm over his Korean reports, I can do no better than quote what I wrote then. I was radio critic on *Le Devoir*, and this is what I wrote in my column of October 6 under the headline "Mr. René Lévesque, a preeminent reporter and commentator."

> I would class the programs I have heard as the most remarkable things to be done on our airwaves in a very long time. In my opinion Mr. Lévesque is radio's revelation of the year, and the best French-language (perhaps English-language too) commentator Canadian radio has ever given us. Some who have not heard Mr. Lévesque may find the praise exaggerated. But I bestow it without reservation after mentally reviewing all the great names in the profession.
>
> ...
>
> Mr. Lévesque had a very precise mission: to inform Canadian listeners about the Korean war, and especially about the life of our troops that are engaged in the fighting, and on the general situation in the countries of the Orient that he had visited. Mr. Lévesque, of course, was not the first to deal with these various subjects! The difficulty for him, then, consisted in avoiding repetition of what others had done, while picking up, where they had left off, the task they had attempted. And I mean the word "attempted," because on hearing Mr. Lévesque's reports one realized with growing admiration

(in the Latin sense of astonishment) that no one, until now, had succeeded in bringing home to us this precursor-war which is festering in those parts like a wound.

· · ·

When he speaks to us, it is not a CBC reporter that we hear, back from his mission; it is a man of our own milieu, a free man, who bore with him to Korea our conscience, our hopes, our fears and our curiosity. What he tells us about are the very things we wanted to know, without knowing what we wanted. And Mr. Lévesque talks with a frankness that is a credit to him, and a credit to the CBC.

Having said this, I would like to quote his text, almost in its entirety, page after page. I should describe at length how Mr. Lévesque wonderfully combines a mastery of broadcasting technique and culture. The technique is never obvious, and the culture is not displayed. But any single passage chosen at random (for example the amazing recording of soldiers chatting in the dark) can afford us a glimpse of a relentless striving for technical excellence, along with the unerring judgment of a man who never confuses propaganda with humanity or play-acting with life.

· · ·

In short, I mean that a real talent for radio is extremely rare. There are any number of semi-talented broadcasters; superior talent is not totally lacking; but real excellence does not turn up once in a year's time. Mr Lévesque achieves it effortlessly in his role as reporter–commentator. It is to be hoped that the CBC will take him out of the International Service, despite the importance of his work there, and allow us more often to hear his comments on what is going on in the world.

I of course expected no reaction from René. To thank a

person for a first encomium smacks of asking for a second. Not at all in Lévesque's line.

But some weeks later, in connection with another column, I received a long letter from him in a handwriting that would later come to be familiar to me: there were traces of the fine, rounded hand typical of a Christian Brothers' school, mixed with the nervous scribble of an impatient man. Lévesque first of all congratulated me on "taking radio seriously enough" to devote a weekly column to it. (As a matter of fact, I was the first Montreal journalist to write such a column in a daily paper.) Then he found fault with me a little for having been too glib in my last article. That was the beginning and the end of all correspondence between us.

But we had agreed on our wish to meet at the first opportunity, which turned out to be a few weeks later.

I have a curious impression of our first conversations. Will anyone believe me if I say there was no mention of politics? And this was not my doing, because since the asbestos strike (1949) and the founding of the review *Cité libre* (1950), the whole group of which I was a part was already deeply involved, not in a party but in a long and demanding political struggle. The Duplessis oppression was at its peak, and clerical conservatism was gloating over its recent victory over Montreal's Archbishop Joseph Charbonneau, who had been *in exile* in Vancouver for the last year. Thus I found René Lévesque to be in a way a stranger to the struggle that was just getting under way. I would not say that he was indifferent, but rather absent, somewhere else, quite absorbed in the practice of his profession and not very interested in politics, except at the international level. We talked about journalism, films, books. His intellectual curiosity knew no bounds. He read everything, starting with a daily pile of Canadian and American newspapers, not to mention a wide variety of periodicals and dozens of books of all kinds. From the bulging pockets of his eternal sport jackets emerged (always) a copy of the *New York Times*— on the right side—and on the left some paperback that he had just bought in a corner bookstore.

I was astonished, as well, at his strange way of looking at one, at the same time penetrating and inattentive. He gave the impression of listening while thinking of something else. He would let loose a flood of words, or rather a long burst from his verbal machine-gun. What he said was rarely trivial, yet one could imagine that as he spoke he was meditating on something else which he shared with no one. Did he find one's remarks interesting? Very hard to say, though he punctuated certain parts of the conversation with a hearty laugh or approving nods.

It was in the old CBC building at the corner of Dorchester and Mackay that I ran across René Lévesque most often. He was always rushing down the corridors at full steam, always in a hurry, his tie, when he wore one, always crooked, his trousers baggy, his long forelock striped across a scalp already bare. He most enjoyed impromptu conversations outside a studio door when he was about to leave, which in no way inhibited him from taking his time, if the subject interested him, nor from supporting his remarks by producing dog's-eared bits of paper, with which his pockets were always crammed, pieces of all sizes, green, white or yellow, covered with his sprawling handwriting.[5]

For several months (perhaps years) in the early days of television, the CBC had a rather small cafeteria where performers liked to meet between rehearsals. I believe it was there that Trudeau and Lévesque first met, or at least where I saw them together for the first time.[6] It must have been in the

---

[5]On November 2, 1977, as Canadian ambassador to France, I went to meet René Lévesque, premier of Quebec, arriving on an official visit to Paris. In the reception hall of Orly airport, before the prime minister of France, a detachment of the *Gardes republicains*, the chief of protocol, and a number of other hangers-on, I saw René pull from his pocket a sheaf of dog's-eared bits of paper. It was his arrival speech, which he had not taken the time to have typed.

[6]On November 5, 1977, having breakfast at the Crillon with Lévesque, I asked him out of the blue (in the presence of Claude Morin and Jean Deschamps): "Do you remember the first time you met Trudeau?" At once he confirmed not only the place I mentioned above, but almost word for word the conversation I have reported.

early fifties, but already René's TV reputation was made and
his face had become public property. Trudeau and I were
discussing the next issue of *Cité libre* (the review had no
home until 1960, and was put together wherever chance
arranged a meeting). Lévesque came over to our table,
slowly for once, because he was holding an overflowing cup
of coffee.

"Hi, guys!"

Handshakes all around. And while René was carefully
setting down his cup, Trudeau assailed him before he could
even sit down: "Hey, Lévesque, you're a hell of a good
speaker, but I'm starting to wonder whether you can write.
We've been after you for a while. When are you going to give
us an article for *Cité libre*?"

Pierre had assumed his "guy from Brébeuf" manner and
Lévesque was put off his stride.

"Writing... writing... How can I find the time?"

"And something to say," added Trudeau, more *Brébeuf*
than ever. "That's essential. But how about making a little
effort one of these days?" Trudeau was smiling, watching
the effect of his provocation on Lévesque, who was suddenly
abashed, smiling uncertainly, puffing on his cigarette, not
knowing what to say or what tone to take.

"Television's all very well," Trudeau went on, "but there's
nothing solid about it, as you know. People watch it when
they have time to kill. Now, if you knew how to write,
maybe with a little effort now and then..."

"If that's what you think," Lévesque exploded, "you can
go peddle your potatoes, you bloody washout of an intellectual!"

That got the conversation going. It went on for a few
minutes in the same tone, at once cordial and acid. If I
remember this occasion so well, it is because the tone of the
dialogue between the two men was to stay the same: half-
serious provocations from Trudeau, reactions from Lévesque in a parody of aggressivity designed to camouflage an
undertone of real irritation.

Years later, Lévesque was to say of Trudeau, in an interview with Peter Desbarats, "He had an inborn talent for making you want to slap his face." But contrary to the legend promoted by Desbarats, René would have taken good care to avoid a dust-up with Pierre (supposing he had ever wanted one), because he was gifted for boxing the way Mohammed Ali is for embroidery, while Trudeau...

But it was also clear from the first moment that the two men held a kind of fascination for each other, which they both unconsciously fought with all their might.

Trudeau watched Lévesque in action with the spellbound admiration one feels watching the tricks of a conjurer. René's vitality, his lively intelligence, his verbal originality, the surprises in his mental processes, his imagination, the breadth and variety of his erudition, his extensive knowledge of history and his disconcerting memory for the slightest facts in current events—all this left Trudeau flabbergasted. He was, nonetheless, irritated by Lévesque's petulance, his biting assertions, his tendency to juggle figures that were more or less well-substantiated or to allow his passion of the moment to distort the realities of which he spoke.

When Lévesque would start off on one of his usual long tirades, riddled with hasty judgments, brilliant, profound or superficial, but always borne along on an irresistible flood of words, Trudeau would withdraw into himself. Slumped in his chair, he would fix on the improviser an Indian eye, in turn skeptical, mistrustful and mocking. At such moments I suspected Trudeau of thinking in secret that a journalist's culture combined with the temperament of a star could only result in a political way of thinking that was adulterated or at least doubtful.

René clearly felt the intensity of that pitiless look, and used to react—probably unconsciously—with language full of a forced vulgarity and a plethora of cusswords rarely equalled in our political annals, which, by the way, have known some experts in the field.[7]

---

[7]Later, in 1960–63, when Lévesque was a minister in Quebec under Jean Lesage,

But he too had a profound if grudging admiration for his interlocutor. In Pierre's presence his assertions were less cock-sure, and he approached certain questions as if he were stalking them, as if he suspected himself of a lack of precise knowledge and refused to admit it. Obviously, Trudeau's political knowledge impressed him. In economics, for example, he sought Pierre's advice and listened carefully to the replies, surprised to find not a man like the rest of us who had gleaned a few notions through haphazard reading or daily life, but one who had been lucky enough to study the subject systematically and reflect upon it for a long time. For Lévesque, Trudeau represented the very type of the scholar whose thorough and solid learning he envied; but he also represented the armchair intellectual who was insensitive to certain realities, the aristocrat of the mind whose ironic banter was a tremendous irritation to René.

If Trudeau won too many points at the beginning of a discussion, Lévesque would often react with a whole evening of verbal excesses and strident raillery. If, on the other hand, it was René who won the first round, it might happen that Pierre retired sulking to his tent, with barely another word from him for hours. Admittedly, this was exceptional. Almost always the conversation between the two men was exciting, electric. Probably neither is fully aware of the fascination they exercised on each other. But many traces of it will appear in the pages that follow.

As for Jean Marchand, he was to have a major influence on both of them. Without him, perhaps neither Trudeau nor Lévesque would today be the men of action they have become.

and Trudeau and he were often at my house with Marchand and Laurendeau, I was no longer the only one to perceive this phenomenon. After one of these late-night meetings, my twelve-year-old son asked innocently, "Do all the ministers swear as much as René Lévesque?"

CHAPTER 3

The Starting-Line

*If we refuse to take over the past, the
past will overtake us.*
GEORGES BERNANOS

F or the men I am speaking about in these pages, the 1950s
were of decisive importance. And not only for them: the
fate of all of us was at stake in that decade.

Just think about it: in 1950 Maurice Duplessis was reign-
ing as the master of Quebec, Louis Saint-Laurent as prime
minister in Ottawa. Ten years later both men had disappeared, taking with them to oblivion political attitudes and
ideas that had been current for a century. At the beginning
of the decade the Quebec clergy was still all-powerful; by
1960 it would be in full flight, and one of the swiftest and
most thorough religious upheavals ever seen would have
taken place in Quebec. And finally, with the coming of
television in 1952 a cultural revolution got under way, one
that is still with us twenty-five years later.

Most chroniclers of our recent evolution place the
starting-line at the beginning of the Quiet Revolution, i.e.,
in 1960. To my mind, this is the finish line. By the end of the

'50s we were already programmed decisively, irreversibly. The play was written; all we had to do was act it out.

But none of that was easy to foresee at the start of the '50s. Quebec seemed frozen for all time in the glaciers of conservatism. We had the impression of living through an endless winter. Nothing gave us any hope of a thaw. There may have been signs of it, but we were too impatient to notice them. It is well known that any kind of militancy blurs the vision of its enthusiasts. When we give ourselves wholeheartedly to a cause, we become so anxious to see it triumph that this very desire blinds us to its progress.[1]

Awareness of Quebec's stagnation did not come at the same moment nor in the same way to all the militants of our post-war period. "A question of the generation gap," people sometimes say to explain the differences observed.

But what, exactly, is a generation? It is a word I am not overly fond of. It is too vague, and refers to ill-defined realities with blurred contours. Yet I cannot find a better one to refer to the group of my contemporaries (another equivocal term). For the purposes of this book, it means all the men and women who reached adulthood just after the Second World War and were already earning a living as the '50s began.

The war had undeniably created a gap between them and their elders who had been involved in the struggle before the war. What an upheaval had taken place between 1935 and 1945! And above all, because of the difference in ages, we had experienced in such a different way the successive cataclysms of the Great Depression and the world conflagration. When these two ordeals came along, the vast majority of our pre-war elders were already imbued with the dominant ideology that had guided Quebec and the French

[1] A very short time ago I had a chance to observe this phenomenon. In Lyon I met a young Acadian militant from Moncton who had trouble admitting the extent to which his people had advanced in the last twenty years. I have known Acadia for forty years, and found it blindingly obvious. But his awareness extended only to the delays and obstacles put in the way of the Acadians' really quite rapid resurgence toward their place in History.

Canadians for the last hundred years. Thus the critical apparatus they had available for interpreting these vast phenomena was rather primitive. They took the measure of these cataclysms by applying the standards of a clerical and theocratic society, motivated by a nationalism of survival which was basically conservative.

What I have just said may seem outrageously simplistic. But when we try to identify the prime factors, the essential aspects of such a complex situation, how can we avoid simplification? No doubt it would be possible to find thousands of people who did not fall within my classification in the 1920s and '30s. Thousands, but not millions. And the clerical–nationalist ideology was certainly the dominant one. Those who opposed it (e.g., T.-D. Bouchard or Jean-Charles Harvey) quickly became a fringe phenomenon, if they were not that from the beginning. Their voices did not succeed in making themselves heard over all the speeches, sermons, teachings and writings, insistent and unanimous, that hammered their message into people's brains the year round.

One might succeed in unsettling one or other of the two pillars of the temple, that is, in attacking either clericalism *or* nationalism, but never both at once. Olivar Asselin, for example, after his condemnation by the Archbishop of Quebec, had ceased publication of his newspaper *L'Ordre* with the famous sally in the last line of the last page: "To be continued under the next cardinal." But in nationalist circles Asselin was very well thought of. Conversely, many politicians openly opposed the nationalist orthodoxy of the time. But they were very careful not to attack the authority of the clergy, even in areas where its presence was unwarranted. The electoral price to be paid for such an undertaking would have been much too high.

In short, the women and men of my generation were faced after the way by a stalled society that put up prodigious resistance to our fondest aspirations. The war and the universal sigh of relief at its termination had left a deep mark on all of us. But Quebec society, its attention absorbed by the war, had unsuspectingly hatched a strange brood. We were different. Even our older brothers and sisters were surprised when they became aware of us. Our concerns were no longer theirs. The young women who came out of the wartime factories, where they had spent the sensitive years of their adolescence, bore little resemblance to their older sisters who, having married in haste in 1940 to exempt their fiancés from military service, had quickly adapted to the traditional cast of the Quebec family. For the first time an authentic labour movement, the JOC,[2] had trained men and women among the young workers to be militants of a new type, socially aware and ready to act. The JEC[3] had done the same thing among the students.

It would take a long essay to explain all the factors that made us a genuinely new generation, one clearly cut off from the preceding one. We had come out of a major industrial revolution which, between 1939 and 1945, had radically transformed Quebec society. But the authorities at the time knew nothing of this, and we ourselves were only dimly aware of it. Only as we entered adult life did we become wide awake.

That life was not a particularly easy one.

*   *   *

Ever since René Lévesque's victory in Quebec, journalists have been seized by a harmless mania that impels them from time to time to go on about our "isolation." Louis-Bernard Robitaille of *La Presse*, for example, asked me in January 1979 whether the men of my age who were partisans of federalism did not feel very lonely among the Quebec nationalists. Were we not cut off from the living forces of the nation? Two months later Denise Bombardier returned to this theme in a television interview: we must be suffering terribly from the loss of all our friends, mustn't we?

I hardly knew what to say in reply to these naive and no

---

[2][JOC: Jeunesse ouvrière catholique (Young Catholic Workers, YCW) Tr.]
[3][JEC: Jeunesse étudiante catholique (Young Catholic Students, YCS). Tr.]

doubt well-intentioned questions.

What friends had I lost? None, so far as I knew. By definition, those who might have edged away from us because of a divergency of opinion could not be considered friends as I understand the word. I quoted the thirteenth-century poet Rutebeuf:

> Ce sont amis que vent emporte.[4]

And why should the secessionist forces in Quebec be more "living" than the others? Why should I feel isolated as long as I have comrades and allies in every sphere of life: militants in the labour movement, the cooperative movement, writers, journalists?

What I did not admit—no doubt to avoid sounding like the grandfather I am—was how ludicrous I found these questions. To talk to men of my generation about their present "isolation" is like deploring a passing shower in front of veterans of the flood. If I wanted to feel isolated now, I would have to forget how we felt just after the war. Those were days in which we were advancing almost alone in an alien world. Our brief experience of life had made us so different that our own community refused to recognize us.

I think of Lieutenant René Lévesque, just out of uniform, telling of his discovery of Dachau, the first death camp liberated by the Allies. "Disgusting propaganda, they've brainwashed you!" cried good nationalist bourgeois, not one of whom had ventured outside Quebec City during all the years of war.

I think of Pierre Trudeau as a student, back in Montreal after Harvard, the London School of Economics and the Paris faculty of Political Science. When he applied for a position as professor, the faculties of the Université de Montréal slammed the door in his face. Yet the teaching of political science there was notoriously weak. In certain disciplines—including Trudeau's specialization—it was non-

---

[4] ["These are but friends that turn with every wind." Tr.]

existent. But was that a reason, in Duplessis's era, for hiring a young graduate who had taken courses from the *communist* Harold Laski, who had carried bad taste to the point of spending a while in Paris when Maurice Thorez was still a member of the French government?

As for Jean Marchand, he was already too solidly established in the labour movement to be easily uprooted. But what an orchestration of calumny accompanied his name! He had *perverted* the unions he led. Peaceful and submissive until his time, the members of the CTCC were turning into dangerous anarchists under his leadership. He was organizing subversion, calling useless strikes and encouraging violence. He was an intellectual. He had insinuated himself under false pretences among honest workers who, unschooled, could not realize what was being done to them. These were the things being said about Marchand.

In my own case, it was with the clergy that I was in trouble. Years of activity within the ranks of the Catholic Action movement didn't clear me with our religious leaders: they merely made me more suspect. Was it not abnormal that I, having been admitted to the inner sanctum, should flaunt opinions that strayed from the official line? I had been close to the clergy and to the bishops, and now I had the ingratitude to say that in a number of areas they were usurping the authority of the laity. These spiritual leaders were unaware that many of their younger priests thought exactly as we did, and feared the consequences such abuses could bring down upon the Church itself. They were so blind (and here exceptions like Archbishop Charbonneau merely prove the rule) that they did not even suspect the danger. A certain bishop reassured himself (after some article we published in *Cité libre*): "They're a timid lot; they'll give in to our first pastoral letter."

But behind these bishops and priests, superiors of orders and communities, behind the rectors of universities, company presidents and factory managers, at the origin of every refusal, every calumny, we always found the same man:

Maurice Duplessis.

In writing this I am not being gulled by any mythology nor giving in to an easy generalization. It would be absurd to attribute to any one man all the complex ills from which our society was suffering. Yet it is perfectly true that we found his spoor and his agency at the origin of every attempt to preserve all that was obsolete in Quebec. Many players were skilful on the instruments of reaction, but he conducted the band. A brilliant manipulator, every kind of conservatism was grist for his political mill: social, religious, philosophical, cultural. He was not the only petty dictator to see freedom as a threat and change as a disaster, but he was the most intelligent, the craftiest, the most astute and the least burdened with scruples.

Not all reactionaries of the day liked Mr. Duplessis, who, by the way, was not a likeable man. But they saw their reflection in him. Their fears were his, and his skill in banishing those fears made him acceptable.

For us, the precise opposite was true. Maurice Duplessis's reign had coincided with our youth. We were emerging from adolescence when he came to power, and we were getting on for forty when he lost it. And during those twenty years it was not only occasional disagreements that found us in opposition to him, but an inevitable, deep and unrelenting rejection of his most cherished assumptions. One might say, in short, that Maurice Duplessis applied, all through his life, the complete opposite of the policies of which we dreamed. Our generation had realized that the collectivity of Quebec was behind the times, and that it must at all costs be brought up to date without delay, accelerating the process the wartime period had begun. But Duplessis and his cronies leaned hard with all their considerable weight on every available brake.

It was inevitable that the first confrontation should come in the trade union area, first of all because manual labourers were the chief victims of our collective backwardness. The working class was just beginning to come out of the veritable hell it had experienced in the depression of the '30s: massive unemployment and starvation wages,[5] urban slums, an infant mortality rate which reached a nightmare level in the working-class areas of Montreal, poor primary education and the lowest school attendance rate in Canada. This litany of misery would be almost endless if we undertook to recite it in its entirety.

Worst of all, our society got along very well with this state of affairs, for the simple reason that it had never given it a thought. In our official ideology at that time there was just no place for the working class. Factory workers were intruders in the scheme of things. They had the bad taste to exist. Wouldn't it have been easier for everyone if they had remained farmers, as in the beginning, minding their own business out there in the countryside (except in 1837), or if they had joined the middle class! At least one would have been able to talk to them. As things now stood, our traditional thinkers had nothing to say to these masses of uprooted country folk who set up some kind of housekeeping in the rather sordid discomfort of our working-class suburbs. Why the devil did they have to turn up there?

All through my childhood, in school and in church, I had listened *ad nauseam* to condemnations of city life—it was the source of all evil, the chosen breeding ground of every vice, a laboratory culture of all the sins, starting with alcoholism. This preaching was so persistent that one ended up wondering why all those fools of manual labourers had left their country paradise for an urban hell. Was it stupidity on their part, or mischief? We could think of no other possible motives. The official ideology played down rural poverty. If young people were thronging into the cities, it was because they rejected the austerity of rural life; they were lazy, and attracted by the mirage of an easy city life.

Some of our teachers at Nicolet, in the first college of my adolescence, made no secret of their contempt for the status

---

[5]A textile worker in 1936 worked 25 to 50 hours to buy a pair of shoes, at rates of 10 to 20 cents an hour.

of the working man. A boy from Asbestos, whose monthly report card left much to be desired, was told in public, when the marks were read out, that he deserved to be sent back to the mine, to "pick cotton" with his father and brothers because that was about all he was good for. In view of the dominant ideology, factory life had no dignity of its own; it was useful only to set off the bucolic charms of working on the farm. I can recall not a single sermon or speech that extolled work in industry or even recognized its social utility.

In short, our ideology turned its back on the industrial world, in which our people had actually been involved for nearly a hundred years. The ideology cultivated agriculturalism. In the trough of the Great Depression, it had no other remedy to propose for the utter poverty of the workers but a "back to the land" movement, the settlement of Abitibi and other outlying regions of Quebec. But the living conditions of those settlers had to be seen to be believed. Our skiing expeditions, when I was studying at Mont-Laurier in 1938–39, allowed me to see them at first hand.

It often happened that, when the cold grew too intense, we would knock at the door of some young farmer newly established in the region, who would invite us inside to get warm. I will never forget the meticulous cleanliness of those houses, nor their frightful poverty. Bedcovers hung on lines served as partitions. If we happened to arrive during a meal, we, the well-fed students from the Collège de la Santé,[6] were shamed by the sight of the meatless meal on the table: the potatoes or buckwheat cakes that were the staple food of these "conquerors of the soil" glorified by the official propaganda. Later, as a union worker, I was to rediscover at Normétal sons of Abitibi settlers whom the war had turned into underground miners. One evening during a strike, I asked one of them what had prompted his family to uproot itself from the east end of Montreal in the thirties.

---

[6]Our institution was so-called because it accepted "in the good mountain air" those students threatened by tuberculosis.

"We never came up here to get rich," he replied. "We knew it wasn't going to be easy, landing in the middle of the bush and having to do work we'd forgotten how to do years before. You know, I think my parents came *to hide their poverty* in Abitibi. They didn't expect much more than that."

Our generation had become aware of that poverty by degrees, thanks to the depression and, after it, the war. It was a physical poverty, but, even more, intellectual and spiritual. When Father Henri Roy, the rather eccentric visionary who founded the Canadian YCW, cried out in 1935: "Let us *help* the helpless," we all understood at once. It was obvious that he was talking about a whole generation of youth in rags, leaving school at the age of twelve and pounding the streets of our cities all through our endless winters, searching for work that was not there. But he also meant boys and girls who were really on their own, looked after and cared about by no one. If they were not orphans, bastards or diseased, the good works of the clergy were not destined for them. Poverty in those days was living the normal life of a young unemployed worker. The Jesuits' ACJC,[7] which was Catholic and nationalist, had a helping hand only for the middle class or for college students about to join that class. In any case the young workers would have understood nothing of the literary works of that ACJC with its campaigns for "speaking proper French" or for bilingual stamps and money. The working class had other things to worry about.

The workers were paying for Quebec's long inaction in social welfare legislation. By the time our first industrial safety legislation was adopted, Ontario had had its own for twenty-seven years. The same applied to compulsory schooling, the women's vote, and Quebec's first steps against industrial illnesses. The middle class cannot be said to have suffered from this long delay. On the contrary, it

---

[7][*Association catholique de la jeunesse canadienne*: Catholic Association of Canadian Youth. Tr.]

spontaneously reacted to each innovation in the field, however late in coming, as if it were a threat to our traditions, to our "French and Catholic" way of life, or a grave danger to provincial autonomy within Confederation.

In this connection, one reads with amazement in the memoirs of Lionel Groulx his pages on the establishment of family allowances and old-age pensions by the Canadian government. Not for a moment does the good Canon linger over the merits of the Act. The poverty of large families, the fate of the underprivileged, the slavery of mothers in working-class neighbourhoods—these are not worthy of his attention. All that concerns him is the federal encroachment on the province's constitutional territory. Friends of his organize a vehement protest against the Act. They try to persuade Joseph Charbonneau, Archbishop of Montreal, to speak out publicly against the measure. And when the Archbishop replies: "There is poverty to be relieved; I don't care a fig where the money comes from," the Canon wonders, "Where are these maunderings going to lead him?"[8] Not once does he question the propriety of his own stubborn attempt to rouse the Archbishop against a government that had offended neither against morality nor the doctrine of the Church.

Are we dreaming?

Not at all. That was the spirit of the times. The episode took place toward the mid-1940s. In Quebec the Godbout government—identified with the war, with conscription, and the paternalistic federalism practised by Ottawa, but also with some progressive measures—was in its last days. Maurice Duplessis would soon be in power. A first timid movement toward modernization would be taken in hand by the new premier. And suffocated.

With Duplessis, Quebec entered on a long period of reactionary government. Unsettled by six years in a state of war, worried by the early signs of change, our clerical–nationalist middle class rallied almost entirely around the

---

[8] Lionel Groulx, *Mes mémoires* (Montreal: Fides, 1974), Vol. IV, p. 269.

tough leader it had chosen. Gone was the time of even the most tentative thrusts toward the modernization of society. Of course there was no question of abolishing the women's vote or compulsory schooling, or any of the other few liberal measures adopted by the Godbout government. The *Chef* was too cunning to show his colours so openly. It was better first to extol the values of the past, glorify traditions without question, and slowly create a climate that would later make it possible to reject any kind of progress, in the name of our history, our imperishable values and the struggle against communism.

It must be admitted that in the early days of his reign, Mr. Duplessis had the benefit of a protracted want of vigilance on our part. And to tell the truth, if we had been wide awake it would not have greatly changed the course of events. Our generation was on the way to the front, but not yet in position. Of the names I have in mind, only Jean Marchand was already in action, but on the periphery, rather far from the centre. Pierre Trudeau was studying in London and Paris, then touring the world with a rucksack. René Lévesque, when he was demobilized from the American army, joined the CBC's International Service, which meant that his voice, that strange, husky voice, would be known in Africa before it became familiar in Canada.

My memory identifies two landmarks from the early days of this regime.

The first was the summer of '44. My wife and I were running a camp for young people that year at Saint-Jovite, north of Montreal, set up for the summer in the splendour of the Laurentians. Cut off from the world, surrounded by students of both sexes who had come to discuss cooperatives, journalism and the uses of leisure, we were barely aware of the provincial election that was storming through Quebec. It took an excursion to Quebec City to bring me back to political reality. Pierre Juneau and I had struck out together on a July morning. As we were hitchhiking just outside Joliette in the early afternoon, chance would have it that we were picked up by Antonio Barrette, a Union Nationale member of the legislative assembly.

Though he didn't know us from Adam, he at once stated the purpose of his trip to the capital: "I smell cabinet down that way," he declared, obviously elated. "I'm going to see if there isn't a portfolio for me!"

Only then did I remember that Duplessis had come to power two days before. And I still recall, not without astonishment, that this new development had left me cold, as did the long monologue served up to us that day in his car by Mr. Barrette, future minister of Labour and future premier. All I remember of it is his diatribe against the *Bloc populaire*, André Laurendeau's party, which, according to the victorious member, had "distorted the election results" by its participation.

"Do you realize," fulminated Mr. Barrette, "that those so-called nationalists, a minority party and beaten before they started, might have lost us the election? You can see what they were up to. They defeated one of our people in Mercier, Edouard Asselin, a great nationalist. Laurendeau must be proud of himself. He barely managed to get elected. But the results show what a dreamer he was. The real nationalists, that's us, the Union Nationale. Who needed that *Bloc populaire*?"

I failed to find Mr. Barrette's indignation infectious. I knew Laurendeau, and respected him more than any other politician. I also knew that the Union Nationale, to pull off its victory, had (like the Liberals) showered the province copiously with election funds. But its rise to power left me quite indifferent.

It was to take three years, two of them spent in Europe, for me to become brutally aware of the consequences of this—unfortunately—major event.

In the spring of 1947, an edition of *Le Devoir*, already old when I laid hands on it in Paris, awoke me out of my somnolence. It contained an editorial by Gérard Filion, the new publisher of the newspaper. This article, entitled "Social justice dispensed by the truncheon,"[9] launched the *social* opposition to Maurice Duplessis in Quebec. In it, Filion commented on the use of the Provincial Police against the strikers at the Ayerst factory in Lachute. This was the face-off for an open struggle against Duplessis's reactionary forces, a struggle in which we ourselves were soon to be involved up to our necks—much sooner than we could foresee.

It was also the beginning of the *Grande noirceur*, the Great Darkness, as we later called this period of our history. For the time being the windows that had been opened a crack by the war were closed again. The Authorities were settling their accounts with the champions of progress. And of course the blows rained down first on the heads of the most deprived: the textile workers.

From that date onward Mr. Duplessis relentlessly stepped up his efforts against the rise of the union movement. In 1948 there was the episode of Bill 5, a veritable legal straitjacket which he tried to impose on trade unionism. But the unions had already smelled danger. For the first time all the rival federations, Canadian and American, formed a united front. They even got the unhoped-for support of a sacerdotal commission set up by the episcopate of Quebec to advise the Church on social questions. This time, Mr. Duplessis had acted without thinking. The resistance surprised him. He was not ready to face up to a united union movement (it must first be divided against itself) or a minority in the Church (he would have to find a way to discredit it). He retreated. But a year later, in February 1949, the asbestos strike broke out.

The Great Darkness, then, had a social origin. The prime objective was to keep Quebec workers in their place. But their *place* did not exist. I have already mentioned that the dominant ideology did not assign them a place. It ignored them. Mr. Duplessis himself, who professed the social doc-

---

[9]*Le Devoir*, Montreal, May 17, 1947. [*La justice sociale à coups de matraque.* Tr.]

trines of a nineteenth-century country notary, held to his conservatism with a religious fervour. For him, the workers' movement represented evil and subversion. He must have known that wages in Quebec were among the lowest in the whole of North America, that housing conditions in our cities were deplorable, and that the worker's life was still a very hard one, despite post-war prosperity. But that seemed normal to him.

During his first mandate as premier (1936–39), he had given Quebec the Reasonable Wage Bill, which was simply a minimum wage law. And this step, in his eyes, had settled the question once and for all.

Any improvement in the worker's position, and the very idea of a modern system of social security, were in his view a defiance of law and order. He could not imagine that this kind of progress was compatible with a prosperous economy and a peaceful society. Those who promoted such measures were a danger to property, religion and social harmony. Mr. Duplessis believed this profoundly. He was capable of duplicity on any other subject: his religious practice had a theatrical side, his nationalism was no more than an instrument of power to which he was attached as the master is to his dog, by a leash of variable length, according to the needs of the moment. But no one could call in question the sincerity of his basic conservatism. The *Chef*, where that was concerned, never swerved from his path.

To be sure, the Duplessis regime was never totalitarian in the full sense of the word. Quebec's imbrication with Canada, and the atmosphere that prevailed after the war in the Western world, made that kind of adventure impractical. But it is well known that extreme conservatism engenders intolerance, which leads to repression. After the union leaders, who were the great aversion of the regime, the next targets were the intellectuals, or, as the *Chef* called them, the "piano players." His little joke caught on quickly in the Union Nationale. It was convenient because of its imprecision, which allowed it to be applied indiscriminately to the

most ignorant reporter or the most learned professor, as well
as to artists or teachers or anyone who might be seen
sneaking into a library. The term "intellectual," already in
disrepute, became the favourite insult employed by our
rulers.

Any opponent of Mr. Duplessis, unless he was an illiterate
or a travelling salesman, became by the very fact of his
opposition an intellectual and a communist. According to
this usage one might have thought the two terms were
synonymous. It was only logical that the premier himself
strenuously avoided any suspect activity of the mind. He
proclaimed one day before the whole Assembly that he had
"never read a book since he left college." Was he clowning?
No. This was a profound stratagem. The politician was
counting on the inveterate mistrust in which the average
Quebecer, who still had only a modicum of schooling, held
those who had noticeably more. To be sure, the *Chef* was, as
Olivar Asselin quipped, "a lawyer like everybody else." But
this was precisely why, in order to be forgiven for his
privileged status and to make people forget it, he had to
show that he set no store by it. In any case it was part of his
performance to encourage the basest prejudices. He never
failed to do so, for he was certain that for him they were the
surest weapons against his critics. There was one, for example, that he was to cultivate all his life with the greatest care:
the anti-French prejudice.

Duplessis knew exactly how emotionally ambivalent
French-speaking Quebecers were toward France. On the
one hand it was their mother-country, "the old country," the
land of their origin which they had never forgotten or ceased
to love. But it was also the promised land of culture, seat of
every kind of elegance, including that of language—the one
in which we were most lacking. Compared with our transat-
lantic cousins who came to Canada as visitors or immigrants, the Quebecer of the '40s often felt like a bumpkin,
dull and uncouth. This, of course, made him aggressive
toward his rich relative, who was more cultivated, a better

talker and more worldly-wise than he. We have not left very far behind us this defensive reaction of the *Canadien* to the verbal sparkle, the gift of the gab, and the self-assurance of the "damned Frenchman." How much ambiguity was hidden in that common term of abuse, tinged with envy and grudging affection!

The *Chef*, on the contrary, always paraded a somewhat overdone superiority complex. To a French writer who had just given an inoffensive lecture in Montreal on "Reading: The Unpunished Vice," Duplessis one day publicly served up his favourite lesson in comparative civilization.

Quebecers, he explained with utter seriousness, were improved Frenchmen. Why, because their educational system, the best in the world, gave first place to the teaching of religion. And because the Church had, throughout their history, protected them from all revolutionary ferment, while France was now succumbing to socialism, the antechamber of communism. (Mr. Duplessis was very fond of this "antechamber," and considered it one of his best verbal conceits.) Moreover, France had been infected for centuries by the microbe of atheism, source of all social contagions. (He was equally fond of his "contagions.") Quebec was sorry for poor France, on which the freethinkers, that contemporary revolutionary plague, had inflicted two wars in twenty years.

Launched on his favourite theme, Mr. Duplessis knew no caution. Head thrown back, paunch protruding, his voice grown shrill and his glance sly and mischievous, he recited his tirade to the bitter end, waving his short arms under the nose of his flabbergasted guest. The audience of the *Société d'études et de conférences* (study and lecture society) was most upset. Their invitation to the premier had no doubt been issued in the hope of obtaining a grant. The *Chef* had given them a tedious sermon.

This kind of humbug was good for a laugh. On this occasion André Laurendeau jumped at the opportunity. In *Le Devoir* he published a mocking, cruel little article which explained Mr. Duplessis's performance under the title, "Non-reading: the vice receives its punishment." Unfortunately one had to take Duplessis's historical analysis seriously to the extent that it inspired the basic attitude of our rulers. It was in the name of this thesis that the regime persecuted freedom of thought, fought the intellectuals, held culture in contempt and dreaded all contact with the plague-bearer, France.

If the doctrine of the regime as expressed by the *Chef* was coarse-grained and primitive, it was even more grotesque in the versions one heard from his ministers.

The Provincial Secretary, for example, who acted as minister of Cultural Affairs, refused to consider the disheartening level of school attendance as a problem. In a speech in Montreal's Plateau Hall, he advised his critics "...rather to be grateful to Providence for keeping our children out of school: they might have learned English." And the minister of Youth (oh, yes! Mr. Paul Sauvé himself) on the radio one day denounced the champions of free education. They were, he said, trying to bring misfortune on the people. "If they had their way, do you think taxi-drivers would be happier with a degree in literature?"

But there were others besides the ministers; a whole pack of subaltern sycophants added its cries to those of the ministerial hounds. When Mr. Duplessis had his film censors ban Marcel Carné's marvellous *Enfants du Paradis* a journalist close to the government commented, paraphrasing the Bible: "We asked our motherland for bread: France gave us a—scandalous—stone!" Thus encouraged, they chopped away with a will at all the great films, especially French ones, to the point where *Le Rouge et le Noir*, for example, became utterly incomprehensible because of their senseless amputations.

Freedom of the universities was a special target of the regime. Using the rectors as intermediaries, the authorities harassed anyone who stood up, even timidly, to the shabby conservatism of the *Chef* or the discipline of the clergy. In

Quebec City, the Faculty of Social Sciences and its dean, Father Georges-Henri Lévesque, provided an ideal quarry. A focus of resistance to Duplessis's arch-conservatism, the institution was to pay the price for the nonconformity it fostered. The tale of this persistent persecution is too long to tell here, but I will give just one example of it. At the time of the asbestos strike, the rector of Laval University, Monsignor Vandry, threatened to expel two students, Henri Schmidt and Guy Rocher, who were to deliver strike relief money collected from their fellow students for the Asbestos miners. I was a young reporter for *Le Devoir* at the time, and when I pressed the good prelate to state the reasons for his action, he answered in all innocence:

"But of course this decision was inspired by Mr. Duplessis. Look, you know how the premier feels about this strike. Don't be a fool!"

"I'm not being a fool, I just want to know why the university kowtows to the government. Are you afraid he'll cut off your rations?"

"Not at all. Don't dramatize. Laval is dependent on no one. If I had to, I could get along without the government. And in any case, he couldn't starve us out. That would create a scandal."

"Well, then?"

"Well, what? If we don't behave ourselves, Mr. Duplessis will take his revenge. You know how he is. He'll take it out on small things—fifty thousand dollars for a laboratory, twenty-five thousand for renovating a lecture-room—small subsidies, I grant you, but they mean serious problems if they are cut off. Do you think I'm going to risk such annoyances just to allow two students to visit miners who are out on an *illegal* strike? Not on your life! For that matter, why don't you take the money they collected to Asbestos? You go there often, don't you? Then Schmidt and Rocher can stay here and the Board of the university will not have to consider their expulsion."

"And what about the freedom of the university? What

becomes of that?"

"Freedom? But we *are* free! What are you talking about? One can be free and still have common sense."

Disarming candour in a sixty-year-old churchman. On the surface, a shepherd among wolves. But this apparent good faith, this unctuous simplicity, masked certain less peaceful inclinations. After my article appeared in print, Monsignor Vandry chose the occasion of a reunion of his alumni in Trois-Rivières to issue a public condemnation of *Le Devoir* and launch a subscription-cancellation campaign against the paper.

A decade later, in *Requiem for a clique*,[10] Marcel Rioux commented on the fall of the Union Nationale party:

> We cannot bid farewell to the regime without mentioning the respectable citizens. Where were they, and what were they all doing during that long return to the Middle Ages? ... A large and worthy majority of them sailed a zigzag course, adjusted and adapted to the regime; the more daring among them denounced the leftists. But in the very heat of the struggle those in high places took their precautions, didn't go too far, sheltered behind ambiguities and hedged their bets in dozens of small ways. Among the clergy, only a few lowly priests denounced the regime; the others gave a hearty blessing to the fruits of patronage.

And those who failed to give their blessing, clerics or lay-men, felt the wrath of the secular arm.

Is it known, for example (I have never seen it mentioned), that *Le Devoir* was the object of a remarkably slick variety of persecution? As soon as an industrial or business firm bought advertising space in our pages, it would receive a visit from a tout for the regime. There were no threats, only blandishments.

---

[10]*Cité libre* no. 30, October 1960, pp. 3–4.

"If you withdraw your ad, the government will give you a big contract. Interested?"

Luckily not *too* many advertisers were interested, or the paper would have died. Which, by the way, it almost did anyway. But that is another story. Mr. Duplessis couldn't get over the failure of his operation designed to make *Le Devoir* his creature. It was perhaps his only failure in an undertaking of that kind.

"Getting the bishops to eat out of his hand," as he himself so elegantly put it, proved an easier task. Not all of them ate there. But most of these men, fenced in by the theocratic structures of our society, constrained by the pressing needs of their good works, found themselves defenceless in the face of this sabre-toothed predator. We must remember that at the time in question the Quebec episcopate and the clergy (I am intentionally avoiding the word Church, which suggests quite a different reality) were still in charge of a great many of the normal functions of a modern State. They dominated education, from primary school to university. Through the religious orders they owned or managed almost all the hospitals. Their good works took the place of social security and public welfare for orphans, young delinquents, vagrants, the handicapped, the blind, the deaf and dumb, and many more I could mention. The clergy were into everything, and everywhere powerful.

The trouble was that for a long time private charity had been unable to fill the needs of these voracious undertakings. The bishops, the clergy and the orders, which had originally supplied both personnel and money to innumerable institutions, were now obliged to count on the public purse to keep this immense *private* machinery in motion. The rector of Laval might maintain as he wished that his university was dependent on no one (Louis XIV had endowed the *Petit Seminaire de Québec* royally in the seventeenth century) but his financial autonomy barely sufficed to cover his operating costs. The new campus at Ste-Foy was built with public funds. As for the Université de Montréal, it was at the end of its tether, as were the colleges, the day nurseries, the orphanages and the hospitals. Still powerful in appearance, the bishops, priests and superiors were bound in the future to be dependent on the bounty of the Prince. Thus almost all religious communities were turned into mendicant orders. They *had* to eat out of the hand of the authorities, or see their tens of thousands of dependants die of hunger, or their secular education, already feeble, perish for want of funds.

Our spiritual leaders were thus embroiled, willy-nilly, in permanent negotiations with the political authorities. This was a role for which they were ill prepared. Theology and canon law provided neither the ideal sword or shield with which to confront the cynicism of our political fauna.

The *Chef* liked to repeat that "you don't fight elections with prayers." Influence-peddling was the rule in his government. There was no such thing as a statutory subsidy in his day. Not one was granted as a right under the law. They were all distributed at the arbitrary discretion of partisan politicians. Each grant was treated as an event, with pictures in the papers of smiling prelates expressing their gratitude to Mr. Duplessis. The regime *gave presents*. (Every public subsidy was in fact presented as a "donation," not from the State but from the Union Nationale.) But it gave without generosity or impartiality. The religious personnel in the institutions worked for starvation wages, and the lay employees, almost always serving in subaltern functions, received a bare pittance. The regime found it convenient to put the blame on the clergy for this stinginess. Better still, it demanded in return for its "donations" the support of the religious authorities, or at least a collusive silence on its abuses of power and its misuse of funds.

If some leftist of our kind had the audacity to call for modern hospitalization insurance, Mr. Duplessis would retort: "Why, we have that kind of insurance now. It is provided by our religious communities, whose devotion to duty is questioned only by the agents of subversion. And in any case, the best medical insurance is health."

Thus was established the inevitable collusion between an excessive clericalism and a corrupt regime. Did the bishops and clergy really want this alliance of the throne and the altar? Probably not—not consciously. But the spiritual powers had for a long time exceeded their proper role. By dint of taking over functions that were rightly those of the State, often out of necessity, often in a spirit of service, but often, too, out of ambition, the churchmen had extended their empire well beyond its natural frontiers. Henceforth they would pay the price of this mistake. They were trapped.

Of course it was not the Duplessis regime that gave rise to clericalism. Duplessis discovered it ready-made, the residue of centuries of history. But he knew how to exploit the churchmen's conservatism to the full in order to consolidate his power.

This was the start of an odd one-upmanship in clericalism between the episcopate and the civil authorities. It was the unalterable rule, officially observed by the government, that everything the clergy did was deserving of public approbation. On this point there could be no discussion. But the premier knew that in a day or a month the churchmen would be in his office with outstretched hands. There, safe from curious ears, he would put the screws on them. He would, of course, spare their honour and their dignity. He asked neither for declarations of support nor for compromising flattery, nor yet for public submission to his dictates. All he wanted was their silence.

As Pierre Vadeboncoeur said in another connection: "Not a word. Not even a blessed word."

There were, indeed, a few bishops and priests who identified themselves publicly with the regime and openly supported it. But most of them were only obliging fellow-travellers, silent and efficacious. And those who had the temerity to resist, those few progressive liberals in the episcopate who refused to surrender, were harassed by the government or rendered harmless by their own colleagues.

Jean Marchand said to me one day in the 1950s: "The silence of the bishops is getting scandalous. Yes, I know, it's not their job to denounce the excesses of the government one by one. That's up to us. But when Duplessis turns favouritism into a political *doctrine*, they have no right to keep their mouths shut."

We had just listened to a speech by the *Chef* in which he proclaimed: "I'm warning the voters: the ridings that vote the wrong way [i.e., against the Duplessis candidates] shouldn't expect the government to build them any bridges or improve their roads or modernize their schools and hospitals."

And these were not vain threats. If you drove through the province you could tell by the quality of the roads for whom this or that region had voted. Some stretches on the main highways (for example, the south shore autoroute between Montreal and Quebec City) remained death-traps until the end of the regime, because Saint-Hyacinthe and the Richelieu valley had voted the wrong way. And the town of Shawinigan had to get along with a decrepit, dangerous bridge over the Saint-Maurice River (which divides the town), because the local union members had elected an opposition candidate.

Marchand was right. We were no longer talking about a camouflaged, clandestine practice, but a clearly stated political principle. The public purse was no longer used for the good of the population, but for the preservation of power in the hands of a clique.

Yet the official voices of the Church, those of the bishops, remained silent. Since the exile of Archbishop Charbonneau, "a few lowly priests" were allowed to write and speak, particularly Gérard Dion and Louis O'Neill, who spoke out courageously at their own risk. But at the top of the hierarchy they did not go beyond very general statements or highly anonymous communiqués.

Were we living under a dictatorship? No. Rather under an

absolute monarchy, that of the Sun-King Duplessis, as Réginald Boisvert baptized him in an article in *Cité libre*.

Maurice Duplessis did not say, "L'Etat, c'est moi." He
said, "The State is the Union Nationale." And the Union
Nationale was Duplessis. He was the sole occupant of the
political space. He liked to surround himself with mediocri-
ties. The others, the ones with talent, had to keep it dark or
become suspect. For example, they were forbidden to appear on television because the *Chef* himself avoided the
cameras. Some men of remarkable intelligence, like Daniel
Johnson and Paul Sauvé, accepted silent roles. In this play
only one actor had lines. Sauvé, after the death of the *Chef*,
freely admitted during a press conference: "As a minister I
was responsible neither for the management *nor for the
policy* of the government."[11] His admission says much about
the role of a minister in that team.

Did Mr. Duplessis have an economic policy? Yes, but it
was barely fit to print.

In the early 1950s I made the acquaintance of Herbert
Lank, then president of Dupont of Canada. We were both
taking part in a symposium that the University of Rochester
(N.Y.) had organized on the theme of Canada–U.S. relations. One evening, after a number of glasses of American
bourbon at the Faculty Club, the industrialist told me a
story which has stayed with me in all its details. (I have also
not forgotten the awful hangover with which I woke up next
morning. I still bear a grudge against our southern neigh-
bours' whiskey).

Duplessis had just imposed his direct provincial income
tax, which especially affected industrial management. The
Canadian Chamber of Commerce wanted to make representations to the premier of Quebec.

"But whom could we send? The choice was not easy,"
explained Herbert Lank. "In the first place, the messenger
for all these great unilingual captains of industry had to be
able to speak French. For once, being in the position of

---

[11]CBC press conference, December 29, 1959. Italics are mine.

asking favours, they insisted on that. But our spokesman must also owe nothing to Mr. Duplessis, for that would have changed the game. But all, or almost all, of these gentlemen had asked him for favours, and received them. Their complaint about the new tax would have rung hollow."

(Thanks, no doubt, to the bourbon, Herbert Lank had quite forgotten that he was talking to a militant trade unionist.)

"It just happened," he went on, "that I fulfilled the two conditions. I was born in the States and had studied at the Sorbonne when I was young, and I can get along in your language. [His French was remarkably good.] What was more, I had never asked the premier for anything, nor received anything from him. Nor did I expect anything from his munificence."

"So you accepted the mission."

"Yes, but not very enthusiastically, I assure you. I don't like dealing with men who are crafty and intelligent at the same time. But how could I refuse? Well, I went to Quebec, was admitted to the august presence, and made my little speech. You can imagine how it went: anxiety of industry over this new tax that affected management personnel. It would have the effect of discouraging them. For example, if a firm wanted to move a specially talented young administrator from Winnipeg to Montreal, he would probably refuse the posting because of this new tax that was coming on top of several others. I emphasized, in conclusion, that Quebecers would now be more heavily taxed than the citizens of other provinces: there was no more certain way of frightening the managers away. Mr. Duplessis cut me short and declared in a tone that brooked no contradiction: 'Your managers, Mr. Lank, are materialists. You're in a spiritual province here.' Was he serious? I could hardly believe it. But I had to play his game. 'That may be, Mr. Premier, but just the same it's those materialists you need to develop industry in Quebec.'

"I had touched a raw nerve. Duplessis stood up, wounded to the quick. He walked around his desk until he was standing in front of me, his index finger pointing upward: 'Listen to me, Lank. You're not going to tell me how to develop a province. I know how better than you. In Quebec, we have two ways of attracting industries and keeping them here. The first way: natural resources. That's what counts. That's what you companies want. I know that and so do you. All right. And those natural resources, I don't sell them to you, I don't rent them to you, I give them to you. And your managers complain about a little tax? There's a second way: manpower. Quebec's manpower costs you less and gives you less trouble than any work force in Canada, not to mention the United States. And my government, the Union Nationale, takes care of that for you. And you have the gall to come crying to me, you, the bosses!'"

Herbert Lank could not possibly have invented this dialogue, with its striking and unmistakeable resemblance to Duplessis's style.

So much for his economic policy.

Obviously, not all Quebecers agreed with it at the time. But the *Chef* had a talent for dodging problems that was close to genius. Solidly supported by the leading citizens and most of the clergy, skilful at manipulating passions, rivalries, greed and fear, he managed to keep himself (and us) in a state that was almost devoid of progress. The economy was prosperous, and the workers' movement, still underdeveloped, was mainly dominated by the international unions (i.e., American), offshoots of the American Federation of Labor, business-oriented unions if one ever saw such. Mr. Duplessis, then, had a free hand.

If by any chance a squeak developed in this well-oiled mechanism, the *Chef* had extra lubricants of rare efficiency: nationalism and the guerrilla war against the federal government. For him they served in place of a constitutional policy.

"An old nationalist like me," he loved to repeat, "leader of the *National* Union party." He used nationalism for his own partisan purposes, without respecting either its objectives or its deeper aspirations. Paraphrasing Henri IV, for example, he might have said that an electoral victory was worth a flag.[12] In any case, this was how Quebec came to inherit the fleur-de-lis banner, which from the beginning was endowed with a strange vocation. It was first used to grace election posters in the 1948 campaign, its white cross covering consciences bought and sold, stolen votes and other misdeeds that ran the gamut to violence and shooting. (Under the reign of the Union Nationale I cannot recall a single provincial poll in the riding of Montreal-Saint-Jacques that was not punctuated by revolver shots.) Our flag also became, perforce, the symbol of the lavish electoral spending initiated at that time. The be-lilied propaganda urged us to "Let Duplessis carry on his good works," in French and English, on newsprint and art paper, in black-and-white and colour, on immense billboards that crowded our visual space, and even in lighted signs, their neon lettering streaking the night sky of Montreal. (Here again the *Chef* took his cue from a long tradition. He might not have invented electoral corruption, but he was to perfect it to a point never before attained.)

Had Mr. Duplessis given us a flag, or had he made himself a present of it?[13] This question could be asked about all his "nationalist" initiatives, which never included the slightest promotion of culture, the smallest coherent economic measure encouraging francophones to enter business, or the least support for the French immigration movement that became noticeable in the early '50s.

At a time when the Ontario government was generously subsidizing British immigrants, we had not one cent available to welcome French citizens who were attracted to Que-

---

[12][Henri IV of France, brought up a Protestant, became a Catholic to win the favour (and surrender) of the people of Paris. "Paris vaut une messe!" he remarked (Paris is worth a Mass). Tr.]

[13]The appropriation by a party of symbols which it declares sacred, requiring strict respect from others, seems to be a permanent temptation for nationalist groups—even today.

bec because of the disrupted conditions in post-war France. I remember the efforts of Jean-Marc Léger and his *Accueil franco-canadien* in which I was involved. Not only were we obliged to count on our own resources—almost non-existent—and a few private donations, we were also exposed to the reprobation of the Quebec government.

Indeed, this portrait of the Union Nationale would not be complete if we did not add to all its other charms a mention of its virulent hatred of foreigners. This also belonged to the Duplessis brand of nationalism. Didn't this organization (the *Accueil franco-canadien*) encourage the settling here of Frenchmen, a bad lot by definition because of the godless education they received in France and the communistic atmosphere that prevailed there?

By dint of repeating such trash the *Chef* had come to believe it himself. A friend of mine, a French diplomat and a militant Christian, was posted in Ottawa at the time. As a young counsellor at the Embassy he was interested in the work we were doing in Montreal in aid of his immigrant compatriots, and visited us from time to time. That was how I met him in the early fifties, and we met in Paris again twenty-five years later. He had vivid recollections of his years in Canada. One evening as we were dining with him *en famille* in the summer of '76, he told me about his first visit to Quebec.

Mr. Duplessis had invited him for a meal with a few cabinet members, and the diplomat arrived at the Château Frontenac very curious about this man who had already created his own legend.

"It was a Friday evening. You will see why I remember this detail. The premier was relaxing after a hard week's work, and joking with his colleagues. I remember that his humour was a little too coarse and his laugh too loud, but his good humour seemed to augur well for the negotiation to come. We sit down to dine, and are served a bowl of soup. So far so good. But when the main course comes, I see on all the other plates a filet of sole (I told you that it

was a Friday), while in the middle of mine sits an enormous
steak, very rare. Thinking there must be a mistake, I wait a
few moments for someone to rescue me from this incongruous meat and bring me the prevalent fish. Nothing happens. I call the waiter and whisper in his ear that there must
have been a mistake. But it is not he who replies, it's Mr.
Duplessis. No doubt he had been observing the whole
procedure out of the corner of his eye.

"'You don't like steak, Mr.——?'"

"'Yes, Mr. Premier, but...'

"'Well, eat it, then. In Quebec here, we're practising
Catholics: we eat fish on Friday.'

"'But so do I, Mr. Premier.'

"'You? A Frenchman from France? Don't tell me! Come,
no hypocrisy, now. Eat your steak.'

"'I assure you...'

"'Are you trying to tell me that you, a diplomat, a public
servant of a secularized State like France, do not eat meat
on Fridays? I don't believe you. Eat your steak.'

"'By dint of argument,' concluded my friend, "I got my
fish. But I had the distinct impression that I had not
convinced my host."

Did Mr. Duplessis really think he was defending the
Christian faith when he undertook his campaign against
Ottawa over the "communist eggs" which the federal government had allowed to be imported from Poland? Certainly not. But how could he resist the temptation to mine
for electoral ends such a rich vein of prejudice? He could
count at the same time on the Quebec farmers' mistrust of
foreign competitors, and the bugbear of the Marxist revolution. Any stick was good enough for beating the federal
government, including the xenophobia dormant in the
heart of every man. When Canada's help to the Third
World got under way, a slogan cropped up which gave an
admirable (so to speak) summing-up of the regime's philosophy in international relations: "Ottawa gives to foreigners. Duplessis gives to his own province."

Some people today credit the *Chef* with having "founded the State of Quebec." But what did he found it upon, if indeed this remained to be done? On the fear of foreigners and the fear of change.

And on the stupidity of the federal government of the day. Because the Great Darkness was not only a Quebec phenomenon.

I have always had the most moderate admiration for Mr. Louis Saint-Laurent. Not that the man was without merit, but he lacked imagination and never managed to see the curves in the road ahead. It was he, in fact, who supplied Duplessis with abundant anti-federal ammunition by unreasonably prolonging wartime centralization.

All through the war years, because of the great effort that had to be made, the Canadian government had gathered into its own hands enormous powers, without much concern for the constitutional rules that normally ensure the division of jurisdictions between the two levels of government. As long as hostilities lasted there could be little objection to measures everyone realized were highly centralist but justified by the war effort and the struggle against the barbarity of fascism.

The trouble was that the federal government did not know when to stop. It tackled the post-war problems with all the arrogance and self-assurance to which it had grown accustomed when the bombs were raining on Europe and Asia. "Nothing matters but victory" was the slogan in the early forties. Now Mr. Saint-Laurent seemed to be saying, "Nothing matters but the government in Ottawa." And the government invaded provincial jurisdiction by granting federal subsidies to the universities, monopolized direct taxation country-wide, and acted as if provincial governments were to be held in trusteeship and treated as children under age, or simply tolerated.

What a golden chance for Mr. Duplessis! Ottawa held the shield, and the little king had only to climb upon it to confirm his power. The man whom Lionel Groulx describes in his *Mémoires*[14] as a "man of the robe encrusted in legality" leapt at the opportunity with the alacrity one would expect: a juicy juridical–nationalist dispute in which he was in the right—what unhoped-for good luck!

Mr. Saint-Laurent had accomplished an amazing feat: he had won support for Mr. Duplessis from two men as unlike as Lionel Groulx and Pierre Trudeau. The former greeted the provincial income tax (January 1954) as a "courageous and concrete act of autonomy" which the premier had finally accomplished. The latter condemned the previous fiscal system imposed by Ottawa as the equivalent of highway robbery, with the Quebec taxpayer as victim. "Oh, I know very well," he wrote in *Cité libre*,[15] "that this state of affairs is due to the total incompetence of the Duplessis government in economic affairs.... But the stupidity of the victim cannot be pleaded by the thief as an extenuating circumstance." (In thus supporting provincial rights, Trudeau stood out from a number of intellectuals who were then whole-hearted partisans of federal centralism, and who are today equally dedicated to independence for Quebec.)

There was no doubt about the Duplessis government's "total incompetence in economic affairs." But only critics from Quebec had the courage to say it out loud. Mr. Saint-Laurent, on the contrary, found it more useful to give his public approval to the scandalous mining concessions in Ungava and the *Chef*'s incredible generosity toward American investors. This connivance with big capital, on which Duplessis and Saint-Laurent were in sudden agreement (feuding brothers as they were, engaged to the hilt in the federal–provincial duel)—this also contributed to the Great Darkness.

Even more astonishing, come to think of it, is the posthumous praise bestowed on the *Chef* by his present-day admirers. They make a virtue of the fact that he accom-

---

[14]Groulx, *Mes mémoires*, Vol. VI, p. 336.
[15]*Cité libre* no. 10, October 1954, p. 7.

plished nothing between 1944 and 1960, thus protecting Quebec's credit rating, which Mr. Lesage was later to take advantage of in financing his Quiet Revolution. This attitude amounts to writing off the trials of the whole post-war generation, undereducated, underpaid, and deprived of the most elementary social welfare structures: in a word, sacrificed.

Unfortunately the incompetence was not limited to the economic field. It was general, and resulted mainly from the non-existence in Quebec of a civil service worthy of the name. Recruiting public employees, assuring them of a career and decent pay, protecting them against partisan interference in their daily tasks—these were certainly the least concerns of the Union Nationale, its leader and his ministers. The ruling principles of this function of the State—and all its others—were openly practised favouritism, patronage and nepotism.

A friend of mine, after a long period of study pursued elsewhere on a Quebec government scholarship (yes, a few were granted), wanted to enter the province's public service. He was under no obligation to do so. Nor was he in search of employment as such. But he found it natural to devote at least a few years of his working life to the community that had let him acquire his particular competence.

The question was, how should he go about it? There were no competitions, no examinations of any kind, nothing but a spectral Civil Service Commission, run by a personal friend of the *Chef*, with only the vaguest of mandates. And so he wrote to one of Mr. Duplessis's most senior ministers, who happened also to be one of the most respectable, to tell him of his intentions.

"My young friend," replied the minister," I am touched by the confidence you place in me. But if I have any good advice to give you, it is to give up the notion of becoming a civil servant. A man as brilliant and serious as yourself, leaving Harvard with the degrees you mention in your

letter, has better things to do than enter the public
service. I have a very good friend in Imperial Oil. I am
writing to him at once with the warmest
recommendations. I am sure he will offer you a position
that is more in keeping with your brilliant capabilities, at
a much higher salary. I fail to see why a talented young
man should be contented with a mediocre salary in a
career that leads nowhere. Yours. . . [etc].

Finally, what can one say about the administration, or rather
the manipulation, of justice under the Union Nationale
regime?

We would have to talk about certain laws like the so-
called Padlock Law which scorned the most fundamental
democratic liberties and opened the way to every abuse of
power. And tell of the talent and stubbornness of Frank
Scott pitted against the high-handed *Chef* in the Roncarelli
trial.

People of my age have a vivid memory of this *cause
célèbre*, which provides a perfect illustration of Maurice
Duplessis's attitude to human rights. Roncarelli, a Montreal
restaurant owner, undertook, in the fall of 1946, to go bail
for some Jehovah's Witnesses accused of "distributing a
seditious pamphlet" so that they could be freed until their
trial came up. Was Mr. Roncarelli himself a Witness? I don't
really know, and the question is not important. He felt that
the members of the sect should not expiate in jail their "sin"
of poverty. Any philanthropist, even if he had no sympathy
for the sect, might have done the same thing out of strictly
democratic convictions. And in any case his action was
perfectly legal. But, unfortunately for him, Mr. Roncarelli
held a permit from the Quebec Liquor Commission, and it
was an indispensable condition for the prosperity of his
restaurant. Mr. Duplessis, who possessed to a high degree
an instinct for the jugular, hesitated not a second; having
warned Roncarelli to "stop encouraging a seditious organization," and Roncarelli not having given in, Duplessis with-

drew his licence, which condemned the restaurant owner to ruin, and then confiscated two thousand dollars' worth of spirits from his bar. The *Chef* had considered that a man could not at the same time have the *privilege* of serving drinks and set up *obstacles* to the enforcement of the law.

He had gone too far—perhaps for the thousandth time in his career—but this time he had not foreseen that the victim had the urge and the resources to resist him. The case went to court. Twelve years later (the mills of justice grind slowly) Mr. Duplessis lost the case. His supporters had to take up a public collection to absolve the *Chef* from paying some forty thousand dollars in damages and costs out of his own pocket.

Mr. Duplessis seemed fortified by this encouragement, and the vigorous persecution of his adversaries went on to the end. In the last years of his reign, retroactive laws became his favourite weapon. In particular he put them to work against two trade unionists, Gérard Picard and Léo Guindon, and did it so openly that the measures adopted came to be called the Picard Bill and the Guindon Bill, in the everyday parlance of the parliamentarians.

In all his successive governments, Mr. Duplessis never entrusted the Justice portfolio to anyone but himself. He kept the judicial arsenal in his own hands, and made the most barefaced and unscrupulous use of it. He alone was responsible for appointing the judges of provincial courts. True to the established tradition, he named only tried and true partisans to these positions. A survivor of his era told me in Paris twenty-five years later how he himself had "got his start" in business thanks to the *Chef*: "I had campaigned for him in the election of '44, along with L., a friend who was older than myself. After the victory Duplessis asked us what reward we would like. L. wanted to be made a judge. He was appointed. My reward was a road-building contract, because I hadn't studied law."

One often wondered whether all the magistrates appointed by the *Chef* fulfilled this latter condition: some were total ignoramuses, others manned the bench while drunk, and others handed down made-to-measure judgments ordered up by the government.

There was also, for example, a mobile system of justice, designed for trade unionists, that was very carefully contrived. Whenever a labour conflict had lasted beyond the limits set by the government, Mr. Duplessis would begin by dispatching a few shock units of the Quebec Provincial Police to the site. Incidents resulted, which the police repressed with the utmost brutality. (During the asbestos strike the QPP showed their zeal to the point of torturing a number of strikers. The fact was finally established and recognized by the court. The torturers, however, escaped all punishment; they had taken their precautions, and no one could identify them to the judge's satisfaction.) The next step was the arrest of a few strikers. And to investigate their "misdeeds" along came a single specialized team, the same one for Gaspé or Sherbrooke or Hull, made up of safe friends of the party, tried and tested party workers. Police witnesses perjured themselves cheerfully one after the other; the "evidence," always the same, was built up according to an invariable litany, and a few workers inevitably ended up behind bars for the edification of all right-thinking people.

*   *   *

I must stop here. There is much more that could be told. I have only skimmed the surface of the subject. It was no part of my intention to make a profound analysis of the Duplessis phenomenon, for I am neither a sociologist nor a historian. I merely wanted to call up the atmosphere, the forgotten taste and smell of this rotten regime for which some are busily braiding fresh laurels.

I did not think I would live long enough to see the rehabilitation of Maurice Duplessis. I had to wait less than twenty years.

In the fall of 1977, confined to a hospital bed by an operation, my abdomen tormented by itches and pains, I was witness to a spectacle televised from Quebec on the program *Teléjournal*: the Parti Québécois government was raising a statue to Maurice Duplessis, literally and verbally, on the lawn of the National Assembly. René Lévesque was officiating in person at the enthronement of his predecessor, cast in bronze for the edification of Quebec's posterity.

I could not believe my eyes, and still less my ears. How the devil had we come to this?

An aesthetic motivation? I hardly think so. The full-length statue that now dishonours parliament hill in Quebec is hideous. The sculptor has left nothing out—the detachable collar, the tie, the trousers-fly, everything is there. Only one detail is missing: life. It looks like a display model stolen by tipsy party-goers from the window of a department store. One's first glance is not drawn to either the face or the pose of the subject. What is striking is the three-piece suit.

Could this masterpiece of mediocrity not have been left in some warehouse? Or exiled to the North, in Nouveau-Québec, as Claude Ryan suggested? In this way the taxpayers who footed the bill would at least have been spared the sight of its ugliness.

But the most astonishing thing was beyond a doubt the speech made by the premier, René Lévesque, at the foot of this statue. He said, in substance, that no people can afford to forget any period of its history. It would be absurd to try to wipe out of our memories all traces of the Duplessis regime.

How right René was!

One is tempted to go him one better, and say that today, more than ever, it is important to remind ourselves that in the name of nationalism and religion, Duplessis inflicted upon us a twenty-year reign of lies, injustice and corruption, the systematic misuse of power, the sway of small minds and the triumph of stupidity. We must remember that this man and his regime held back for a quarter of a century Quebec's entry into the modern world. It would be fatal to forget that he did everything possible to turn our population inwards upon itself and isolate it from the world, to convince us that it was better to eat dry bread by ourselves than to share the richest feast with "foreigners." It would actually be dangerous not to recognize that some of these notions lived on in our collective subconscious, and are resurfacing today.

"Hitler? Never heard of him," was the reply of German youth in 1960 to a question in an opinion poll. Other things being equal, the ignorance of young Quebecers is no less great today.

I repeat: René Lévesque is right. It would be wrong of us to forget the evil done to us by that corrupt regime. On the contrary, we must keep it in mind, for fear of slipping again into the same ruts and the same patterns of lies. I do think, however, that there are better ways to perpetuate this memory than by raising a statue and "rehabilitating" the person in question. After all, the Germans have raised no monument to Hitler, nor the French to their Marshall of 1940. As for the Soviets, they began after Stalin's death to dismantle those that the dictator had erected to himself in his own lifetime.

Yet, whatever oratorical precautions and mental reservations may have riddled his speech that day, René was still rendering homage to the memory of the *Chef* and his clique.

CHAPTER 4

The Joys of Opposition

There is nothing more interesting than being able to catch famous people before their glory, while they are still learning.
SAINTE-BEUVE

W hat were you doing in the Blue days?"[1]
This was the caption of a cartoon published by Normand Hudon, early in the sixties. The question was lacking neither in piquancy nor relevance, because Quebec society was then teeming with amnesiacs. Nearly all the friends of the late regime, and especially those who had lived off the fat of it, were crowding toward the turnstiles of forgetfulness. They loudly disowned the dogmas of Duplessis and desperately tried to find room aboard the Quiet Revolution. Employers who had profited from the anti-union laws, union officers who had made deals with the regime to escape its rigours, businessmen who only yesterday had been blessed with juicy contracts, assorted beneficiaries of patronage, all this motley crowd was suddenly touched by the grace of society's renewal. There is no forgetting this procession when one has seen it pass even

---
[1] [Blue: Conservative (party) or, in this case, Union Nationale. Tr.]

67

once, its votive candles burning for new gods.[2]

But we, what had we done in the Blue days?

First, we had to survive, which was not as easy as it may seem nowadays, twenty-five years later. To prosper in silence was not a problem. I have mentioned that the Union Nationale did not expect a public profession of faith. This provincial dictatorship was quite satisfied with silence. At times it even rewarded discretion. (I knew a writer who lived for years, quietly following at the heels of the regime, now in Paris, now in Montreal, with the sole occupation of putting his complete works on paper. The regime paid him fifty dollars a week—a comfortable sum at the time—as publicity man for the Quebec Liquor Commission, which was by statute forbidden to do any advertising. But if by chance you spoke out of turn, you might be sorry for it. And the trouble-makers who had the audacity to openly combat the regime were as good as excommunicated. Because Maurice Duplessis was short on ideas but long on influence.

It so happened that the men about whom I am writing here came together, sooner or later, in the opposition, and one that was not only political. It was first of all directed against a tradition, a dominant ideology and social habits, all of which went much beyond the scope of government. We considered the regime as an outgrowth of our whole collective existence, not as an isolated disorder. In a democracy, people get the government they deserve. We firmly believed this.

Between 1947 and 1950 we were not concerned with ousting the government in power and replacing it with another one. I would even say that we barely thought about this. It was our society that we wanted to change. We devoted all our attention to questions such as religious and cultural development, the transformation of social rela-

---

[2] Pierre Trudeau had other terms to describe this same cortège of those "who formerly crawled on the Union Nationale side and now hasten to crawl in the other direction." (*L'élection du 22 juin 1960, Cité Libre no. 29, August-September 1960, pp. 3–8.*)

tionships, the scientific method, educational reform. Party struggles interested us hardly at all.

But as the government's conservatism fought fiercely against every kind of change, the collision was inevitable. For most of us, it was brought about by the asbestos strike. After the confrontation of 1949, those who had taken sides with the underground miners were, in the eyes of the government, marked men. Those in power had a special resentment toward us, different from their hostility toward parliamentary adversaries. Those who were most astute, starting with the *Chef* himself, quickly saw the danger of an extra-parliamentary opposition.

One Saturday evening in the spring of 1949, when the asbestos conflict was in full swing, when the union's strike fund was exhausted and hunger was threatening the miners' will to resist, we were called together to the archbishop's palace in Montreal by Archbishop Charbonneau. I don't remember why this was a nocturnal rendezvous, but it was after eleven when Gérard Picard, Jean Marchand and I arrived at the prelate's residence, and the conversation ended in the small hours. We had foreseen this, and arranged to meet some union colleagues in a nightclub (the only place in the neighbourhood that stayed open till dawn) to give them the details of our encounter with the archbishop.

But it chanced that in the same club, at a table beside our own, sat a strong, slightly tipsy contingent of government members of the Legislative Assembly, among whom I recognized Daniel Johnson. As soon as he saw us he came over. (He was not in his cups; for that matter, he never was.)

"Well?"

Well, what? We had no intention of telling him about our interview with the archbishop, about the prelate's anguish at the thought of the workers abandoned by Duplessis to the whims of their bosses, and least of all about his question, which had stunned the three of us: "We must take serious measures now: are you strong enough to call a general strike?"

"Well," repeated Daniel, smiling, standing straight, hands on hips, "still the agitators, are you?"

Marchand glowered at him, and Gérard Picard looked up to stare.

"Like to see us quieter, would you Daniel? Or maybe crawling at the feet of your little friends in the Johns Manville Company?[3] Don't count on it, my friend. You could get disappointed."

Daniel, still smiling, threw up his hands: "Come on, let's not dramatize. You're free to do all the stupid things you like. You can call out all the workers in the province against the government if you want. What do we care? But let me give you just one little piece of advice: if you're so anxious to play politics, why don't you get yourselves elected?"

None of us had the heart that night to get into a discussion. We had other worries. But Johnson's phrase was to come back to me often in the years that followed. It grew increasingly obvious that furthering the workers' cause or struggling against the excesses of the clergy or even claiming simple democratic rights put us directly in the way of the course the Union Nationale had chosen. They would try by every means to discredit us and isolate us so that they could more easily brush us aside. If we were members of the opposition we would be exposed to the artillery Maurice Duplessis held aimed at his adversaries in the House: slander, denunciation, insinuation, etc. But the *Chef* kept certain special kinds of revenge as a homage to unelected opponents: witch-hunts, petty judicial harassment, and all kinds of arbitrary measures that power put within his reach.

Those who had believed in the possibility of free trade-union activity or an unfettered journalism; those who had expected to pursue a normal teaching career in the universities, removed from the hurly-burly of politics; even artists, like Paul-Emile Borduas, dedicated to the most specialized

[3] A mining company, American-run, which was mining the deposits at Asbestos.

kind of teaching—all these and many others were soon to be forced to change their tune. We found no shelter against this badgering, remote-controlled from Quebec City. One had either to keep silent and come to terms with the regime, or come out and combat it openly. It was no use searching for neutral ground, some no man's land where one could work in peace or utter, even timidly, opinions that diverged from those of the clergy or the regime.

But there was the Canadian Broadcasting Corporation.

No doubt the existence of the Corporation explains in large part the tardy entry of René Lévesque into the struggle against Duplessis. The premier had no influence inside the Corporation, which was a federal institution, and René, as I said previously, was almost exclusively interested in foreign affairs. If we retrace his career from 1950 onwards, we find nothing that might have brought down the wrath of our temporal or spiritual leaders upon his head in the first five years.

After his reports on the Korean war, the CBC assigned him to cover, successively, a royal visit, the coronation of Elizabeth II in London, the visits to Canada of Haile Selassie and Pierre Mendès France, the Empire and Commonwealth Games (in Vancouver), etc. Lévesque also provided the burgeoning Public Affairs Department with almost daily contributions in the form of interviews and short reports. Incidentally he took part in two very popular radio programs: the *Revue des arts et des lettres*, for which he did film reviews, and *Lettre à une Canadienne*, dealing with women's interests. Nothing very compromising in all that.

But the collision, for Lévesque as for us, was inevitable. It happened in 1955, on his return from a trip to the U.S.S.R. where René had accompanied Lester B. Pearson, then minister of External Affairs. It was not his reports that earned him the opprobrium of the Quebec establishment. If he had confined himself to talking about the Pearson–Khrushchev conversations, no one would have turned a hair. There was the current mood to be taken into account, however: the

Cold War was at its chilliest.

When he came back to Canada everyone wanted to know what this star reporter had observed behind the Iron Curtain. And as Lévesque had not visited the concentration camps of the Gulag, or the prisons, or the forced labour sites in Siberia, he simply reported what he had seen. That, however, did not square with the kind of Russian hell and Soviet horror with which official doctrine fed the North American imagination, and still less with the primitive anti-communism of the Union Nationale.

René's replies, and a number of talks he gave to service clubs and other right-thinking audiences, were enough to trigger indignation. There was a first-class row. After a few weeks he was tossed, rejected, among us; that is, among the leftist clan. A few months later a parochial letter in Montreal enjoined the faithful to pray for the "conversion [sic] of Gérard Pelletier, René Lévesque and Jacques Hébert."

From that day on, respectable journalists never once sang his praises without the preliminary disclaimer: "I do not share Mr. Lévesque's opinions. . . ."

He was not the only one to experience such mortification. A few months after this episode, Gérard Filion, publisher of *Le Devoir*, also returned from a trip into forbidden territory: China. And he too refused to tailor his stories to the official patterns. He took pains to tell just what he had seen and heard, nothing more and nothing less.

He told, for example, how one Sunday in Peking he had gone to a Catholic mass that was celebrated, to all appearances, according to a perfectly orthodox litany. He had even chatted afterward with the celebrant, a Chinese priest whose remarks reflected an exemplary fidelity to the doctrines of the Church.

Filion's talk raised a general uproar. He had barely pronounced the last word when he found himself surrounded by inquisitorial clerics and overwhelmed with objections.

"How can you tell that he was not a false priest or a traitor to the Church?"

"True or false," Filion replied imperturbably, "he celebrated a real mass before my very eyes."

"You say it was real. What do you know about it?"

"Well, you taught me Latin at college, didn't you? And I've been going to mass for thirty years."

"It may have been a sham for the benefit of foreigners."

"I saw some Chinese in the congregation."

"But in a communist country a fake performance could be arranged."

Having had enough after an hour of questioning, Filion resorted to a characteristically mischievous way out of his dilemma:

"Look here, you want irrefutable proof that the mass was the real thing? You want it? [then, after a pause for effect] They took the collection, for god's sake, what more do you want?"

Filion, a nationalist and a product of the very Catholic UCC (*Union catholique des cultivateurs*, the Catholic farmers' union) could afford to crack a little joke like this. Lévesque, an outsider, a man with no diplomas, with precarious roots in Quebec reality (had he not been through the war with the Americans?), a journalist working for a federal institution and belonging to the already suspect circles of the national radio system, was more vulnerable. I had the impression that his rude treatment came as a surprise to him. Unlike Filion, he had no daily paper in which to clarify his point of view. He retired into his tent.

But his tent turned out to be a circus big top. And a few months later, on *Point de mire*, he became a television star. From that moment he had a major influence on public opinion in Quebec.

This influence was mainly brought to bear, however, on questions in the federal area, of Canadian interest. Local opposition to the Duplessis regime was certainly not a matter of indifference to him, but he was not involved in it. During the 1950s Lévesque was wedded to his profession more than to any combat, as he himself has said. And

Gérard Bergeron was to remark, quite accurately, some years later: "During his journalistic career, until the CBC strike in 1959, he [René Lévesque] curbed to the maximum his faculties of impatience and indignation."[4]

His job was to report, not to editorialize. For him the words honesty, competence and respect for realities had a very precise meaning. He was acutely aware of the fact that the CBC provided a public service and belonged to all Canadians. He would not tolerate its becoming an instrument in the service of personal opinions. He did not confuse reporting with preaching. Claude Sylvestre, his producer on *Point de mire* (or was it Judith Jasmin?) told me one day that René had just given a severe dressing-down to a cub reporter who on some news program had begun shamelessly preaching his own ideas:

"Hey!" René shouted at him. "Do you know who owns that microphone you talk into? You don't own it, I don't own it: everybody owns it. And 'everybody' is not interested in what you think: everybody wants to know what happened, what you saw!"

It was in this spirit that Lévesque felt a bond with the Corporation. Though he was now a freelance broadcaster (he had given up his employee status on launching *Point de mire*), his newsman's professional conscience prevented him from also taking part, even as a private citizen, in the tough battles of the time. It seemed to him that his credibility as a journalist (we didn't use this anglicism yet; we called it objectivity) might have suffered. Even at the start of the producers' strike René was to hesitate some time before taking the plunge. He had to be nudged a little. But I'm getting ahead of myself.

For the moment it suffices to say that between 1950 and 1959 he was absent from the fray—from ours, at any rate. We found ourselves shoulder to shoulder with him only in January 1959. In the meantime we would meet him often in the studios of the CBC and in friendly get-togethers, but

4 *Ne bougez plus* (Montreal: Editions du Jour, 1968), p. 148.

never on the picket line or at public meetings.

Jean Marchand, on the contrary, spent every day of those ten years on the firing line, with not a moment of respite. At thirty-three he was already a veteran, experienced militant. He enjoyed great respect in the union movement, not only among his fellow-leaders but among the militant membership.

After I left *Le Devoir* in the spring of 1950 to become a permanent employee of the CTCC (later the CSN), I had the advantage of a closeup view of Marchand in action.

As we emerged from the asbestos struggle we had all learned in a tough school what the coming decade held in store for us. But Jean understood this more clearly than anyone. The man always astonished me with his uncannily sharp perception of social and political realities. He was never a theoretician, never an ideologist, and still less a visionary. He never comes unstuck from reality. When he says of someone, "He hasn't got his feet on the ground," it is the most unflattering judgment he can make.

I asked him one day what he had learned in university. (For my own part I had taken a rather anaemic course in literature as I worked my way through college. Marchand was a graduate of the prestigious School of Social Sciences at Laval.) He gave me the shortest possible answer: "Nothing!"

To be sure, he then admitted that the word was perhaps too sweeping. But the intellectual clutter of the classroom and its high-flown speculations had left little trace on his mind. What he preserved from his years in the School (it was then referred to as Father Lévesque's School) was a certain conception of the problems of change, a certain way of perceiving social reality in its complexity. All the rest (there was a lot of chatter at the time about the "social doctrine of the Church") he had hastened to forget. He still knew how to speak that language, when circumstances called for it. But it was not *his* language.

His language had been forged from that of the workers, at the very base of the union membership. It was rich, but simple, direct and remarkably concrete.

Marchand is one of the men to whom I have listened most, and with the most fascinated attention. I mean not only his union speeches, of which I listened to several hundred and which enriched the life and thought of the Quebec labour movement for twenty-three years. I am thinking mainly about endless nocturnal conversations while we were on the road, at a time when the accidental pattern of developments made nomads of us. Jean's system was to work all day in his office or in select committees, make a speech in the evening to a mass meeting, then travel at night from one city to another. I can remember itineraries that took us in the space of a few days from Montreal to Louiseville, on to Quebec City and Arvida, landing for the weekend in Asbestos or Hull after a stop in Sorel. Marchand did not merely sample the crowd: he lived in it.

It was thrilling. And exhausting.

But at day's end, around eleven or midnight, his mind was as clear and busy as at daybreak. And while the car swallowed up the night by the hundreds of kilometres, I kept my companion talking.

He would think out loud, sharing his observations of our day, his projects and fears, or telling me about the militants we were to meet at the next stop, people I had not yet met.

Then, with no transition, he would start to sing. Out came the *chansons* by Ferré and Piaf, of which Jean knew every word. In general he preferred the most nostalgic and popular songs, the ones that spoke of unhappy loves or celebrated the workers' hopes and struggles or poked fun at society. We were also starting in those days to hum the first Canadian hits by Félix Leclerc, Petel or Raymond Lévesque. Monique Leyrac's voice singing of "the lights of my town," "*Les lumières de ma ville*," sticks in my memory in connection with the asbestos strike, in the little café in Asbestos where he would wolf down a sandwich to the sound of the juke-box before hitting the road again. But Marchand's great classics were "*L'accordéoniste*," "*Que sont mes amis devenus,*" "*Padam,*" "*Le vaisseau espagnol,*" and so many others whose poetry enchanted him.

When he stopped singing we would drive in silence for a few minutes. Then I would start my questioning again. What constitutes the makings of a "natural social leader," a label that Gérard Bergeron, after so many others, pinned on Marchand in his 1968 portrait of the man?[5] That's what I was trying to grasp.

I found, of course, an exceptional mind, but one which could just as well have led Jean to the scientific career he had once dreamed of. Except that in those days, when nothing was free, Jean would have needed financial means that he did not possess in order to follow that path. His father had had the misfortune to die very young, leaving to his wife a flock of lively children and very little money to feed them.

I also discovered an ardent love of action and a passion for work that were really out of the ordinary. Seeing how the man lived, one could not help wondering what unrest he was trying to appease as he forged ahead in a perpetual activity that left no time for leisure or vacations. At that time Marchand's legal residence was in Quebec City, but he spent no more than three or four days a month there. His real address was the road and a few dozen hotel rooms scattered over almost all the cities in the province. All the union leaders I have known, with two or three exceptions, were hard workers. In spite of prevalent legends about labour leaders who lead the life of Riley at the membership's expense, union activity is one of the most demanding professions. To see Marchand in action you would have thought that the ultimate fate of the working class depended on what would happen that day.

What Makes Sammy Run? was the title of an American best-selling novel in the 1940s. I used to ask myself the same question about Jean. It certainly wasn't money, because the little he earned was quickly spent. Ambition? In the noble sense of the word, certainly. He was conscious of his own

---

[5] Bergeron, *Ne bougez plus*, p. 76.

worth, and meant to leave his mark. One had to make something of one's life, something useful, serious, something that made sense.

But Jean Marchand's real passion was for justice. I know how commonplace that statement may sound. Nobody likes injustice. But when I talk here about a passion I am weighing my words. I know of no more constant quality of his, nor any motivation more profound, than his love of justice and his detestation of its opposite. Nothing shocks him more violently than to see the oppression of the weak, the abuse of power, and especially the massive, placid injustice that is perpetrated by the privileged. I found this passion so strong and decisive in him, and at times so exasperated, that I was surprised not to hear Marchand preach revolution.

What held him back from taking that last step? First, a natural distaste for violence. Though he was combative, impetuous, irrepressibly hot-headed, and endowed with unusual physical courage, he found the use of force repugnant, no doubt because of his democratic convictions but also because he knew that violence is blind. He once said: "People who talk about a revolution in Quebec make me sick. Either they're showing off or, if they're sincere, they haven't thought it through. They don't know."

"I know some who think they know. Daniel Johnson, for one. I remember a crack of his, back in the conscription crisis. 'Quebecers?' he said, 'starting a revolution? Come on! They can't even stay up for two nights in a row.'"

"Johnson doesn't know his working class. I do. Believe me, you wouldn't have to push very hard. But it would be absurd. When you can do without violence, it's criminal to resort to it. And we can do without it. Sure, it has its attraction, violence has. I like a scrap myself. But in the end it would be the workers who would pay for it. We have no right talking revolution if we're not ready to go all the way."

Marchand always saw the transformation of society as a series of *stages* to be gone through. The word kept cropping up in his speeches. He liked it, no doubt because it combines the notion of movement with that of a precise objective, and is open to the future. "We have just completed an important stage. And here is how I see the next one. . . .

He usually saw it clearly. Speaking of poets, Cocteau said, "They are people who find first and search afterwards." In these terms, Marchand must be a poet of action. He *feels* what he has to do; a kind of instinct warns him, and is rarely wrong. But once he has "found," he has to begin to search, that is, to gradually refine his arguments and discover the *reasons* behind his intuitions. Strange alchemy! But this instinct exists in all the men of action I ever knew. It is even indispensable when the pressure of events leaves no time for analysis and calls for a quick decision.

In Jean this gift goes with a rare ability to perceive, to *feel* the reality around him, and with a kind of slightly cynical realism that for a long time I found surprising. For him all morality revolves around justice. What one might call moral decorum was less important. Marital infidelity, for example, was in his eyes a problem only as a gross injustice toward the wife or children. He never felt it necessary to close his eyes to the weaknesses of his friends (still less those of his adversaries) or to their shortcomings.

If I reproached him with sparing no one, and with pronouncing the most cold-blooded judgments on his closest associates, he would reply: "That doesn't prevent me from liking them. But when you're in action you can't afford not to see clearly. Seeing men through rose-coloured glasses can be costly."

"You could be a little tolerant . . ."

"Failure to see is not tolerance. It's blindness."

Does the ability to see clearly, in a man of action, always lead to cynicism? In any case, his cool judgment never prevented Marchand from communicating an intense human warmth to those around him.

This is not, by the way, the only paradox in his personality: this militant, this organizer, this stirring public speaker is also a pessimist. By this I mean that when launching some project, he always assumes the worst about its possible outcome. How often have I heard him, before a strike was called, describing to the assembled workers the trials they could expect. At the risk of discouraging them, he refused to leave them under the slightest illusion.

In the same way, on the verge of the 1950s, Marchand knew very well what lay ahead of all of us as a result of the choice we had made. He was fully aware that the labour movement could not win its freedom of action (and the working class its most basic rights) without a long and arduous struggle. I doubt very much whether the School of Social Sciences gave him this conviction ready-made. He had come to it from his own personal analysis. Between Sherbrooke and Quebec, on the night of a strike in the spring of 1949, he said, with exemplary lucidity:

"You know, Pelletier, this government will never be able to recognize that the union movement is legitimate. For Duplessis we'll always be the enemy. Not adversaries, the *enemy*. The adversary, for them, is the Liberal opposition in Parliament. It will try to come to power and form a new government, but that's all part of the game. We, on the other hand—and Duplessis knows it, or feels it—want to change society. And to prevent that, he'll go as far as repression by the police. What we've been through in Asbestos was only a start. It's going to continue. And the regime won't lack for allies, that I'll swear."

"You mean the employers?"

"I mean *all* the leading citizens. We're living under the reign of those people. The government is based on them, on their interests, their prejudices, their blind conservatism. And God knows the regime is clever about encouraging those prejudices and looking after their interests."

"In that case, Jean, we should be acting at the political level. We can't change society through strikes."

"No? That remains to be seen. What I do know is the strength of the union movement right now, and the weakness of the opposition in the Assembly. For the time being union power is the only one the regime can't control or take over. It has managed to get hold of a portion of it, but the greater part of the movement has not given in. Let's not give up the substance for the shadow. Unionism sooner or later will make a proper parliamentary opposition possible. But the time isn't ripe. And anyway, would you leave guys like Rodolphe Hamel or Larivée or Daniel Lessard in the lurch to put yourself at the service of a party?"

Marchand knew in advance what I would say. By naming those miners whose struggle we had just shared, he was introducing a personal note into a line of reasoning I tended to pursue in the abstract. He was facing me with an immediate union job to be done in response to the real and urgent needs of flesh-and-blood people oppressed by the permanent collusion among employers, "leading citizens" and our provincial rulers. In and through unionism we could begin at once to make some changes, however modest the results of our actions might seem to us.

Marchand's analysis seemed most convincing to me. That the leading citizens identified with Duplessis's regime had recently been proven to me beyond a doubt. All the professionals of Asbestos—doctors, lawyers, notaries, dentists—instinctively lined up on the side of the employers and the government, from the very first days of the conflict.

"You know," a doctor said to me, "the Company managers are patients of mine."

It took several months of the strike and a dizzying drop in their incomes for them to realize that the miners, and not only the Company managers, contributed to the standard of living of professionals.

A few years later, in 1956, a member of the cabinet and pillar of the Union Nationale admitted to a friend on the eve of the elections: "It's going to be harder this time. *We can't afford to lose the support of a single churchwarden.*"

What with the churchwardens, the notables of the province, the bishops, the big employers and assorted manipulators, a whole clerical–nationalist machine was busily organizing the defence of the Union Nationale and the perpetuation of its power. The party had no philosophy other than this efficient conservatism combined with an impotent nationalism. To oppose the Union Nationale in depth, as Marchand saw clearly, was to challenge the dominant ideology and Quebec society itself. What political party would have been equal to that task? What party, in those days, was ready for such an undertaking?

In 1978, Jean Lacouture's *Léon Blum* showed me that the moving spirits of the Popular Front in France had been able to distinguish, in 1936, between the conquest of the *government* and the conquest of *power*, between a political plan and a plan for society.

It was something like this of which Marchand had an inkling, even if he had not yet found the words to express it. And events proved him right, far beyond what he had foreseen.

About the reality of the extra-parliamentary opposition, Trudeau wrote about the 1950s ten years later:

> When the provincial Liberal Party was a nonentity
> ('There were only eight of us . . .' 'Yes, the illitereight!')
> and was annihilated under the tutelage of the all-
> powerful King and Saint-Laurent governments; when it
> was the time of non-aggression pacts with Duplessism
> both in Ottawa and the administration of Montreal;
> when Saint-Laurent gave his benediction to Duplessis's
> policy in Ungava; when the party as a man declared
> against the provincial income tax; when Mr. Lesage was
> a centralist federal cabinet minister; when Mr. Lapalme,
> put in by Ottawa to oust Godbout, was still struggling
> desperately to free himself from the reactionary clique;
> when the progressive line of a Jean-Louis Gagnon was
> considered an embarrassment; when a Hector Langevin
> was ill thought of by the party for lending his name to a
> subscription campaign for *Le Devoir*; when the Liberal
> Federation was still in its infancy; when the Liberal

newspaper *Le Canada* disappeared for lack of readers, lack of backers, and lack of an ideology; when, in brief— and this is not so many years ago—the provincial Liberal party was still no more than a heavy body with no soul, and Isocrates[6] talked about his "last chance Convention," there was, nonetheless, an opposition to Duplessism in the province. But it was neither in the Assembly nor within the Liberal party that it exploded with vehemence, courage and determination.[7]

It exploded first within the labour movement. And in bringing about that explosion Jean Marchand was doubtless mainly responsible: the most active, the most visible and the most clear-sighted. I mean that he was the first to give up any illusions about the possibility of peaceful coexistence between the regime and the unions. He did not go looking for a political fight, but he knew it was inevitable. He had understood that any policy is the result of a relationship of forces. And as he knew Quebec society from top to bottom, it was obvious to him that the forces at play in 1950 were moving toward an all-out struggle between a working class in search of its place in the sun, and a government dedicated by its very nature to preventing the emergence of a popular will that would upset the traditional order.

Marchand was the spokesman for this new force. He also assisted at its birth. To realize this, one had only to see him in action before an audience of miners or metal workers or weavers. His speeches were not samples of rhetoric but the unpolished reflections of a man thinking out loud.

I can still see the smoke-filled halls, always overheated, packed with workers, half of whom had only standing room. I see the checked shirts, the leather windbreakers, the faces, tanned or pale, unshaven or clean-shaven according to the shift that was called to the meeting: the one leaving the factory or the one that would start work after the meeting.

[6] [Isocrates (Isocrate in Fr.) was Gérard Bergeron's pen-name. Tr.]
[7] *Cité libre* no. 29, August–September 1960.

I hear the good-natured heckling:

"What are you going to tell us, Jean?"

"Don't talk too long, we had a hard day!"

"Any good news tonight?"

And I see the inevitable "old faithful" (there was at least one in every factory) go up to Marchand to shake his hand or slap him on the back and say: "Remember, Jean, that strike meeting in Thetford?" Or Sorel or Sherbrooke or Chicoutimi...

(I was astonished to hear in the stage performance of *Charbonneau and the Chef*[8] how actors playing working-men's roles referred to *Mister* Marchand. In real life he was never Mister to the workers; they always treated him as one of their own.)

I remember particularly the respectful silence that set in as Marchand approached the microphone. I can see his sturdy form and his ever-unruly hair. I hear his clear, ringing voice, which carried to the farthest corner of any hall, as I weigh the effect of his words on the hundreds of tense and curious faces.

Jean's remarks always started out with facts—a collective agreement to be reached, some arbitration process, an incident in a factory—but he always went beyond the facts and put them in the broader context of social, economic and political life. Marchand explained and showed the inner workings of the forces at play in those chess games in which the workers were pawns. He did this in simple terms, never choosing a word that was not in common use. Yet he managed to deal with the most complex problems with a fiery passion that was contagious. His speeches were not university lectures. They broadened the listener's horizon, but above all they were stirring, they incited to action and combat, they provided weapons for all these workers engaged by choice or necessity in a struggle for which nothing, except poverty and humiliation, had prepared them.

[8] A play by John Thomas McDonough, performed at the Théâtre Port-Royal by the Compagnie Jean Duceppe from 1973 to 1975.

Fifteen years later in the House of Commons I would observe the startled looks of English-speaking members subjected to the shock treatment of a speech by Jean. Surprised and moved, they were more than a little scandalized by the indecency of a style that hardly tallied with the somewhat starchy traditions of that very British institution. They reproached Marchand (aloud from the opposition, *sotto voce* from certain government benches) with making his speeches too emotional, a word that in their vocabulary was a thinly veiled insult. Until the day when a New Democratic member from Toronto, John Harney, made the distinction between emotional and impassioned, and made it stick.

But Marchand's style of speaking went straight to the hearts and minds of the workers. For that matter, trade unionism in general proved to be a most effective kind of civic education. Thanks to it, the workers in Quebec quickly acquired a training in democracy which other groups remained deprived of for a long time. Our schools, colleges and universities at that time looked to a single autocratic model for their mode of operation. They taught their charges how to obey like monks or soldiers, not like members of a free society.

In the labour movement, thanks to the interaction of deliberative assemblies, committees, and elections at every level, life more and more took on the appearance of that organized freedom that constitutes democracy. It was thus reasonable to hope that political awareness might be awakened within it sooner than in other sectors of society.

This was a hope that Pierre Trudeau shared wholeheartedly with many of his friends in the union movement.

Was he involved in the action of the early fifties? Intellectually he had always been involved. But it was to be a few years before he arrived at a concrete commitment, the point where his ideas could intersect with social realities. Already in 1950 he had had a taste of the federal Civil Service in the Privy Council in Ottawa. I doubt very much that he ever

seriously considered a career as a civil servant. But of course
he plunged into the work with all his energy, because he
never did things by halves.

At almost any hour of the day, and often the night, he
could be found in the attic of the East Block, in the dusty
office he shared with a young colleague. Surrounded by
heaps of files, he would cover page after page with his
minuscule handwriting. Exactly who was destined to read
it, I never knew nor much cared. To tell the truth, I didn't
really understand what he was doing there. I was too
ignorant of governmental mechanisms to grasp the importance of his work, and he, bound by professional secrecy,
talked little about it. From a long conversation we had at
that time, as we picnicked on the well-groomed lawn of
Parliament Hill one summer day, I gathered mainly that he
was uncomfortable serving policies of whose timidity he
disapproved.

I also remember that this official position kept him too
isolated for his taste from the concrete action he aspired to.
Or am I interpreting his remarks in the light of my own
prejudices? Trudeau as a civil servant? The equation seemed
false to me. And that he was a civil servant in Ottawa was, I
thought, an aggravating circumstance. There was so much
to be done in Quebec, and so few of us to carry on the
struggle, that I was unwilling to see Pierre stay out of it. I put
all my persuasive powers to work, trying to convince him
that his place was in Montreal, serving in the labour movement. I also talked to him about an undertaking that was
afoot in our little group, an undertaking that as yet had no
name, but which was to become the review called *Cité libre*.
This latter lure got an immediate bite from Trudeau. As of
spring 1950, he was to be found every weekend with us in
Montreal for the preparatory meetings of which I'll have
more to say later.

But I still don't know what made him decide, the following year, to leave the Privy Council. It was not the attraction
of a particular job in Montreal, because he held no such job

for the next ten years. He did many things, very important things, but always as a freelance, à la carte, according to the inspiration or need of the moment. There was a question for a long time of his joining us as a technical advisor to the CTCC. Marchand had made overtures to him on the subject, but nothing ever came of it. During the decade Pierre was to plead a number of causes for the union movement, but on contract, without ever becoming the employee of an affiliated group of unions, nor a partner in any firm that specialized in labour law.

Throughout those ten years Trudeau could have described himself as being a committed outsider.

His fundamental choices were never in doubt. We knew very well where his sympathies lay. But his financial independence made it unnecessary for him to hold a steady job. He cherished his freedom so jealously that some took him for a man about town, a playboy who would never do anything worthwhile. One of his oldest college friends expressed this feeling one day with the quip: "What are you going to do when you grow up, Trudeau?" Pierre was already over thirty, and I'm not sure that he appreciated the joke. Because, despite his appearance of being a man of leisure, he was in on every struggle and never shirked a difficult task. He did not sulk in his tent when there was a cause to be served. But between battles he would take off without warning for Europe or Asia or Africa, for an indeterminate time. This was, of course, a luxury that none of the rest of us could afford. Jean-Paul Desbiens once wrote: "People think that Trudeau is lazy because he doesn't take his holidays at the same time as everybody else."

His independence was not merely a convenience to the globe-trotter's whims. It also allowed Trudeau to take on any case he felt was important, with no more notice than a simple phone call. But he consistently refused any request if there was the slightest hint that he was considered an idler.

As I recall his activities in those days, I can identify the three main lines followed in his involvement in Quebec public affairs. Along the first fall the many tasks, always promptly performed, which he undertook for the labour or human rights movements. Whether he had to represent a particular federation in an important arbitration case, or prepare for another group a statement on equalization payments to the Canadian provinces, or join the picket line of striking metalworkers at Murdochville in the Gaspé, Pierre was on the job, going strong for as long as he was needed.

In the same way, his response was automatic when he had the opportunity to act in the judicial area. He never, I think, considered practising law in a conventional way. But from his university reading he had preserved an acute sense of the citizen's prerogatives in a democracy. Nothing aroused his ire like an abuse of power, especially in the administration of justice. He often indulged in the luxury of pleading causes which did not concern him, but which raised important questions of civil rights and personal freedom. In this he obeyed an imperative logic he could not escape. He too, like Jean Marchand, was endowed with unusual pugnacity, which he had some difficulty keeping under control. It was certainly not apathy that led him to reject the idea of violence, but the conviction that it was unjustifiable in a free society. Accordingly, he renounced it absolutely, but with difficulty. Thus, respect for the democratic process and human rights took on in his view a very fundamental importance. If government did not want the citizens to take up arms, it had to pay scrupulous respect to their right to act, to protest and to make legal claims. From this viewpoint, any attempt to silence a minority or impose order on peaceful non-conformists seemed monstrous to him.

The problems of terrorism and organized violence did not yet exist in Canada at the time. It was only in the early sixties that the first FLQ bombs began to explode in garbage cans and letter boxes or at the entrances to military armouries in Montreal. But the problem did exist elsewhere in the world, particularly in Algeria, in a form that could not leave us indifferent.

Despite our distance from it, the struggle of the Algerian FLN was the subject of debates in Montreal which, if they did not interest the masses, were nonetheless very lively. On the one hand, the Quebec nationalists of those days felt no sympathy, as a rule, for the Arab terrorists in their struggle against the French regime. They were particularly indignant, and not without reason, about the blind terrorism unleashed against the civilian population of Algiers. It was not easy to explain away events like the Milk Bar massacre: a bomb thrown from the street into a family restaurant had killed a large number of customers—men, women and children—who were sipping their evening apéritif. The shooting at La Corniche was no less barbarous: machine-gun fire from a clump of trees overlooking a beach was directed at bathers on a hot, sunny afternoon. The terrorists' only defence was that they had no recourse in peaceful means or a normal military operation. They were struggling to be free, to put an end to the colonial oppression which, in fact, was blocking any possible peaceful political solution. Their political parties had been condemned without the slightest justification.

Their moderate national leaders were exiled or imprisoned. This was the fact that too many Quebec nationalists did not know, or pretended not to know. Their press devoted its space to condemning the atrocious violence of the FLN and remained silent on the no less atrocious poverty of the Algerian *fellahin*. It condemned terrorism and neglected to condemn French massacres likes that at Sétif, or the fierce repression of all the peaceful movements that had tried to end the colonial regime through negotiation.

In union circles in Quebec at the time we were very interested in the national liberation movements that were announcing the last days of colonialism. The fact that the Algerian colonists were French, and were supported by the French military, certainly did not make things easier for us. But in the debate that was raging in Paris, almost all our French friends, starting with those on the review *Esprit*, had taken sides with the FLN. Like them we indulged in a long process of reflection on the legitimacy of the fight for decolonization and on the recourse to violence. We soon made contact in New York with Mohammed Yazid who headed the FLN's lobby at the United Nations. After the five-year war that was still very much in our minds, our first instinct was to reject all use of force, whatever the cause that was to be defended. I believe, for example, that André Laurendeau, without mentioning the fact in his articles, had already adopted the stand of absolute pacifism which he later professed. But the war had also taught us the price of freedom, a horror of all oppression, and the necessity of fighting to preserve the former, while loosening the grip of the latter. We realized, in taking up the cause of the FLN, that we were implicitly condoning the recourse to violence. In certain well-defined circumstances, to be sure, and only under excessive oppression. But we condoned it just the same. We renounced Gandhi's non-violence, for example. And this was not an easy step for our generation, whose adolescence had been touched by the grace of the Indian liberator.

In weighing these distinctions thirty years later, I cannot forget a recent article by Guy Cormier. He maintained that we had had the tables turned on us because we had, with all our energy and against a hostile public opinion at the time, supported the liberation of Algeria, only to be attacked at a later date by Quebec's apostles of independence, a stand which we rejected with like vehemence.

The tables were turned on us? Yes, and without moderation, first by the prophets of *Québec libre* and then by its militants. But how could anyone pretend that Quebec's terrorists ever had the same reasons the Algerians had for their recourse to violence? The two situations were comparable only in the fevered imaginations of adolescent setters of bombs. And if the Algerian situation explained the use of terrorism (the only arm available), no one ever tried to defend our hothead militants. The Parti Québécois, moreover, was to prove that it was possible within Canadian federalism to build up in less than ten years, without violence and using only democratic means, an electoral force that was openly based on a platform of secession, to lead this party to power, and to hold in perfect legality a referendum on the objective of sovereignty. If the FLN had enjoyed that kind of freedom, the war in Algeria would never have taken place.

What is more, our reaction to the Algerian war was not nationalist in its inspiration. I already mentioned that in large part Quebec's nationalists at that time—and France's nationalists even more so—had spontaneously come out in favour of French colonial power. In the debate this war gave rise to among us, what we demanded for the Algerians were basic human rights, rights which we in Quebec had enjoyed for almost a century. And we found the efforts of certain Montreal intellectuals to prove that we were living in a colonial situation within the Canadian federation somewhat futile, to say the least. With great doses of Jacques Berque and Frantz Fanon they concocted analyses and demonstrations that had little to do with the real world, and even very little to do with the authors by whom they pretended to be inspired.[9]

Trudeau's second line of action, of course, was political, and constantly intersected the first. As soon as he had left the Privy Council, Pierre Trudeau made his presence felt in Quebec's public forum, and never ceased to do so until he went into federal politics fifteen years later.

He probably relished the joys of opposing the government more than any of us. He showed an undisguised pleasure in taking on the powerful men of the period. I mentioned earlier that he disliked appearing on television. Was he

---

[9] "...*Les damnés de la terre* of which...our counter-revolutionaries say it is their bedside reading. Which leads me to believe that they read as little in bed as they do anywhere else...." (Pierre Elliott Trudeau, *Les séparatistes: des contre-révolutionnaires, Cité libre* no. 67, May 1964, pp. 2–6.)
[*Les Damnés de la Terre*, by Frantz Fanon, Eng. title *The Wretched of the Earth* (New York: Grove, 1965). Tr.]

unsure of himself in front of the cameras? Perhaps. Trudeau never was a talkative man, and he may have believed (before he himself proved the contrary) that the art of being telegenic was a matter of flooding the screen with words. But he never missed a chance of discomfiting a government spokesman on a question near to his heart.

I have been unable to find, among my too-numerous papers, an article by the columnist André Roche, written toward the end of the fifties, on a televised debate between Trudeau and two Union Nationale militants, one of whom later became a judge. "They were quite unsuspecting," wrote the critic, in substance, "but when Pierre Trudeau began to speak you could see the thunderclouds forming over their heads. Toward the end of the program, the lightning struck." Pierre was already a master of the art of parliamentary debate, of the logical snare laid for the adversary, the unexpected argument that would pounce upon him the moment he felt himself in safety.

More than the other members of our team, who had to preserve the non-partisan stance of full-time union staff, Trudeau periodically took part in direct electoral activity. On a number of occasions he spoke in support of the NDP in federal and provincial elections. But he never consented to become a member of the party, in spite of repeated invitations to do so from Thérèse Casgrain, its Quebec leader in the early fifties. Not only did she want to enlist him in the party, she would have liked him to replace her as head of the Quebec group.

And what a group it was! One would have had to possess Thérèse's sustained indignation and blind faith to accept such a position. In Quebec the party was in a larval, even theoretical state: it had not the shadow of a popular membership, nor any means for effective action. And above all (I will come back to this point in a later chapter), on certain vital political questions its positions were incompatible with some of our most profound convictions. But Thérèse Casgrain never despaired of persuading Trudeau. She used to invite our group to cozy consultations in her Côte Saint-Luc apartment. There we went about our discussions hammer and tongs. Thérèse would begin by describing the political situation of the day, which she always found to be "abominable" (it was her favourite epithet), and invariably ended up begging Pierre: "Take it on, why don't you? You're the only one that can do it. Take it, Pierre."

In her plea, "it" referred to the party itself; she dreamed of seeing Trudeau take it over, to relieve her of a responsibility which was becoming too heavy for her. But Pierre merely smiled, well aware of the vanity of a leadership thus offered to him on a platter. It was Michel Chartrand who eventually took it on and became Thérèse's successor as party leader in Quebec.

Along Trudeau's third line of action we find his written, reflective works, which occupied a very special place in his life. When I read today under Pierre Bourgault's signature that "... Trudeau clings to his dictionary of quotations, he is not a cultured man,"[10] I cannot believe my eyes. A sad incredulity, by the way, because of my friendship for Bourgault, whose natural generosity seems in this case to have been suppressed by political passion or by an eccentric definition of culture.

Trudeau, uncultured? His political learning alone should make Bourgault envious if he were in the least aware of it. Trudeau had read and studied Tocqueville, Gibbon, Marx and Acton, not to mention Aristotle or contemporary thinkers, before his detractor suspected their existence. Indeed, the striking thing about the many essays he published over the years is his thorough knowledge of the authors he deals with. He almost never calls on "famous quotations" of the dictionary variety. How many readers saw him for the first time in his writings some mention of works about which our schools in those days—even schools of higher learning—had never breathed a word? (But Pierre Bourgault, when he

[10] Andrée LeBel, *Le plaisir de la liberté* (Montreal: Editions Nouvelle Optique, 1983), p. 157.

writes about Trudeau, is barely coherent. Three lines away from one another, on the page I just quoted, we find the following three statements: "I despise him.... When Trudeau decides to go places, he goes.... This makes him a winner, and I respect winners." It is a strange contempt, indeed, that is no sooner expressed than it turns to respect.)

I don't believe that Pierre Trudeau ever wrote anything just for pleasure. Even his retaliatory pieces (I am thinking of certain disputations with his former schoolmasters, the Jesuits of the review *Relations*) cost him much hard work. He wrote well, but not easily. His most transparent prose— and I could quote many passages that seem clear as spring-water—called for a laborious effort on his part. He would spend hours on the slightest of his weekly columns for the newspaper *Vrai*. And very often, as I personally witnessed, he would rush to the printer's at the last possible moment to change a word or a turn of phrase that did not satisfy him. Jacques Hébert and I, both professional journalists and all-around writers on the side, would look at each other and grin.

But when I re-read those short pieces today, to my surprise I find in them a quality that has survived the passage of time. The reason is that Trudeau, as a journalist, did not write journalistic articles but political theory and analysis. Current events were merely an excuse or springboard.

In 1956, when he published his long introduction to *The Asbestos Strike*,[11] his vigorous cross-examination of our traditional social, economic and political thought caused quite a splash in our intellectual backwater. As usual, those who squealed the loudest had not read the essay. What they were condemning was the undertaking itself, the very idea of a man attacking accepted ideas, many of which were held sacred. He even went back in time to jolt on their pedestals certain monuments that years ago had been cast in the bronze of our official history. This sacrilege had to be denounced without even examining its motives.

[11] *La grève de l'amiante* (Montreal: Editions de Cité libre, 1956).

Other critics had read the essay, and were all the more furious because they realized how deeply Trudeau had laid his mines. They were not pacified by the fact that this iconoclast was attacking their idols with a style and method that were highly civilized. Mentioning the theoreticians of nationalism, he wrote:

"I think . . . it should be said that almost without exception these men deserve respect. They were not lacking in rectitude in their intentions nor courage in their undertakings, nor steadfastness in their resolution; nor were they always wanting in originality in the solutions they proposed. In the midst of a materialist civilization, pitted against politicians with no sense of decency, the nationalist school was almost alone in producing a *body of thought*."[12]

But out of that thought Trudeau selected for attention "particularly those elements that are now an encumbrance for the present, and stand in the way of free and direct action." His indictment was severe, but calmly stated. On re-reading it now, one is surprised that it triggered such extreme reactions. Even Canon Groulx, who until then had paid little attention to *Cité libre*, emerged from his reserve to give us an indignant scolding on the radio. I remember listening to his diatribe as I was driving home from work one evening. I never subsequently saw the text of his talk, but the impression I have is that it came from a man trying in vain to conceal his distress. He was too intelligent not to realize that his citadel had been mined at its foundation by a man who had read and analyzed Garneau, Etienne Parent and Edmond de Nevers among the nineteenth-century writers, and Bouchette, Paquet, Montpetit and Minville from the present century, not to mention the torrential works of Groulx himself. That evening on the radio he was pronouncing what he refers to in his *Mémoires* as "My pitiless judgment

[12] Trudeau, *La grève de l'amiante.*

on a certain group among the young."[13]

But not all judgments, even those of the nationalists, were so ill-tempered. Some of them were beginning to realize—no doubt assisted by Trudeau's careful reasoning—that a particular kind of abstract idealism had had its day, along with the monolithic character of social thought in French Canada.

A few weeks after the book appeared, André Laurendeau phoned to give me his impression of it. I knew in advance that he would not call down fire and brimstone on Trudeau's head, but the enthusiasm of his reaction astonished me just the same.

He said, in substance: "You can imagine that I'm not in agreement with all of Pierre's opinions. But you have no idea how much I approve of what he is undertaking. It's time that our critics followed their thoughts to a logical conclusion, tackling *all* the problems and coming out with *all* the things with which they disagree, sparing no one's feelings. Trudeau goes straight to the point, and he didn't lose my attention for a second. I read his essay from beginning to end at one sitting. Mind you, it's never pleasant to see things questioned that one has seldom or never doubted all one's life. But I told myself with each page that it was healthy to have my certainties and thinking habits shaken up, especially by a mind of this quality. Do you see what I mean? I wish that all those among us who have something to say would say it with the verve, the frankness and the clarity of this text. The angry shouting doesn't matter: that's the price of creating a true intellectual climate."

Laurendeau was not averse to being challenged, and saw in Trudeau a challenger of great class. I can think of no better way to end this chapter than to transcribe here André's last remarks on a subject that had often cropped up in our conversations. This one took place on February 16, 1968, barely three months before his death. That morning, Trudeau had announced his candidacy for the leadership of

---

[13] Lionel Groulx, *Mes mémoires* (Montreal: Fides, 1974), Vol. IV, p. 302.

the Liberal party. André was in Ottawa, and we had previously arranged to meet at noon. Among my papers I find the following notes, written up that same afternoon while our talk was still fresh in my mind.

Just had lunch with A.L. at the Cercle Universitaire.

Of course the great topic is Trudeau's candidacy. André is against it. There is no question about either his friendship or his admiration for Pierre. His objections bear on three points. And as always his analysis is penetrating. It goes to the heart of the matter.

"I was born," he told me, "of parents who had been brought up on Maurras and *L'Action Française*.[14] This is why, in politics, I am apprehensive about a highly intelligent man whose logic is unswerving. I'm afraid that Pierre's anti-nationalism may have become a dogma for him."

And again: "One has the impression that for Trudeau the sociological dimension does not exist. I know very well that this is a confused field, dense and unclear; and I know the kind of jargon sociologists use. And yet this dimension does exist. Now, it seems to me that Trudeau's intellectual rigour does not take it into account at all, that he leaves no room for it in his political calculations."

And finally: "It's astounding how Trudeau resembles Henri Bourassa: his cult of intelligence, his aristocratic style of thinking, his impatience with certain attitudes (an impatience that verges on intolerance) and his inability to resist a flash of wit, whatever the consequences for him later. Bourassa was like that too; and I wonder if one can be a party leader (and above all a head of government) with a mind that works that way."

On the other hand, André understands perfectly Trudeau's power of attraction. He read Pierre's book,

---

[14] [Charles Maurras—French writer and politician, dogmatic nationalist, monarchist—contributed to *L'Action Française*, a monthly review of which he became the editor, and which he transformed into a daily in 1908. Tr.]

Federalism and the French-Canadians, with fascination and great pleasure. "Even when you don't agree with him," he says, "you can't help admiring him. And he writes so well, the wretch! But what a supreme absurdity to accuse him, as some do, of having been indoctrinated by the Anglos since coming to Ottawa! The man has not wavered an inch in the last twenty years."

CHAPTER 5

The Birth of Cité libre

*"My friend," said he, leading me back
past the old pear tree still in healthy
bloom, "to please the fashionable wits,
you speak rather lightly of your early
philosophy. I pity any man who in his
youth did not have a passion either for or
against liberty."*
CHARLES PÉGUY

W hen I look back and wonder what impelled us thirty
years ago to launch a review when we already had our
hands full with a hundred other tasks, a few lines written
eleven years later by Pierre Trudeau come to mind.
Why *Cité libre*? Because

we were painfully aware of what needed to be done in
Quebec in every domain: we had to replace the
superstructures, laicize civic life, make politics
democratic, pay attention to economics, re-learn our
French, rid the faculties of those who were incompetent,
and open our frontiers to culture and our minds to
progress.[1]

It is clear that our project did not err on the side of
modesty. Even if we had been planning a high-circulation

---

[1] Pierre Elliott Trudeau, *De l'inconvénient d'être catholique* [On the disadvantage
of being Catholic, Tr.], *Cité libre* no. 35, March 1961, pp. 20–21.

magazine with a super-efficient distribution system and a phalanx of top specialists as contributors, this list of tasks— and the illusion that they could be carried to fruition— would have smacked of madness. *Cité libre*, however, was nothing more than a hesitant idea, ill-defined, shared by a tiny group of people. At the very beginning we ourselves didn't know what we wanted to start: a review, a movement, a magazine, or all three at once!

But we knew that a certain silence must be broken, that too many serious and urgent questions were remaining unanswered because no one dared even to ask them. We found this silence oppressive; it had lasted too long. The need of a new forum for discussion was self-evident to the members of our group. But not everyone outside that group shared our opinion. Yet another periodical, destined for a public that was lukewarm to the existing publications... What a slender hope!

When I first tried out the idea on a few friends, I was rather disappointed. I spoke about it to Claude Ryan, for example, as we regaled ourselves on a thirty-five-cent spaghetti plate in a sorry little restaurant on Saint Catherine Street. His reaction was as cool as the spaghetti. "It sounds to me like a case of writer's itch, and you of all people should be wary of it," he said, in those very words, without looking up from his plate. And Gérard Filion, publisher of *Le Devoir*, my boss at the time, described the project as "adolescent," but I never knew whether this was a condemnation or a joke. The interest he later showed in our adventure makes me lean toward the second hypothesis. Filion often affected skepticism about his journalists' projects, but only to test their practicality, not to discourage their proponents. Like a good "*habitant* from the Ile-Verte," as he used to describe himself, he was suspicious of ideas that were too fancy or high-flown.

The high-flown idea in question was, rather, a great dream with vague outlines, cherished for a long time by the members of our team, though it did not have the same origins for all.

The majority faction, if I may call it that, came from the Young Catholic Students movement. Guy Cormier, Réginald Boisvert, Pauline Lamy, Jean-Paul Geoffroy, Renée Desmarais, Pierre Juneau, Fernande Martin, Alec Leduc and I had all done a stint at the movement's head office doing a variety of jobs. But, more important, we had been united by a strong camaraderie, and had done some important work (in our eyes at least) among the student body. We developed a spirit of teamwork and common purpose that we later found hard to give up. At a very early age we had shared the desire and possessed the means to influence our contemporaries, not only in Montreal but in the province and the country as a whole. We came from the Eastern Townships, la Mauricie, Rigaud, the Saguenay, les Bois-Francs. There were more country folk among us than Montrealers. It was the Young Catholic Students that had brought us together in the big city as employees at its headquarters, and made it possible for us to travel from Halifax to Vancouver and make contact south of the border with young Americans of our generation, from New York to Cleveland, Notre Dame (Indiana) and Chicago. After the war, through the same movement, we came together with our French, Belgian, Swiss and Latin-American comrades: we had founded the international of the YCS.

But once we had turned the corner into adulthood we had no desire to stay in youth movements. Were we nostalgic about this first apprenticeship? I don't believe so. We were too impatient about getting on with our lives. But we also wanted to pursue the work we had begun. The YCS had given us a taste for changing the society in which we lived. It had revealed to us the needs, the lags, the weaknesses, but also the possibilities and sleeping forces which we dreamed of awakening. What troubled us was not the thought of leaving the cradle, but the awareness of our lack of means to accomplish the urgent tasks that awaited us. We were working as teachers, union employees or journalists, at the modest level that suited our age. Most of us already had family responsibilities. How could we again manage to have the kind of influence the YCS had allowed us to exert? How could we reestablish contact with our generation to ensure that the work we had begun in the student movement would be carried on?

We obviously wanted to give meaning to our lives. At thirty this is a major concern. For us it took on a special acuteness because of what we had experienced together. Were we henceforth to be scattered and separated, each of us partitioned off into his or her own chosen domain? Was the team going to break up for good, and were our ideas to disappear with it?

It would be hard to explain how these preoccupations led us to publish a review if I did not mention here the influence of Emmanuel Mounier and the review *Esprit*. We discovered both more or less by chance. It was in 1942, when Mounier had only a handful of readers in Montreal, and his review, like all French periodicals, became unobtainable in Canada.

Where on earth had Alec Leduc dug up the already yellowing issue of *Esprit* that she handed me just a few months before we were married? She herself doesn't remember. And all that I recall is the uncanny talent she had (and still has) for discovering unsuspected treasures under the most uninviting piles of papers.

Esprit? The name meant nothing to me. We were familiar with *Les Etudes* and *La Vie Intellectuelle*, published in France, the former by Jesuits and the latter by the Dominicans, and distributed in Canada by their respective Orders. Unlike these two, Mounier's Christian review was, by design, fiercely secular. It had no clerical group in Montreal to publicize it. As Alec leafed through the copy she had unearthed, an article on History by Henri Marrou caught her attention. Little did we suspect that Marrou would become for us a mentor and a friend; but we found his essay—and several others in the review—most impressive. What we were discovering (we had also barely heard of the weekly

Sept, which was unknown in our colleges) was the existence of an intellectual fraternity that came to be known after the war as the "Christian left." Had the expression existed in 1942, it would have held no precise connotation for us. Not only was our political ignorance abysmal, but Quebec politics in general were in their infancy. They would not have distinguished right from left, even if there had been a left. But what was revealed to us in those pages was more significant than any labels inspired by politics.

In *Esprit* we discovered a line of thought for which we had been groping ever since we became interested in the Young Catholic Student movement in our adolescence. We learned that not all Christians were handed down a heritage of hidebound conservatism. We also learned that Christian thought is not by its nature hostile to the innovations and values of the modern world, and that it does not look at History through a rear-view mirror but as part of a resolute approach to the future. The impassioned reasoning that filled the pages of *Esprit* answered certain questions we had only half-formulated in our minds. At a more or less conscious level, they still troubled us. The articles in *Esprit* opened new horizons to us.

Other old issues of the review (we had discovered several of them) began to circulate in the YCS head office on Sherbrooke Street. Articles that had appeared several years before gave rise to endless discussions among us. That they were not recent, that they were unknown outside our circle, made little difference to us. The ideas were new and alive, and that was all that counted. Later, arriving in a liberated Paris, we found that in France and well beyond its frontiers *Esprit* and Mounier's works were very influential. The review's circulation at that time—unusually large for a periodical of its intellectual level—testified to the fact that the articles by Mounier himself, by Marrou, Jean Lacroix, Domenach, Ricoeur and others not only answered the questions we were asking, but dealt with the most pressing concerns of our contemporaries.

One of the first concerns on arriving in France was to make contact with *Esprit* and the movement it represented. But with what precautions and respect we did so! I still reproach myself for the absurd shyness that prevented me from going straight to the rue Jacob to see Mounier, one of the people I most admired in the whole world. That, of course, was the trouble: I admired him too much to take up his time, even with a meeting a few minutes long. I settled for going to hear him speak, religiously reading everything he had written, and getting to know some of his young contributors. Fortunately, other members of the Canadian YCS—Guy Rocher, for example—were not victims of this exaggerated reverence. Nor was Pierre Trudeau intimidated. He was not in the YCS, but he was then undertaking an exploration of Paris that was not limited to its museums and its historic stones.

When we met again in Montreal, we found that we shared a high esteem not only for the ideas behind *Esprit* but for Mounier's audacity. We marvelled at this man who, with no more material means or prestige in 1932 than we had in 1950, had calmly undertaken to "repeat the Renaissance."[2]

Not that any of us took himself for another Emmanuel Mounier. The rebirth we dreamed of was more modest: it consisted in giving rise to a way of thinking in harmony with the needs of our community, and restoring a then much mistreated liberty.

Some of us were mainly preoccupied with religious, or rather ecclesiastical, questions. We had been active in the YCS, dreamed of a renewal of Christianity, and rejected the view that it was incapable of change. But *Cité libre* never had a theological calling. The Church problems that interested us were peripheral, on the boundary that separates the religious institution from secular society. In our YCS days we had asked only to fill that place and role in the Church's everyday life which belonged by right to ordinary believers.

---

[2] *Refaire la Renaissance*, title of the manifesto that launched the first issue of *Esprit*.

At the same time, however, we had become aware of the ambition that led the clergy to dominate everything, to keep whole sectors of purely secular activities under its thumb.

Blithely oblivious to consequences, they thus perpetuated in Quebec society an infantile overdependence, with which they themselves reproached their flocks. We had sworn to put an end to this abuse, not out of hostility to the Church but because of our love for and attachment to it. To us it seemed obvious that an overly protective clergy, along with the prelates secure in their privileges, was leading our Christian community toward disaster. Not purposely, of course: how could they have become aware of their errors when no one dared raise a voice in protest?

Cité libre, as we saw it, should give priority to attacking such a state of affairs. During the time we had spent within the framework of the *Action catholique* we had raised these problems only in private, champing at the bit. But now we felt the time had come to tackle the question of clericalism head-on and in public. For those of us in the YCS this was a long-standing resolve, a well-ripened project. But none of our new friends could remain indifferent to it. "Omnipresent and omnipotent," as we used to murmur, exaggerating ever so lightly, the clergy's activities in those days affected the lives of every citizen. It was not hard to escape its spiritual influence, of course, but one could not easily avoid the authority it exercised over civic and political institutions, not to mention the business world.

The middle class took this tyranny in its stride. People with money could always find some escape. They found Quebec's intellectual climate stultifying, but no one said it out loud. Why endanger your business or your position in the University or the next election, when you could afford a few weeks of letting off steam in Paris or New York every year? There were other safety valves, such as muttered complaints and low-risk anti-clerical jokes at cocktail parties.

Cité libre wanted to put an end to drawing-room anti-

lism. Our denunciations would be public and clearly
lated, in the name of principles we had learned from
urch itself. Those in our team who had not come from
... :s agreed on this intention from the start. They also
shared our "social conscience," as we used to call it. No
member of the group was indifferent to the situation of the
working class. That, along with a sense for freedom, constituted, I believe, the common ground and preestablished
harmony that was never in dispute among us.

When Trudeau talked politics or Maurice Blain culture,
when Roger Rolland waxed indignant about the stagnation
in education, or Charles Lussier gave us a legal standpoint,
or Jean-Paul Geoffroy outlined his trade union projects,
there were healthy exchanges of abuse. In full agreement
about principles, we indulged in the luxury of hard-hitting
disagreement as to form. There was Pierre Vadeboncoeur,
already patiently digging away at his political–mystical
furrow—no one then could guess where it would lead him—
who fascinated some and irritated others by his extremes,
his paradoxes and his ambiguities. If a reader balked at one
of his articles we would cite the case of the young Péguy (at
the time of the *Cahiers*) who had also discouraged his
public. We were never at a loss for a far-out comparison to
defend our writers.

But I'm getting ahead of myself. At this point in my story
we were still founding a review.

By January 1950, we had been talking about it for almost
a year. It was now Geoffroy, now Réginald Boisvert that I
would badger on the subject; or from time to time Guy
Cormier would grow impatient in Moncton, where he was
teaching in Acadian country, and write inviting us to take the
leap or give up, one or the other. There is some pathos in
these letters in which he makes a brave effort, despite the
distance, to put together the first issue of a review "which is
not yet born," as he cautioned. "Let us not make any rash
assumptions."

Yet who would have been rash enough to assume that

Cormier alone, by mail, would be able to accomplish this task, or rather perform this feat? Apparently all the above-mentioned friends must be held responsible for a decision that was sheer madness. Guy was in Montreal for a visit at New Year's and we unanimously appointed him editorial secretary. After that he redoubled his epistolary efforts.

Here are some excerpts from a letter of his, dated January 20, 1950, to Réginald Boisvert:

> I'm writing to Pierre Trudeau. I found a passage in
> Harold Laski I'm asking him to meditate on.... I've
> written (it's done already) to the Sauvés. I asked them to
> do a letter for the review.[3] ... I thought you might do a
> piece on *Esprit* for those who don't know *Esprit*. It
> would be symbolic, in a way, for the first issue of the
> review and that would be good.... We're still counting
> on Pelletier to write what we pompously call a mani-
> festo...but it will be one!... Geoffroy, called Jean-Paul,
> was to write a "Letter to a young bourgeois." I beg you
> to phone him. I'm also writing to Fernand Cadieux. I
> doubt very much, however, if my letter will find him in
> Montreal.... I'm working on a piece myself. And then
> there's the "*Flèches de tout bois*"[4] department. You don't
> think I'm going to do this on my own? It's still pretty
> light, so far as quantity goes at least. Our review has no
> name. Here is my final suggestion: *Exercices*.

It turned out that the question of a name was not so urgent, as the review did not appear for several months. But Cormier was asking for copy to be in by March 1, as the end of his letter shows, "so that it can be at the printer's at the latest by March 20." By April 23 he still had no copy, and was still struggling with the combined problems of our chronic lack of discipline and postal delays which had their picturesque side.

---

[3] Jeanne and Maurice Sauvé were then studying in London.
[4] [Literally, "arrows of all kinds of wood," meaning roughly "grist for the mill." Tr.]

"Your letter reached me only Saturday evening," he wrote. "It must have spent some time in the Post Office. When letters for the University are addressed to Saint-Joseph, they take a few days' rest there before going on their way. The postmaster waits until the 'pile' is big enough to send it on to the University...."

It's clear that the project wasn't quite ready, to say the least. Would it be a review or a mimeographed bulletin? Would it be called *Exercices*, according to Cormier's last-chance suggestion? (Several others had been put forward, among them *Terre promise*, *Lest*, *Raccordements* and *Ville ouverte*,[5] as I discovered in an old file.) And would the "bulletin" bear the address of the Young Catholic Students movement?

Clearly, there were some decisions to be made, but others were already settled: Trudeau would write the political pieces, Boisvert and Geoffroy would share social affairs, Cormier himself would exercise his caustic wit in the *Flèches de tout bois*—it was already on paper—and I was to write a manifesto. In the months that followed everything fell into place. The editorial team began to meet more or less regularly in Montreal, and the project took shape...far from our friend Cormier.

The review was to be called *Cité libre*. It was Alec Pelletier who had invented this name, a variant on the *Ville ouverte* suggested by Jean-Paul Geoffroy. He and his wife Renée, in charge of distribution, would use their own apartment address for the review: 3834 Prud'homme Street, Montreal.

At last, in the spring of 1950, the embryo of an editorial team was there. A year later, with the addition of Charles Lussier and Pierre Vadeboncoeur, we would have the ten editors we had envisaged from the start.

Why ten? No doubt because round figures are reassuring, but also for other reasons. All the participants were close to thirty years of age, and were busy earning a living. We had to make up in numbers for the limited effort each of us could

---

[5] [*Promised Land, Ballast, Connections, Open City.* Tr.]

devote to the review. And the same principle applied to the financing of the undertaking. As we were determined not to be dependent on the Jesuits, or the Dominicans, or the Oblates, or any other patron in publishing the review, but on ourselves alone, we had to pay the price.

In the preliminary note to the first issue (which was not a manifesto, despite Guy Cormier's prediction), we announced: "Each of the contributors to *Cité libre* will share in the ownership of the review. To know the names of the owners, it suffices to read the signatures of the articles. A cooperative review? No: communal."

In plain language, that meant we had been obliged, in order to get a run of five hundred copies of the first issue, to fork out two hundred and fifty dollars to the printer. Thus the ten founders had put in twenty-five dollars each. As it sold for fifty cents a copy, the economics of the project began to look more and more like the business methods of the legendary seller of clay pipes. He sold his pipes at cost, and declared that he made good his losses on broken pipes. We made good our losses on the 30 percent discount we had to give the bookstores.

But the commercial absurdity of the project failed to impress us. The main thing was to avoid being taken over by the "clerical clergy" (as people nowadays refer to politicians' politics) or by any other party of that time. And from this point of view our strange financial system turned out to be most effective.

But when I think back, I must admit that *all* our systems seem rather strange.

At that time *Cité libre* had no publisher. It was written by a team, and as the operation still remained as small as it had been at the beginning, there was no danger involved in giving free rein to our shared aversion to imposed authority.

This team spirit that we swore by, however, put us through some strenuous intellectual gymnastics. No individual, of course, had the last word on what was to be printed. The team alone could decide to reject an article or publish it.

That meant the collective reading (and criticism) of every piece, before all the editors. Whence the need for frequent *Cité libre* meetings: they took up much of our lives from 1950 onwards without ever ensuring the magazine's regular publication.

But we had a lot of fun.

Almost every fortnight the group came together at the home of one or other of its members. These were not male gatherings. Wives and girlfriends were a part of the team, and some of them contributed to the review.

In the spring of 1950 it was at Ile Perrot that the first delivery was prepared. The Pelletier and Geoffroy families had just moved there to share a big stone house which we rented for the season. Our windows looked out on an immense lawn beside the Lake of Two Mountains. Our children ran themselves tired there all day in the sun, free as the wind, so that when night fell and the visitors arrived from Montreal, the young ones were fast asleep. Neither the racket of Trudeau's motorcycle (he rode there from Ottawa), nor the loudest discussions could begin to wake them: dead-tired from exercise and fresh air, they slumbered away, indifferent to their elders' occupations, which were perhaps more intellectual than their own, but just as noisy.

Indeed, we argued hammer and tongs at those meetings, which, as Jean Le Moyne said, "obeyed no orders of the day but only the disorders of the night." For the first hour, once settled on our rather rudimentary seats and armchairs, we rarely did more than try to reinvent the wheel.

What was a review? Did we want to publish a traditional periodical or develop a new formula? And had we the means, in any case? (I refer, of course, to intellectual means.) Was a review possible without a leading figure like Sartre or Mounier? We had no such figure. (We were still obsessed by the great French models.)[6] And finally, were we really sure

---

[6] Thirteen years later the founders of *Parti pris* were still obsessed by those models: "André Brochu knew Pierre Maheu, and said of him: 'He is the Sartre of Quebec. His dream is to create the *Temps modernes* here.'" (Jean-Marc Piotte, *Perspectives*, October 7, 1978.)

that we had something to say?

How many evenings did we squander talking about the obvious! Yet this work had its useful side. The *Cité libre* adventure lasted fifteen years. For a review of its kind in Quebec, that is a long life-span. Had it not been for the patient calibration and the endless process of adjustment that took place in the early days, it would likely have died an early death. This was not a "mainly literary" endeavour, whatever Guy Cormier says.[7] Collective thought was much more important in it than writing as such; and literature properly so-called was a poor relation compared with politics, social questions and religious problems.

The introductory note quoted above stated: "*Cité libre* will hold seminars and working sessions: it is at the starting point of an action."

In my old papers I find a document that explains this sentence. It is the account of a meeting in June 1950, written, or rather taken down, by Alec as the discussion went on. The first issue of the review was well under way at this time, as shown by the titles of a number of articles listed before the notes begin. Then, following the name of each speaker, come a few sentences summing up his remarks.

What was causing us concern on this occasion was the danger of isolation, not as a group, but individually, with each of us inside his own professional ghetto. We wanted to develop a common outlook that would be broader and more accessible than the sum of our professional limitations allowed.

GEOFFROY: If you want this idea to take shape, we'd have to set up real connections with other people, other organizations outside our own team.

PELLETIER: That's just how I see it. We need groups everywhere taking part in our effort: in

---

[7] Guy Cormier, *Un théâtre d'ombres* ["A Theatre of Shadows." Tr.], *Le Devoir*, January 14, 1978.

Sherbrooke, in Trois Rivières, in Quebec City, as in the YCS days.

GEOFFROY: We mustn't found a review just for the fun of doing so, and that's what will happen if we aren't linked to groups with specific needs.

BOISVERT: But that presupposes a whole movement, a platform, a technique...

GEOFFROY: Yes, with regular summer meetings, following a program developed by the central group.

PELLETIER: You're thinking of the *Esprit* movement, in France.

GEOFFROY: Every generation needs a group to represent it. The way the *Jeune Canada* group represented Laurendeau's generation. That leads to working together later on. Most of the *Jeune Canada* people are now in strategic positions.

TRUDEAU: Well, I'm just a novice in your group, but I don't really know what you have in mind when you talk about your summer meetings. We're writing first of all for ourselves, aren't we? The public, for a start, is ourselves. Then other people will recognize themselves in what we print, and they'll come to us. The group will grow by osmosis. But it has to exist first. It's not true that we're fundamentally in agreement about everything. For this first summer, we should be the group, working, and exploring our affinities and divergencies.

Trudeau was right. On the one hand, he really was a novice among us, still grudgingly accepted by our team, several of whom barely knew him. On the other hand, he was vitally interested in our undertaking, which was to allow him, after several years' absence, to find his place again in his generation, and in a circle that was broader than the one to which he belonged. But his personality did not always smooth the way for him. I knew him somewhat better, and noted with some anxiety the reactions of some of my friends of longer standing. They were fascinated by Trudeau, aware of his strength and often dazzled by his intelligence. But something in them resisted him. Pierre's Outremont origins, the rumour which whispered that he was *very* rich (certainly the first millionaire we had ever known), the fact that his religious thinking was inspired by Cardinal Newman rather than by our familiar authors—all these things made him certainly not an intruder (he was the best company in the world), but a kind of come-by-chance. He was a disturbing influence, as he has continued to be throughout his life.

In a recent article,[8] Guy Cormier recalls this feeling of unease, which luckily did not last.

> The first issue [of *Cité libre*] was passed around during the evening of July 14, 1950, in a cottage on the Ile Perrot. Toward midnight a courteous but very lively discussion broke out concerning the participation of Pierre Trudeau.
>
> The original nucleus of *Cité libre* was made up of former YCS workers. One of them made the following pronouncement: "I don't want to see Trudeau on the team. He's not with our people, he never will be with our people."
>
> Pelletier said he had had enough of cliques and coteries, wanted an all-round team. His point of view prevailed, and Trudeau stayed in the group.

How well I remember that discussion! It was the only one of its kind we ever had within our team, for we were not afflicted with the wretched mania of trials and expulsions. Trudeau, of course, was not there when the subject was

---

[8] Cormier, *Un théâtre d'ombres*.

raised. Four or five of us were standing in the middle of the large kitchen, glasses in hand. It was well past midnight, closer, in fact, to dawn. We were having a quiet post-mortem on the evening's discussion when suddenly the thing that had been incubating for months gave the conversation an unexpected turn. It was not Trudeau's ideas that were questioned by my friends, but his origins, his circle, his society connections. He wasn't one of us. He had been in school at a Jesuit shop where the YCS had never even set foot.

On one important point in his article, Cormier's memory was faulty. In 1950, in fact, we didn't speak among our-selves of *our* people, but of *the* people. Our vocabulary was not nationalist: we left that to Duplessis, to Canon Groulx, François-Albert Angers and the Saint Jean-Baptiste Society. Our fads had more to do with the working class, as did our convictions and our feelings. Thus, the reproaches directed at Trudeau were inspired by the vague socialism that for us took the place of a body of political thought. And the friend who made the remark was afraid that Trudeau would betray a social class, not an ethnic group. "We want to be on the side of the people. So does Trudeau. But his origins will always stand in the way. When you're born into the upper middle class, you stay there: you have no choice." That was what our friend said. And it was no doubt unconsciously that Guy Cormier distorted his remarks, giving our preoccu-pations of that time a colouring of today.

In the same way, some people deduced from the date (July 14) chosen for *Cité libre*'s launching that some nameless nostalgia for France had turned us into stay-at-home emi-grants. Nothing could be more wrong. What actually in-spired this choice was the theory of the meaningful paradox. To celebrate the fall of the Bastille was to turn our backs on our whole clerical–nationalist education, which never tired of abusing the French Revolution (responsible for all the evils in the Western world) and considered *The Declaration of the Rights of Man* a highly suspect document. Our celebrations were not nostalgic but turned toward the future. We attacked a censorship that spared no form of liberty. (I remember that in 1950 Quebec proudly banned the tribute we wanted to pay to a *bad* author on the centenary of his death: Balzac!)

But we carried on our attack with good humour, glasses of red wine in our hands. Every year for the next twenty summers a group that was constantly growing came together, first at Lac-en-Coeur and later at Lac Ouareau, for a whole night of singing, dancing and drinking, ending at dawn with a dip in the icy Laurentian water.

On that morning of July 15, 1950, there was certainly nothing very frightening about us. Our team was not a large one. Putting together the first issue of *Cité libre* had been hard work. Every text published had involved long haggling with the author and endless discussions among us. Luckily the team's enthusiasm was high enough to surmount these obstacles, and the future was to show us shortly that we had arrived just in time.

Barely had our poor five hundred copies been distributed (and that in mid-summer) when the reactions began to flow in. Nothing could have pleased our youth and impatience more. We had been fighting for a long time against the greyness, the boredom and suffocation of a society ruled by too many martinets; now we hoped to awaken many echoes. The first words of our first issue were revealing on this point: "We have been here, hundreds of us, for some years now, suffering from a certain silence; and that is why *Cité libre* now sees the light of day."

We had broken the silence. We had reactions from everywhere. It mattered very little to us whether the answers held praise, contradictions or insults. We had hit the target. Only the absence of any reaction, or even the organized silence to which some of our predecessors had been treated, could have discouraged us. On the contrary, our readers responded as if they were touched to the quick of their feelings or convictions. The reactions fell into two main classes: an enthusiastic reception or angry disapproval.

A student wrote to us from Paris, where he was attending university:

I received the review this morning, I have skimmed through it, and I began to love my country as I never thought I could. Because our Quebec is a country in distress.... When will some great social observer give us a psychoanalysis of Quebec, as a great sociologist wrote a psychoanalysis of Alsace? While we wait for this great healer to appear, I think that *Cité libre* can lead us on to certain breathing exercises that may save us from asphyxia.

As I re-read this rediscovered letter, I can better understand how Mr. Georges-Émile Lapalme could say today: "*Cité libre* never played any role, anywhere."[9] Because our correspondent's reaction is not one that a politician, vintage 1950, could ever understand.

But a good orthodox Jesuit, solidly seated at the heart of the immense power his Order wielded in Quebec society in those days, interpreted the impact of the review in quite a different way. For him it was not Quebec that was sick, it was the publishers of *Cité libre*. In the review *Relations*[10] the Reverend Joseph-Marie d'Anjou turned his gaze upon our little magazine.

As I re-read his article today, I can hardly believe my eyes. The author saw in our articles only "the stirring of uneasy souls prey to deep-seated complexes and a glaring aggressivity. A reader with no more than the rudiments of psychology could in a brief perusal get the impression that he had been handed a psychological case-book...." Despite this diagnosis, Father d'Anjou did not prescribe psychoanalysis for us. Less anxious to treat our "case" than to preserve morality and dogma from our impious attacks, he mobilized in Indian file Saint Paul, Pope Boniface VIII, Archbishop Léger

---

[9] Georges-Émile Lapalme, Mario Cardinal, Vincent Lemieux, Florian Sauvageau, *Si l'Union nationale m'était contée* (Montreal: Boréal Express, 1978), p. 236.

[10] *Relations*, March 1951.

(not yet a cardinal), Borromeo, Pope Pius v and Ignatius Loyola.

How can one explain today why our articles (very well-behaved articles, as we knew) could cause such acute irritation to educated, intelligent priests at the very summit of clerical power in our community?

It was André Laurendeau (once again) who gave the clearest answer to this question, simply noting in *Action nationale* the existence of certain problems "that *Cité libre* did not invent but had undertaken to bring to light." He had first emphasized that "as a number of subjects seem to be more or less taboo, we hear no mention of them anywhere, or such muted mention that it becomes inaudible."

But if there were hundreds to deplore that it became inaudible, there were thousands of others, not only to rejoice in this state of affairs but to make sure that even the faintest mention of these subjects was stifled. For example, when the Archbishop of Montreal was forced by the Vatican to "resign," this self-censorship was automatically applied. No one imposed it formally, but no one dared to breach it. The official version of a "resignation for reasons of health" appeared everywhere in the press, while everybody and his brother knew that it was false. Still worse, when Archbishop Charbonneau himself from his Vancouver exile assured the *Canadian Press* that he was in the pink of health, *no one* had the courage to pick up this flagrant contradiction in public except *Cité libre*. But the tone of our remarks was far from reflecting the "glaring aggressivity" *Relations* had found in them.

Here is a sample:

> Why [we asked], was it necessary to surround the departure of our archbishop with this shameful silence and these clumsy lies which deceive no one? Is this really a necessity of ecclesiastical policy? Any true version, however distressing, would have seemed preferable to us....[11]

---

[11] *Cité libre* no. 1, January 1950, p. 39

"Quebec," said our friend Guy Cormier at the time, "is a college. The day pupils are in Montreal." We had resolved to exploit to the full our freedom of expression as outsiders or day pupils, but the great majority of Montrealers went on behaving like boarders. Just think: our first issue contained praise of Léon Blum and Harold Laski. In the next issue, Trudeau's political article talked of a "Quebec where we are educated to have the reflexes of slaves before the powers that be. We ourselves must again become the authorities," he wrote, "and let the disciplinarians and the police go back to their proper place as servants. Premiers do not hold their positions by divine right, nor do bishops. They have authority over us only by our consent."

The phrase "divine right" was to lead us directly to the Archbishopric of Montreal. Archbishop Léger let me know via his secretary that he wanted to meet Trudeau and myself "to touch on certain subjects relative to *Cité libre*."

It was near the end of summer 1951. We had an early evening appointment. I remember the two of us walking across the Place du Canada after a quick dinner in some barbecue on St. Catherine Street. We were not worried, but rather stimulated by the prospect of the kind of tough discussion we had always wanted. We had no idea of the form the discussion might take; we knew only that our review might die of it before it was rightly born. If the Archbishop was as angry as we feared and rumour reported, the irreparable could take place, because we had no intention of retracting a single word. Was he going to tackle certain questions in the tone of a discussion, an exchange of ideas, or announce to us at once the blow that would put an end to *Cité libre*? Either event was possible in the mood of the times, and what we knew of his Grace's temper was not reassuring. Paul-Emile Léger did not belong to the race of lambs, nor even to that of timid shepherds. Since his arrival in Montreal there had been no sign that he wanted to slacken the clerical vise: quite the contrary.

Icon of the Great Darkness. "Duplessis inflicted upon us a
twenty-year reign of lies, injustice and corruption, the systematic
misuse of power, the sway of small minds and the
triumph of stupidity."

Le Chef, Maurice Duplessis. "We found his spoor and his agency at the origin of every attempt to preserve all that was obsolete in Quebec. Many players were skilled on the instruments of reaction, but he conducted the band."

Louis Saint-Laurent *(left)*. "Not that the man was without merit, but he lacked imagination and never managed to see the curves in the road ahead."

Future Premiers. Paul Sauvé *(left)*. As Minister of Youth, he "denounced the champions of free education. They were, he said, trying to bring misfortune on the people." Antonio Barrette *(right)*. "'The real nationalists, that's us, the Union Nationale. Who needed that *Bloc populaire*?'" Daniel Johnson *(below)*. "He told us, 'If you're so anxious to play politics, why don't you get elected?'"

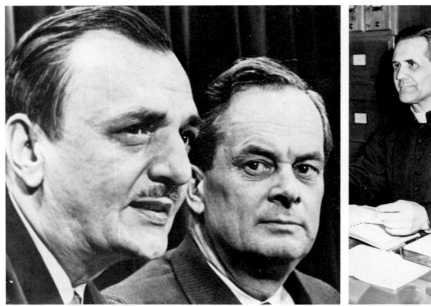

André Laurendeau *(left)*. Active in the *Bloc populaire* and later editor of
Le Devoir, he "watched the generation that followed his with a sharp
but friendly eye." Paul-Émile Léger *(right)*. "He did not belong to the race
of lambs, nor even to that of timid shepherds."

Arthur Tremblay *(left)*. By 1953, "he was already obsessed by the
grand design that was to occupy his lifetime: educational reform."
Félix Leclerc *(right)*. "Only a few of his friends were acquainted in those days
with his rough-hewn poetry. Yet he was already in the process of launching
Canada's contribution to the contemporary French *chanson*."

Pierre Trudeau in Paris, 1947. "He was the only one to have already begun reflecting on the evolution of politics in Quebec and in Canada."

Jean Drapeau *(left)*. "We have all had time to forget that he often, and to many people, appeared as a possible recourse to Duplessis in the fifties...a more likely one than Jean Lesage." Réal Caouette *(right)*. "A terror of the airwaves, with disconcerting virtuosity he wielded everyday speech, popular imagery and the disarming comparison."

Asbestos, 1949. Food trucks arrive to bring relief to the miners.

Jean Marchand *(below).* ''His speeches were stirring, they incited to action and combat, they provided weapons for all those workers engaged by choice or necessity in a struggle for which nothing, except poverty and humiliation, had prepared them.''

René Lévesque. "He was one of the few TV stars who appealed to the audience's understanding rather than to its emotion." "René possessed a very rare quality: the gift of communicating his knowledge and insights."

The CBC Producers Strike, 1959. "André Laurendeau wondered, 'Is this René's Road to Damascus?'"

September 10, 1965. Pierre Trudeau *(left)*, Jean Marchand and Gérard Pelletier. "René phoned us from Newfoundland to beg us, in the name of his own experience, not to join the Liberal party in scattered order but to go in 'at least three at once' as a team."

What was waiting for us on the other side of the door where we were now ringing? First of all, a grumpy old porter who ushered us into a parlour and immediately disappeared. "Here we are, back in college," Trudeau whispered, glancing around at the antiquated furniture. From their high frames a number of pontiffs stared coldly down at us. The armchairs were ugly, stiff and uncomfortable as they inevitably are in the parlours of Christendom.

The Archbishop made his entrance. There were the usual greetings and handshakes, then ... nothing. An embarrassed silence on both sides. A bad start. Why was our host, normally at no loss for words, sitting there and smiling at us? Was he expecting explanations from us before they were even asked for? As Trudeau didn't let out a peep, I screwed up my courage and said:

"You called us in, your Grace ... "

He shifted in his chair.

"I invited you," he corrected me. "This is not a summons. I invited you, first of all to make your acquaintance and then to draw your attention to certain points ... of doctrine raised by your articles. You see...."

He was launched. The ice was broken. To say our conversation was cordial would be overdoing it. The Archbishop remained tense, and so did we. But our discussion was polite and reasonable. Obviously, Trudeau's "divine right of bishops" was the main subject. Trudeau put the expression in its context and defended his position so sharply that the Archbishop was moved to say: "If I were to condemn the review for this proposition—and several others—it would be with great regret, believe me."

"And we," interrupted Trudeau, "would appeal to the universal Church, as is our right."

The Archbishop, disconcerted, stared strangely at Trudeau. He hesitated a moment, then went on to his next point. I have a lively recollection of those few seconds during which, I believe, the fate of *Cité libre* was decided in the incredible atmosphere of a medieval dispute.

That was Quebec in those days. It was to take several years before the religious authorities fully accepted our role as critics.[12] For the next ten years we were to deal in turn with almost all the questions that people felt it was more appropriate to ignore, especially those having to do with freedom of expression, religious freedom, political freedom and freedom itself.

If we had followed our natural bent we would no doubt have resorted to the overt provocation that had brought down the wrath of bishops and cardinals on our great predecessors such as Olivar Asselin. But we were men of action. We wanted to reach a specific objective: an improvement in Quebec's intellectual climate. And we knew that condemnation by the religious authorities would put an end to our venture. It was thus important to know how far to go.

Two French friends, professors Henri Marrou and Paul Vignaux, gave us invaluable advice on this score. It was normal that the *Cité libre* team often tried to kick over the traces. It was tempting to forget all caution and vituperate against oppression by the clergy, instead of sticking to the rational tone we had adopted at the start. But our two mentors, who came from Paris every autumn to give courses at the University of Montreal, protected us from our own indiscretion.

Marrou, the historian, reminded us of the disaster of the *Sillon*, a movement of young Christian progressives whose condemnation by Rome at the beginning of the century had delayed by a whole generation the emergence of a Christian left in France.

Vignaux, the trade-unionist and philosopher, gave us more secular examples. "You should remember," he told us, half-bantering, half-serious, "Lenin's question at the time of Brest–Litovsk. Lenin asked those who objected to the shame

---

[12]Ten years later, in January 1961, Cardinal Léger invited us for dinner to his house in Lachine: Pierre Trudeau, Jacques Hébert and myself. It was a friendly encounter. The tension in our relationship had disappeared, and from that day on there was increasing trust between us, right up to the Cardinal's departure for Africa.

of a separate peace between imperial Germany and the Russian revolution: 'Are we here to die with honour or to save the proletariat?' It would be very easy in your case to die with honour," Vignaux went on. "Just give in to your impatience, publish a few imprudent articles, and the Church authorities will pronounce some kind of condemnation against you, and there you are. You would either cease to exist or become so marginal that you don't count any more.

"The hard thing for you is simply to last. In order to do so you must take certain precautions. I know it's not easy, moderating your tone when you would like to shout, sounding reasonable when you are burning with anger. No, it's not easy. But only by so doing will you succeed in what you want to do."

Marrou put it even more strongly: "Your *originality*, the reason *Cité libre* is disconcerting, is that your criticisms are made by Christians. You are a voice *within* the Church, and that makes all the difference. If you are pushed outside it, no one will listen to you except the tiny group of declared non-believers."

Jacques Perrault[13] gave us the same advice. And some of the clergy as well, such as Father Germain Lalande, an old friend, and the Dominican Louis Régis, a more recent acquaintance. But the prestige of Marrou and Vignaux, comrades-in-arms of Emmanuel Mounier since the first days of the review *Esprit*, impressed us even more.

Of course the "tiny group of declared non-believers" did their best to play the part of provocateurs for our benefit. They had no reason to fear a condemnation from us.

In the same old file, I find a strange document that I had completely forgotten. It is a letter from the writer Claude Gauvreau. It is dated January 27, 1951.

---

[13]Prominent Montreal lawyer and legal adviser to *Le Devoir* Jacques Perrault had developed a gently humorous theory of the "meaningful paradox." Though he was the attorney of the Archbishopric he also supported the cause of the left.

Dear Gérard Pelletier,

Do you believe in freedom of speech? No, of course not. And this is the proof of it: The article I enclose has been refused by another publication. You also will lack the independence, the force and the moral courage to publish it.

What a less hostile paper than yours was so cowardly as to deny me, your paper will consciously refuse me as your enemy.

You will not assume either the right or the responsibility to discuss openly the ideas my article contains.

Of course!

You will not lack for excuses: too long, poor style, repetitions etc.

Please be so cynical as to make your list.

In full awareness of my inalienable superiority,

Claude Gauvreau.

He was right about one thing: *Cité libre* never published the piece he sent us. I believe the article has still not been published. Its title is "Spellman, Rossellini and Censorship." It begins with the following two paragraphs:

Cardinal Spellman, this obese individual with the sharp, shifty eyes, was no doubt hungry for the bright lights of publicity. No one was talking about him any more. The professional blarney-merchants of American journalism had turned their filial apple-polishing away from his haloed head. He felt neglected. Cardinal Spellman, this obese individual with the obstinate features of a Machiavellian hypocrite, has declared war on Roberto Rossellini.

A boycott of the film *The Miracle* has been ordered.

The Legion of Decency—that organization of creeping blackmail, fabricator of multi-morphous inhibitions exploitable for mystical sublimation, began by wagging all its spidery limbs: the hysterical, the moonstruck, the simple-minded, the ambitious, the cuckolds, gamblers backing the altar, speculators—all these co-ordinated the rhythm of their nauseous oscillations. Because the obvious can only be defeated by obscurantism!

The rest of the text is also in this vein.

I cannot imagine why Claude Gauvreau thought he was (or that we thought he was) an enemy. That had never crossed our minds. I had taken the liberty, in a critical piece for *Le Devoir*, of making gentle fun of him, but not in an ill-humoured way, I think. The oddest passage in his letter, however, is the one in which he assumes we will condemn his article for its length, its poor style, his repetitions, etc. We did not make a habit of being pedantic or obsessed with grammar. If there was a certain emphasis on handling the language with care (thanks to Pauline Lamy who kept an eye on our participles) it would never have occurred to us to tell others how to write, and above all to use grammatical errors as an excuse for rejecting an article when we had other reasons for doing so.

I don't remember our reply to Claude Gauvreau, and can find no trace of it in my files. But if, despite the dislike of censorship we shared with him, we did not publish his article, it was because we rejected verbal violence. *Cité libre* was not a broadsheet.

On the other hand, we had neither the leisure nor the competence to make it a truly serious review. We were green with envy of our French, English and American counter-parts who could snap their fingers and collect three econo-mists, six political writers or a dozen psychiatrists ready to write an expert article on any given subject. Whom did we have to deal with the grave and complex problems from which our society was suffering? A handful of young people keen for action, not all of whom had even graduated from university.

The uneasiness engendered by this awareness of our weaknesses was expressed in the second issue of *Cité libre*.

Many readers, we wrote,

> mistrust our venture. Some go so far as to refuse us all
> credibility, and hold as condemned from the start a
> project in which, according to them, competence must
> inevitably be replaced by good intentions.
>
> This is certainly the objection that strikes closest to
> home.... With every step we take, we feel the lack of a
> specialist who would be really on top of a given subject.
>
> Thus it would be very easy just to give up the under-
> taking.... We could have limited *Cité libre* to a single
> issue devoted to proving that it was impossible in French
> Canada to publish a truly serious review.
>
> But we thought it was better to give it a try.[14]

In the episode related above, about the team's hesitation
to accept Trudeau, the feeling of our inadequacy played an
important part. And when Guy Cormier wrote that "Pelletier's point of view prevailed... and Trudeau stayed," he
gives me too much credit. It was Pierre's intellectual bag-
gage that was his passport to the group and finally won
their confidence.

In mid-September 1950 (our second issue did not appear
until February 1951), I received a letter from Trudeau in
Ottawa about a special issue the team had asked him to
plan. He was still working in the Privy Council, whence the
scruples he mentions, which finally led him to return to
Montreal a year later.

> Ottawa, September 17, 1950.
> Dear Gérard,
> I'm sending you the four-part plan of an issue on war
> and peace. All kinds of real preoccupations prevented
> me from doing it earlier, and even from giving it the
> thought it deserves.
>
> Look at it as soon as you can. By the way, you will

[14]*Cité libre confesse ses intentions, Cité libre* no. 2, February 1951, p. 7.

have to resign yourself to many meetings without me in future. I'm prepared to go as often as previously, but that is not enough, especially as Saturday is not always the best day for you.

I don't know if you'll find the plan I'm submitting workable. The four articles will need a lot of effort, but that's a minimum if we want to do an issue on the subject.

. . .

Before deciding on the portion to be assigned to me, I must ask you to realize that my role here is becoming more and more delicate. As long as I am in the Civil Service I have to obey the rules of the game. This week I had some long conversations with a lawyer for the Civil Service Commission to clear up the situation. It seems I would be very imprudent to write anything that touched on political controversy.

. . .

So, to sum up, briefly, in a word...the only article you could assign to me would be the first one on the theory of peace, and even then I would have to remain very theoretical.

. . .

I can't think why I didn't explain this to you last Saturday. It was perfectly obvious that of all possible subjects, the foreign policy of our government was the one I could least afford to discuss at this stage of international developments. The fact that I didn't think of this at once proves that I still don't have a bureaucrat's reflexes.

If there is a meeting Saturday let me know. If it's on the Ile Perrot, I'll stop in on the way from Ottawa. And damn it, let's try to get started before ten o'clock!

Peace and fraternity,

Pierre.

The special issue never appeared. Trudeau's article was

the only one of the four that got written (it was a remarkable piece, by the way), and it was published in May 1951, signed "*Cité libre*." The subject, of course, was the Korean war, the prelude to the Cold War. After that article, not only was Pierre accepted fully as a member of the editorial team, he became an indispensable stimulation for us all. An issue of the review without his name on the page of contents seemed dull even to our least demanding readers.

I might say as well that he was more faithful to *Cité libre* than to any other undertaking in his life, except, of course, the political project that has occupied him almost twenty years.

By the end of 1951 the review was well under way. It was beginning its hectic, chaotic existence—a review that was really different!

I already mentioned that in eight years we published only twenty issues instead of the thirty-two expected of a quarterly. Why so irregular? I suppose that there is a different explanation for every year, such as a strike in Louiseville, a long stay in Europe for Trudeau, the cancellation of a special number because too many contributors had failed to come through with their articles. And how many other reasons? Our structures, as people say nowadays, were so fragile that the slightest incident could set them trembling.

The amazing thing was that the review was able to provoke such a stir in spite of its bad publication habits. A friend who was teaching abroad in the fifties wrote to me on this subject: "Really, I can't understand it. All the Quebec papers I get here allude to *Cité libre* so often, you'd think it was a daily, though you can't even manage to come out four times a year!"

The explanation of this phenomenon is doubtless that we refused to play the game of obedient silence. One voice is enough to break a silence. The weak voice of *Cité libre*, despite our low circulation, was enough to place a problem before the public. Once the problem was posed, everyone felt the need to talk about it. The conservative or out-and-out reactionary publications, such as Quebec City's *Action catholique* or Montreal's *Notre Temps*, flew to the aid of the Church, or Law and Order which they saw as threatened. Other periodicals often took advantage of a breach opened by *Cité libre* to slide in their own comments. And as they laid the full blame on us for having broken the silence, or rather took us as an excuse for attacking other taboo subjects in their turn, we were cited in a great many articles.

Finally, in religious circles, publicity by word of mouth still had the extraordinary efficiency of the bush telephone. Starting with its second issue, *Cité libre* began to circulate (clandestinely, of course) in the colleges, convents and seminaries where our whole intelligentsia was educated. A lawyer chum of ours supplied the Jesuit theological school, then attended by several hundred students. As it was a boarding school, they had to wait for their first holiday before their couriers could go to our friend's office and pick up the two copies reserved for them.

As for the diocesan clergy, we had many friends among them because of our years in the YCS. They signed up for subscriptions in good faith, which did not fail to irritate certain bishops. Quicker on the riposte than most of his confrères, Archbishop Philippe Desranleau of Sherbrooke honoured us with a few sentences in one of his pastoral letters. He warned priests not to read *Cité libre* and advised those who had already subscribed to cancel their orders without delay. But a careful check of our lists in the following months revealed that not only had our readers remained faithful to us, but a number of Sherbrooke priests, who had previously shown no interest, quietly became subscribers in the weeks that followed.

It would be false to say that we were unconcerned about whether the review was influential or not. If that had been true, why take the trouble to publish it? But the question did not preoccupy us unduly. None of us counted on *Cité libre* for notoriety. We had access to other papers, and to radio and television. We were neither suffering from obscurity nor running for public office. And our energies had ample outlet in other tasks.

But there was another explanation for our capricious publication dates and the lack of order in our administration and distribution processes. *Cité libre* was the place where we could write and think at our best. We might rush an article for a newspaper, but for the review we gave nothing less than our best. That "best" may seem a little pathetic today to those of us who look back at our texts. But if we recall those days carefully, we can testify retroactively to the severe vigilance and care we exercised. We never hesitated to delay the publication of an issue if it seemed possible to improve its quality by a few weeks' additional work.

Such scruples surprised some of our contemporaries, and still more our juniors. I can still see the expression of panic and astonishment on the face of a very young man who happened to be invited to one of our meetings. He was passing through Montreal, between two university terms in Paris. I don't remember who had brought him along to Charles Lussier's place on Rockland Street, to the big basement flat where we often met. Our usual group was there, as well as Anne Hébert who had just published in *Cité libre* her poem *Le Tombeau des Rois*. As we took our places I was watching our young guest out of the corner of an eye. He had brought a text with him, but didn't know to whom to give it. He held it awkwardly on his knees, as if impatient to be rid of it.

The meeting started.

If I remember rightly, it was Maurice Blain who was presenting a long article for the next issue that evening. After a short preamble he began reading it aloud, according to the established ritual. Everyone listened with close attention, including our guest, who seemed puzzled by this procedure. He kept looking around the room, more interested in the behaviour of the company than in Blain's reading.

But it was at the end of that reading that he seemed to lose his bearings as all of us, men and women, took turns at criticizing what we had just heard. The team was already broken in by this time, and we didn't pull our punches in formulating our points of view. Comments flew in all directions, praise and blame mixed together with a minimum of mincing words.

My young neighbour couldn't get over it. Was Maurice Blain going to stuff his article back in his briefcase and go out slamming the door?

Not at all. The process went on. The author accepted even the most abrupt remarks with good humour. Sometimes he would make note of a remark on a pad which he held on his knees. Sometimes he would argue, defending his piece and rejecting our interpretations. On some points his critics would beat a retreat, convinced by Maurice and his patient explanations calmly expressed in a voice never raised in irritation.

After a good half-hour of this exchange on "A Dynamics for Our Culture," it was my turn to read my contribution. I think it was called "Crisis of Authority or Crisis for Freedom?" It went through the mill. I can still hear Trudeau opening fire, asking where I got my mania for titles ending in a question mark. And later, during the page-by-page challenges, it was Trudeau again who reproached me with killing my ideas in my conclusion, "as all of us have a tendency to do, as if we lost courage on the way, and were afraid to pursue our logic to the end and rejected the consequences of our own premises."

The young visitor was dumbfounded. When our working session ended and we were having the no less ritual drink that wound up our meetings, I saw him coming toward me, glass in hand, shy and obviously anxious.

"Do you always work this way?"

"Yes. Always."

"Do you tear all your articles in the review apart like that?"

"All the important ones, yes. But sometimes they're better

than mine and don't arouse so many objections."

"Really . . ." he said, musingly. "I wonder if I could submit to the rule. And what about the friendships among you? Don't they suffer in the process?"

"Friendships? No. Vanity sometimes. But we get over it quickly, precisely because we're friends."

"Really . . ." he murmured again, as he left.

And I noticed that he had put back in his pocket the article he brought for us.

This young man's name was Hubert Aquin.

CHAPTER 6
Vox Populi

*There are no breaks in History. We can
never declare ourselves out of the game.*
P.-L. LANDSBERG

P aname, Sunday, March 16, 1952.[1]
Dear Friend, or rather, Sir,
If your question was so precise, it was because you failed
to include any of the elements that would have allowed
me to make an intelligent answer. On the other hand,
this deficiency in your letter makes an immediate reply
possible. A thought-provoking missive from you would
have taken time.

Well then!... Yes, I "would be interested in running in
a provincial election, probably *in asbestos country*, with
the *total support* of the unions and our friends, of
course." It would interest me because I have never in my
life felt so unattached, physically and morally; because
I'm ready to commit the greatest follies; and because, all
in all, I am just now in a rather pitiable state. I was going
to leave around mid-April to vegetate and write in the

---
[1] Paname: affectionate, admiring *argot* for "Paris."

Sicilian sun for an unspecified time. All things considered, however, I wouldn't mind going over there to vegetate, where the Duplessis sun king shines. The advantage
of Sicily is that the number of follies I could commit
there is limited. Whereas the adventure you're
suggesting—if it is badly run—could compromise certain
ideas, and the futures of several people.

I count on your friendship not to make me commit a
folly when I'm in a state of hypnosis. Don't wonder
about whether I'm serious—I am. The only thing that
makes me reply affirmatively to your "feeler" is an act of
faith in your judgment. But if you want a candidate who
is something more than a straw man, who has become a
candidate freely and acts intelligently, you have to make
me an intelligent proposal.

1. Do you have in mind a general election or a by-
   election?
2. Will there be a number of union candidates? Who?
3. In what ridings? Have people started *working* on
   those ridings?
4. What is "the total support of the unions"? The
   CCT, the CMT, the CTCC?
5. Is the CTCC officially abandoning its apolitical
   constitution?
6. Is there a precise electoral platform? Is this being
   worked on?
7. Is there an electoral machine at the disposal of
   candidates (e.g., will the union leaders be
   encouraged to campaign actively?).
8. Where will the money come from?
9. Who are the 4 or 5 chums who are in on the plot, for
   whom "this is a very serious proposal."
10. Does my candidature (for better or for worse) exclude
    the possibility of my becoming a "technical advisor"
    to the CTCC (the job that Marchand once offered me)?
11. Did you write mainly because "Marchand wants to

know . . ." or because you yourself feel vitally committed to the scheme?

I leave you, wishing that your next letter would be less simplistic. And tell Alec to drop a friendly line. When is Anne-Marie's first communion? If it's soon I won't be able to bring back the things you asked for in time.

. . .

If the Economic Conference in Moscow is on, I may leave Paris in six days' time so as to be able to stop off in Austria and Czechoslovakia on the way. So I won't be back in Paris until mid-April, and I want news from you before that.

Zig heil! Skalski!

Trudienko.

I have no trouble recalling today the genesis of this letter posted from Paris by Pierre Trudeau in answer to my own.

Daniel Johnson had told us three years earlier, "If you're so anxious to play politics, why don't you get elected?" In fact, we were not anxious to "play politics," but we refused to live in a stalled society. And it was becoming obvious in the early fifties that every social sphere in Quebec was ready for a change, except the political milieu itself.

The employers, for example, were beginning to evolve. Though small businesses and the industrial sectors that were in difficulty still sought shelter under the wings of religious arch-conservatism and other reactionary groups, the big employers feared an explosion and were trying to forestall it. No doubt they would exploit to the full the benefits a retrograde regime still offered them, but they now understood that this situation could not last forever. They could foresee the end of certain privileges. They were getting ready to negotiate with the unions in Quebec, which were becoming ever more assertive. There were still to be tough strikes and many attempts to deny the right of association; nothing had yet been won, but the change was beginning.

Also, despite its antiquated structures, the educational system was starting to stir. Compulsory schooling and a sudden rise in the birth-rate just after the war were having their effect. The schools were literally overflowing with students, and the religious communities, with their decreasing membership, felt their monopoly slipping because of the mass influx of lay teachers. In the colleges and universities there were signs of a demand for free secondary education, easier access to university, and a reform of teaching methods. To be sure, the old structures were resisting. It would be another ten years before the reforms came into effect. But the movement was already under way. Not only secular voices were raised in its favour: many open minds within the old clerical system were ready for the change.

The clergy as a whole were questioning their own positions: their role, their usurped power, their traditional omnipotence, which they felt was growing weaker. The ferment of action by laymen within the Church had challenged the clergy's confiscation of responsibilities that were not their own.

The change at first took the form of Byzantine controversies which it's hard to believe engaged the passions of reasonable men halfway through the twentieth century. These disputes were not over theological questions. The argument was not over the addition of *filioque* to the Apostle's creed in A.D. 589, but over problems that had long been solved in the majority of Western societies.

There was wrangling, for example, about the religious affiliation of cooperatives and trade unions. The traditionalists violently denounced the neutrality of these institutions (meaning their freedom from direct control by the clergy) as treason to the Christian faith. They also maintained that the Church had established for believers a social doctrine as obligatory as the most sacred religious principles, which dictated in advance certain political choices.

In the domain of education, should girls be given access to the classical humanities, or should all female students be confined within an apprenticeship for maternity or "household science"? Could the bishops accept that Quebec, like other States, should acquire a minister of education? Was it conceivable that our pontifical universities (which they all were) would ever be under the direction of a lay rector?

These questions were not only asked, they were the subject of endless disputes among the bishops. And the great religious orders joined noisily in the strife: Jesuits on the right, Dominicans on the left. As a rule the discussion never reached the general public. It was rarely that one found any reference to it in the daily press, except in some oblique editorial allusion.

But at times a more irritable bishop would indulge in open warfare. Archbishop Philippe Desranleau of Sherbrooke once published a pastoral letter in which he denounced non-denominational service clubs and forbade his diocesans to join them. Apparently his episcopal city was infested with Lions, Moose and Elk. It was not Christian, the prelate remarked in passing, to endow human beings with such animals' names. That belonged, he said, to a pagan mentality. There was no lack of mischievous priests to dig out of the Bible the Lion of Judah, the Lamb of God, etc.

But that did not settle another aspect of the question: Should the Richelieu Clubs, of Christian origin, ask their bishops to appoint chaplains, or should they not?

How was one to react to these controversies? Watch them and sneer? Brush them aside contemptuously? Have a good laugh at the expense of the protagonists? That would have been a mistake.

We had little desire to get mixed up in them. But the scope of the phenomenon seemed to us significant. This threshing in the underbrush had to be stilled before the real problems could be faced. What was more, these debates were shaking the pillars of the clerical temple. Its monolithic nature was our enemy, and as soon as people stopped thinking in unison, freedom began to have a chance. The slightest crack in the solid block of the dominant ideology brought a ray of hope. As it turned out, this effervescence, grotesque as it may have appeared to some, was the forerunner of developments with extraordinary implications.

But there was not a single swallow to herald the most timid political springtime. On the contrary, the Duplessis government was defending its positions more obstinately. It took refuge in a fierce rejection of all change, backed by a constant appeal to our traditions, the worst and the best of them, but mainly the worst. We heard it sung in every key, with the regime's characteristic emphasis, that we had the best educational system in the world, that social peace reigned in Quebec as nowhere else in the world, that we were free of the evils from which France and the United States were perishing, that we alone had preserved those Christian values that were scoffed at and flouted elsewhere, and so on and so forth.

All that was nauseating. But the question began to arise insistently: how on earth would we ever achieve the social changes that were necessary if Maurice Duplessis remained obdurately in the seat of power? It was he who was blocking the horizon. And his regime as yet had showed no sign of faltering. Seriously shaken by the asbestos strike in 1949, the Union Nationale had made a quick recovery. Barely a year after the end of the conflict, the people of Thetford had brought back as mayor a Duplessis MLA who had not lifted a finger to help the hungry, strike-bound town. He had, on the contrary, supported the government's repressive actions. All over Quebec, leading citizens of all shades and hues were closing ranks around the *Chef*. The parliamentary opposition was still searching for a platform and a fighting stance. The federal government, except on the question of autonomy, seemed quite ready to get along with a masked dictatorship that was preventing Quebec from advancing into the twentieth century.

In short, the new forces at work had at their service only a marginal and ill-defined political expression. As a general election was approaching we were looking desperately for a way to make a breakthrough, however modest, into the political field. We realized now that this was the only way, and that trade union or social action could never accomplish their goals as long as the levers of political power remained in the hands of a clique mainly concerned with self-perpetuation.

What means were at our disposal?

There was no question of undertaking a major campaign. The Quebec Liberal party was not yet that of the Quiet Revolution. Its liberalism, wrote Pierre Vadeboncoeur in *Cité libre*, "is not revolutionary, it is out of date." Should we join it, and change it from within? Perhaps we were wrong not to choose this path, which René Lévesque successfully took in 1960. But that seemed impossible to us. The Liberals at that time were no more likely to accept us, and not much more concerned about democracy, than the Union Nationale itself. And above all, our troops, a handful of militants, were totally involved in a labour movement that professed to be strictly apolitical. As for the CCF, the labour party of those days, in Quebec it did not have a French name or the embryo of an organization; nor did it arouse the slightest interest.

"Just the same," said Jean Marchand after our gloomiest analysis of the situation, "we can't simply sit on our thumbs. The boys in Asbestos didn't fight for nothing. We have to find a way to prove that not everybody goes along with Duplessis. The labour movement needs a voice in Quebec's parliament."

From that was conceived the (stillborn) idea of three or four union candidates for the summer election. Pierre Trudeau, in the letter I quoted above, was reacting from Paris to the proposal Marchand had asked me to transmit. I no longer recall the exact terms of my epistle, and no doubt Trudeau the nomad (as he then was) left it in the wastebasket of some hotel room. But I remember the main points of the project. It involved choosing a few working-class ridings where unionism already had some muscle (for example, Asbestos, Shawinigan and Thetford) and putting up union-backed candidates who were independent of existing parties. Marchand guaranteed to supply a team of union staff people to run the campaign and mobilize the membership to support the venture.

Clearly there was no question of beating the government. The Liberals themselves knew (and privately admitted) that they had no chance of doing so. But if we could get a few men elected, or even one, the workers would have a voice in Quebec City. Duplessis would not be able to accuse them of all the accumulated sins of forty years of power committed by pre-war Liberal governments. Nor could he write them off, as he had done to the nationalist Members of the defunct *Bloc populaire*, by proclaiming that "only the Union Nationale could claim to be heir to the great patriots of the past." Behind our handful of candidates would be the growing strength of the labour movement. They could not be dismissed without some people taking to the street. Asbestos had proved that.

We were dreaming.

When I say we, I don't mean only Marchand and myself but the whole progressive wing of the CTCC. Gérard Picard listened to us with interest. Jean-Paul Geoffroy and Jacques Archambault were behind the project. And among the union militants of the time, Rodolphe Hamel, the veteran of Asbestos, Daniel Lessard of Thetford, Lavergne and Brûlé of Shawinigan, Adrien Plourde of Arvida and Marcel Pépin in Quebec were for it, along with many others. Outside the labour movement the idea attracted a few journalists (including the whole team of *Cité libre*) and a number of university professors. But how many reservations were expressed when it came to concrete action!

From Paris, Pierre Trudeau had seen them clearly. Except for the first question in his letter (general or by-election?)

which sounded as if it came from Mars, given the expiry date of the government's mandate, his questions were sharp and relevant.

I don't remember how I answered him, but no doubt my second letter gave me a good deal of trouble.

Yes, we were thinking about several candidates, but apart from him had no one really in mind. No, there had been no preliminary work done in the ridings. And did we, in fact, know what was involved in that kind of work? I'm afraid not. We were utterly lacking in experience with elections, and had nothing but contempt for the traditional election workers typical of the Union Nationale machine, half crook, half bully. We may have tended to confuse union organizing with electoral campaigning, and failed to make the distinctions dictated by reality.

But where Pierre touched the heart of the matter was in asking if the "total support of the unions" included participation by the American internationals affiliated to the AFL and the CIO. Because in Quebec there prevailed an atmosphere in the labour movement that was frankly schismatic. In a pinch the CTCC and the CTC (CIO) could envisage working together. But the AFL affiliates (the FTQ), old-fashioned trade unions, kept up a barely dissimulated flirtation with Maurice Duplessis and his government. They were not ashamed to be classed as dollar-minded unions. Their president told me one day at a public debate in which we were both taking part, "There is no principle I am not prepared to sacrifice in negotiation for an hourly raise of ten or fifteen cents." Moreover, the spectacular rise of the CTCC in the forties and its new militantism were very disquieting to a Quebec AFL that had long grown passive and blasé. Who could believe that it would get into a political adventure that was hazardous to say the least and certain to interrupt its recent honeymoon with the government in power?

Moreover, right inside the CTCC there was no lack of old militants who would throw up their hands at the very mention of political activity. Though the unions hesitated to work on the ridings, Duplessis's men had been working on the unions for a long time, without the slightest scruple. By handing out modest favours and insignificant privileges (they kept the big money and sinecures for the leading citizens), the party in power had infiltrated certain professional federations. Within their ranks the party had reliable friends who did their best to resist any reform. The debate on political activity, which was open in the CTCC after the asbestos strike, had as yet led only to very timid steps. We were far from being able to count on an involvement of the movement itself, with contributions of men and resources, in an electoral undertaking. If the leadership of the CTCC— not to mention the FTQ (AFL) or the CTC (CIO)—had officially encouraged its members to get into politics, there would have been serious repercussions in the movement.

It was acceptable to attack openly this or that government measure, and the leaders certainly took advantage of this. But to go as far as openly supporting a particular candidate was something else again.

What Trudeau called our "scheme" was aimed precisely at crossing that line, while trying not to provoke such waves as would ruin the undertaking. This was why we had thought of acting outside the parties, putting up specifically union candidates. But what precise platform would these men have? Could they ignore all other problems and concentrate solely on the labour or union aspects of Quebec politics?

*　*　*

Trudeau came back to Canada. The discussion his letter had touched off went on for a few weeks, but the project never got off the ground. If I mention it here, it is because it led to a process of intense reflection, no longer merely on the general goals of our political action, but also on the concrete and practical means of ensuring its success. Perhaps for the first time men of our generation and cast of mind were seriously thinking about running for public office. Also for the first time, Pierre Trudeau and Jean Marchand came together to plan a common project. This was the beginning of a long association. Thirteen years were to pass before it led to a final commitment by the two men and their firm resolution to be elected.

If I cannot recall exactly the circumstances that surrounded the abandonment of the project, it's because there were so many others equally short-lived. I spoke earlier about the joys of the opposition: we were to enjoy them for a long time.

I see this whole period as a series of triumphal victories for the forces of Duplessis and humiliations for their adversaries. At the federal level the outlook was not much more encouraging. How could it have been, for us? Our idea of federalism implied participation by a modern and vital Quebec. As long as the country's main francophone component remained silent and withdrawn, as long as it refused to follow the changing times, how could it play its part in Canada and leave its own mark—as Ontario was doing—on this country in full development? And how could the other French-speaking communities scattered across the country resist the pressures, the prejudices and the cultural intolerance of the anglophone majority without the indispensable leadership of Quebec?

Mobilized for the struggle in Quebec, we had little time to think of Canada as a whole. Without giving up hope for the needed reforms in the central government, we felt they were impossible to carry out if Quebec did not first emerge from its stagnation. For us that was the absolute priority and the indispensable prerequisite.

Our union activity, however, brought us in frequent contact with the government in Ottawa. Every year the CTCC submitted a brief to the federal authorities, and current business also led us to see this or that minister to make representations on particular and urgent matters.

While our visits to Quebec City were dominated by the coarse rebuffs, the puns[2] and buffoonery of Mr. Duplessis,

---

[2]Gérard Picard was president of the CTCC, and Canon Henri Pichette was its

our pilgrimages to Ottawa had the cold, starchy and solemn atmosphere of a Protestant church service. Simultaneous translation was not yet in use in the federal capital. The few anglophone ministers in Mr. Saint-Laurent's entourage stared at us with dead, fish-like eyes as we set forth for them (in French) our annual demands. Only the French-speaking members of the cabinet seemed to be following. And it was the Prime Minister himself, of course, who led the debate, though he often appeared to be ill-informed on the problems that concerned us.

One year, after we had deplored the stagnation in the textile industry, Mr. Saint-Laurent took the trouble to explain to us the deeper causes of this decline. In his harsh French he began by noting the drop in consumption:

"People are buying less cloth than they used to," he said in the laboured tone of an adult explaining to a child the mystery of a four-holed button. "People don't dress the way they used to. They say young women no longer wear undershirts."

During this monologue I had been watching our union officials. They seemed not to understand, not having read *Madame Bovary*. And the Prime Minister never suspected that he had that morning revealed to us an unexpected secret touching on the antiquated vestimentary habits of Madame Saint-Laurent.

The official attitude of the federal government to the union movement was polite, in no way aggressive, but clumsily paternalistic, in vivid contrast with the blustering, scolding contempt of the premier of Quebec. But the avuncular calm of Mr. Saint-Laurent did not rub off on all his ministers. A visit to Mr. C.D. Howe sticks in my memory. Some leaders of the CTCC had joined with their confrères of the CLC in submitting to the minister of Defence Production

---

chaplain. After a discussion the *Chef* concluded: "To interpret the Church's social principles I'd rather rely on Pie XI and Pie XII than on Pichette and Picard." [Pie = Pius. Tr.]

certain requests concerning the wartime factories, which were still running at nearly full steam in the early fifties. Pat Conroy, one of the most remarkable leaders of the CLC, made the presentation. Mr. Howe listened, leaning heavily on his desk, his eyes half-closed.

Conroy spoke with rare precision, and with all the eloquence of his convictions. C.D., as he was called, punctuated the speech with muffled grunts whose meaning was a mystery. It became clear, however, when our friend had finished his plea and formulated his conclusions. Without moving, Howe said distinctly, unanswerably, "My reply is no. Thank you gentlemen." And he stood up as a sign that the meeting was ended.

On the political side, it was our contacts with the CCF that kept us in touch with federal matters, because we were trying at that time to interest the party in the realities of Quebec. As I mentioned earlier, the group in Quebec was about as robust as a ghost. I think I am right in saying that it had more anglophone than francophone members in the province, and as its constitution at the time made it a highly centralized organization, its party workers in Quebec always had the disagreeable impression that their activities, even at the provincial level, were remote-controlled from Ottawa.

A great deal of nonsense has been talked to the effect that the men I'm writing about belonged to the CCF. In fact, none of them was ever a member of that party. If public opinion associated them all with it (except René Lévesque, who was not in the circle) it was for certain reasons that are interesting for what they tell about the political situation in those days.

As the only left-wing party in Canada, always reviled by the most authoritarian clergy of Quebec,[3] it was natural that the CCF should attract those for whom the word socialism was no longer a bugbear. I would even suggest that the

---

[3]Archbishop Georges Gauthier of Montreal had condemned the CCF in the thirties.

unanimous hostility it inspired in our reactionaries of all shades was enough to make it attractive to us. The phenomenon is familiar to all men of action: one is spontaneously drawn, even without knowing them, to those who are persecuted by a common adversary.

An extreme case of this negative magnetization comes to mind. At the time of the ephemeral Federation of youth movements of Quebec, which, toward the end of the forties, united all young people's groups, I made the acquaintance of a stalwart, good-natured and blunt young man from the Beauce, a farmer's son who, in the Federation, represented the Quebec Communist Party. Flanked by a young French girl who occasionally whispered in his ear the answers to our questions, he liked to provoke us into impassioned discussions on the world revolution, the dictatorship of the proletariat and the influence of Stalinism in Eastern Europe. The girl's militancy did not surprise me. A doctor's daughter, vaguely Amazonian and remarkably well-read, this beautiful, ardently eloquent girl reminded me of certain prototypes of keen communists I had run into in Europe in 1946.

The case of the boy from the Beauce, however, was a mystery to me. Where on earth had this young rustic, product of a countrified, ultra-Catholic background, as *Canayen* as they came, caught the Marxist–Stalinist virus? Quebec in those days had no more than a handful of communists. How had he found his way to them? After a meeting one night, drinking a beer in the Ontario Tavern, I asked him this point-blank. He was not surprised. He laughed, looked me straight in the eye, fidgeted on his chair for a moment and said:

You've been wanting to ask me that for a long time, I know. The answer is easier than you think. Pelletier, do you know what a country parish is like? Compulsory high mass every Sunday? Lenten retreats? Sermons an hour and a half long? Well, I know what it's like. A bossy priest, an intolerant mayor. Holy Virgin, they made me sick, the lot of them. And as you can imagine, they were all talking against communism all the time, the priest and the vicar and the notary and the MLA. What was communism? I had no idea. In Saint-X in the Beauce? So when I decided to revolt, my reasoning was very simple. If all those guys are against it, I said to myself, there must be something good about that party. That's how I became a communist. Not in the Beauce! There weren't any communists around home. I had to come to Montreal to find some.

Our approach to the CCF was not quite so simplistic. But when the CCF came to us in search of French-speaking members, a similar reaction was triggered off in us. And if other factors had not been there to confuse the issue, perhaps our whole generation would have joined this party whose labour-oriented platform was made to measure for us. What was it that held us back? Simply, the CCF's obvious lack of understanding of questions that were very important to us. We disagreed about the nature of Canadian federalism and the basic complexity of Canada as a country. Moreover, the party's federal leaders knew little about Quebec, and less about Quebec's francophones.

In the fall of 1947, fresh from my European experiences, I met David Lewis at Professor Frank Scott's place in Montreal. From that long conversation with David I remember just one of his replies to the questions I peppered him with. When I enquired about his party's position on Mr. Duplessis's autonomist attitudes (the only point on which I was close to the *Chef*) I received a decisive reply: "We don't cater to Quebec nationalism."

One reason why I'm sure that my memory of that short phrase is accurate, is the fact that I had heard the English verb "to cater" for the first time that day. That evening I had to look up its exact meaning in my dictionary. My research revealed that David Lewis was missing the train. According to him, it seemed, anyone who demanded that the federal government should respect the constitution was automatically the kind of Quebec nationalist his party did not wish to encourage. The division of powers between the levels of government, that keystone of the Canadian system, was not even worth attentive examination. And by implication I, who had raised the questions, was one of those Duplessis-style Quebec nationalists that were not to be catered to.

To say that I was put off would be an understatement. If this incident had later turned out to be a misunderstanding or a purely personal attitude of David Lewis's, I would gladly have reversed my judgment. But no: the federal leadership of the CCF, and of its successors, the Social Democratic Party and the New Democratic Party, never missed a chance to show its insensitivity to the heart of the Canadian problem as we saw it. On this matter the Party line has had its ups and downs, from the obtuse centralism of the post-war period to the near-separatism of the Quebec wing in the early sixties. But that's another story.

The reader may wonder why, in view of this obvious and basic lack of understanding, we later agreed on several occasions to associate ourselves publicly with initiatives of the CCF.

No doubt we were not lacking in conceit, the pet vice of young men who think they can change everything and bend all things to their will. But we were not so presumptuous, after all, as to commit ourselves deeply before clearing up the misunderstanding. Our failure to do so explains the arm's-length distance that we afterwards maintained.

But these reservations did not prevent us from cooperating with the party, as long as we still hoped an understanding would some day be reached. And then, in a period of masked dictatorship, when the opposition was small and mistreated, one is not so particular. There were so few possible allies that all democrats felt the need to stick together, despite their divergencies.

However, the CCF party was unable to win more than a few hundred votes from French-speaking Quebecers in any riding, and not even that in all ridings—far from it. On one election night (was it 1952 or 1956?) some of their candidates got fewer than a dozen votes. I remember that Pierre Juneau jokingly remarked that it took some heroism to vote under those conditions. "There should be a medal," he said, "for electors whose candidate received fewer than ten votes."

Nevertheless, the CCF constituted a political voice. There was nothing discreditable in supporting it on occasion. There was agreement on the broad lines of its platform. This, no doubt, was why Pierre Trudeau campaigned several times for CCF, SDP or NDP candidates, but with no illusions—to that I can testify—and without ever becoming a member of a party which would have welcomed him with joy.

Politically, then, there was nowhere to go.

From this state of affairs was born, in 1956, a movement that will certainly not attract the attention of historians: the *Rassemblement*.[4] On the evening when it was founded, David Lewis had predicted its future in four words and a smile: "It will peter out." And Trudeau, Marchand, Laurendeau and I laughed with David. We all knew, I think, that the *Rassemblement* would have a short life. None of us ever believed that it would resist the wear of centuries or singlehandedly transform the political life of Quebec.

A few hundred women and men, however, took the trouble of getting the movement under way. They spent their energy and their money and their leisure too, simply because at that moment it was the only thing to do, the only possible thing, and the most immediately necessary. And so they agreed to set up an organization that was fragile, but allowed them to act despite the current constraints. They had understood that in politics inaction is the worst of evils, especially the verbose and whining inaction of an intelligentsia bereft of power.

---

[4][*Rassemblement*: rallying point, gathering. Tr.]

And that was what threatened us in Quebec toward the mid-1950s.

On the one hand, as I have pointed out, the breakthrough of unionism was progressing, despite the obstacles put in its way by the Quebec government. On the other hand, an increasing number of *intellectuals*—professors, writers, senior civil servants, students, members of the clergy and the liberal professions—were growing aware of our stagnation and the urgency of putting an end to it.

The most aware, the less timid ones and those who had no personal ties to the regime had just established (in 1954) the Institute of Public Affairs. Every year, thanks to an agreement with the Canadian Broadcasting Corporation, the Institute gathered a few hundred people together in a Laurentian hotel for a seminar, as we would say today, on a current problem. For three days we listened to prominent speakers and held lively discussions, while the main sessions were broadcast live across the country, thanks to the French Network of the Corporation.

This initiative was not without merit. The annual meeting allowed many people to get to know each other, people who would otherwise have remained strangers deprived of a common vocabulary and a common approach. In an atmosphere of a struggle toward the most elementary democracy, which was the atmosphere of the period, it was quite useful for combatants of all shades of opinion to come together once a year, regardless of origin, tendencies and generations, to take their bearings on the state of the Quebec and Canadian societies.

The nationalists from *Le Devoir* could rub elbows with those with social interests from the Laval Social Sciences faculty; the political types from Ottawa and Quebec City met union leaders, journalists and a few writers. Marcel Faribault and Léon Lortie met Jeanne Lapointe, Jacques Hébert or Judith Jasmin. Maurice Lamontagne, Jean-Louis Gagnon and Father Georges-Henri Lévesque, who were among the Institute's founders, never missed a session. In order to lower the average age of the participants, subsidies ensured the presence of student delegations from all the universities. And finally, a few representatives of the English language sister organization came each year from Toronto to join the debates.

Every year one saw new faces. The gathering was like an intellectual festival, an exhibition-hall of ideas, not limited to a single school. You went in there as into a mill. I remember, for example, the slim (oh, yes!) dark silhouette of the young Jacques Parizeau turning up at Sainte-Adèle one fall, fresh from his studies in London and Paris. He had a clear, elegant and precise way of speaking, and an intelligence as lively as it was decisive. No one knew him yet, except the small circle of his students from the Hautes Etudes Commerciales. I see also Jean-Pierre Goyer taking his first steps in public affairs, Robert Cliche, Bruno Meloche and how many others! I think I first met Léon Dion there. He was just beginning to establish his reputation as a professor.

The beauty of the arrangement between the Institute and the CBC French Network was that the Corporation provided funds to invite foreign speakers to every session. In this way we came to know Raymond Aron, François Perroux, René Rémond, Hubert Beuve-Méry, Alfred Sauvy, Paul Ricoeur and several other important European thinkers of the day. But the Institute's principal merit was no doubt the introduction in Quebec of the practice of face-to-face dialogue in public, and civilized discourse among people of the most varied and contrary opinions. (In case the reader wonders whether this tradition survived, I must say that the Institute gave up the ghost toward the end of the sixties, a victim of the dogmatism that had begun to return after ten years of absence from our political scene. The truce had not lasted long.)

After every session we found that we were better informed about our problems, less wanting in theoretical solutions, more up-to-date on the currents of contemporary thought on questions as vital as education, economics, Third World development or international affairs. This was not a slender achievement. But so far as action was concerned, the results were negligible.

The most noticeable effect of these debates on the participants was that they exacerbated each one's discontent. The conservatives, partisans of the regime and the established order of things (they didn't come in crowds, but they came) left with the certainty that these warped intellectuals were fomenting revolution. And those same intellectuals were dying of frustration, having realized their powerlessness. Some naively deplored the apathy of the masses, though the masses were much more active than the university elites. Others lamented loudly that they would never see Quebec throw off its reactionary yoke, but they were counting on those same "apathetic masses" to give the first push.

It was high time to provide this vague but profound discontent with a more effective safety-valve than mere words. The intellectuals and liberal bourgeois were no more ready than the workers for direct electoral action. We would have to prepare a transitional phase, and develop a formula halfway between idle talk and party campaigning.

We also had to define a common objective capable of rallying the discontented of all kinds, who constituted a highly varied fauna. Like all oppositions, this one was profoundly divided. Bakunin said of the revolutionary movement of his day that it grew like the cellular mass of a living body, by dividing itself to infinity. So it was with the anti-Duplessis forces in the mid-fifties. What platform would unite everyone? What positive goal could we all agree to pursue together, without wasting too much time in preliminary discussions?

It was not an easy problem to solve. As I always had a liking for concrete approaches, I tried, for my part, to personalize the question. I would ask myself, for example, thinking of three of our friends, "What common denominator is there between Pierre Dansereau, Jean-Marie Bédard and Noël Pérusse?" This exercise often looked like an attempt to square the circle.

Pierre Dansereau, a distinguished professor, a scientist, a product of the nationalism of the thirties and the Jeune-Canada movement, a man who also had wide international experience gathered in his botanizing excursions around the world—Pierre Dansereau was the eminent incarnation of our intellectual middle class.[5] He lived in Outremont. His speech was polished, with a touch of an Outremont accent that was slightly precious. His father was a friend of Duplessis. He never identified himself with any political group, except perhaps for a furtive attachment to his friend André Laurendeau's *Bloc populaire*. His natural habitat was the university. In fact, I was not aware that he had any well-defined opinions on the future (or the present) of Quebec. I knew only that it made him furious to think that we were governed by a man who was totally estranged from the contemporary realities that he, Dansereau, had observed on the six continents, including Oceania.

Jean-Marie Bédard was as far removed from Pierre Dansereau as a man could be. Nothing about him was reminiscent of his rural origins. Squat and a little on the stout side, rough-mannered at times, a staff member of an American union, he anticipated the typical romantic leftist with whom we were to become familiar in the sixties. One would have taken him at once for a factory worker. He lived modestly, affected a worker's manners, and looked like the neighbourhood tough guy. Gifted with a powerful voice and a strangely old-fashioned eloquence that was none the less effective, he was always conspicuous at meetings. For him, communism was already a thing of the past. "Jean-Marie," said his friend Marchand, "has gone without any transition from Léon Bloy to Trotsky!" He

---

[5]If I speak in the past tense of the people in question here, it is merely to indicate the time at which I came to know them. They are all, thank God, in the land of the living as I write these lines.

preached an absolute radicalism, was carried away by anarchist songs, loved to indulge in all kinds of provocation, and never missed a chance to denounce "the regime" in language so crude it would have sent a bishop into a fit.

As for Noël Pérusse, he was several years younger than the other two. He, too, worked as a staff member of a union, but his style differed from Bédard's. Son of a civil servant, a university graduate, with a quick mind and an impatient tone, he was the complete technocrat, down to his meticulous way of dressing, his well-combed hair and his metallic voice. I believe he was the first *intellectual* to work for the FTQ. He had made his choice: he was a militant Social Democrat (formerly CCF) and found it hard to understand that others had reservations about his group. He maintained that all power would emanate from Ottawa the day the CCF–SDP won a national election.

I could go on forever with the list of disparate personalities that were attracted to the *Rassemblement*. It would not be hard to show that the movement was already moribund from its internal divisions before it saw the light of day.

Yet there was a common denominator among all those people. They were all aware of the threat to democracy in Quebec that came from the Union Nationale's regime. That democracy was still in its infancy, despite a century of representative government. They did not, of course, fear a turn to fascism, still less a military dictatorship. The very idea of Maurice Duplessis in uniform, with his paunch and his short arms, his nose as pointed as a 1914 bayonet, was enough to dissolve such a project in laughter.

But we already had a masked dictatorship, with its petty authoritarianism, its sabotage of democracy by corruption. If I'm not mistaken, it was Pierre Trudeau who first developed this theme, which the *Rassemblement* had the merit of publicizing. We do not, he said, have a true tradition of democracy:

History shows us that French-Canadians never really

believed in democracy for themselves, and the English-Canadians never really wanted it for others.[6]

With truths taken out of context, such as "All authority comes from God," some of the clergy have made us forget that the people is sovereign. Through an educational system based on theocracy, the citizens of Quebec are prepared and conditioned to live under authoritarian regimes. Mr. Duplessis's genius lies in having realized this. And if we fail to become aware of this danger, we will be slowly but surely deprived of our democratic rights by the very fact that we neglected to use them, or refused to defend them. The process, by the way, is already far advanced.[7]

And Trudeau went on to invite all the regime's opponents to forget their differences on questions which might indeed be important, but which did not involve dangers as serious as the Duplessis government's attacks on the very foundations of political liberty.

One would think such a simple proposal, based on such obvious realities, would have had no difficulty in uniting most of the opposition groups. But the climate of the times was unpropitious.

Three weeks after the convention that founded the *Rassemblement* (which several hundred people had attended in September 1956), the press of the regime opened fire. One may wonder why this new-born movement constituted a target for the Duplessis artillery. The founders had simply identified the *Rassemblement* as an organization with no party ties, dedicated solely to the political education of the

---

[6]*De quelques obstacles à la démocratie au Québec*, in *Le fédéralisme et la société canadienne-française* (Montreal: HMH, 1967), p. 107.

[7]This kind of analysis led a certain Denis Monière to state in 1977 that Trudeau (and *Cité libre*) were ruled "by one postulate: we (the French-Canadians) are *congenitally* inferior and powerless." This shameless distortion of the stated positions of others seems hard to reconcile with the notion of social *science*. Yet this Monière formerly taught social science at Ottawa University. Denis Monière, *Le developpement des idéologies au Québec* (Montreal: Editions Québec-Amérique, 1977), p. 138.

citizenry and the improvement of Quebec's political climate by the promotion of democratic values. They had adopted a strongly worded declaration of principles, but those could have been defused easily by the most authoritarian politicians of the government simply by adopting them, as they had, for example, adopted the Church's social doctrine. To Mr. Duplessis, a few principles more or less made little difference, as he felt bound by none.

But the reaction was not so restrained.

Already on the second of October, Mr. Clément Brown was writing in *Le Droit*:

> The *Rassemblement* sets itself up as a school devoted to the social and democratic education of the people. The high-sounding declaration of principles it has been so kind as to give us, the vagueness of its doctrines, the lack of precision in its attitudes, the poor quality of its leaders and the disturbing character of some of its protagonists—none of this is likely to encourage support from those who would like "something new" without sacrificing what has been acquired.[8]

A few days later, the unofficial mouthpiece of the Union Nationale, *Montréal-Matin*, reproduced these remarks, and *Le Temps* in Québec, its official mouthpiece, commented on them with a heavy hand, asking: "Are we moving toward secularization and democratization?"[9] For *Le Temps*, of course, which went on at length on the subject, democratization was a grave danger.

As for *Nouvelles et Potins*,[10] another newspaper (if one may stretch the term) that performed the lowest tasks for the Duplessis party and indulged in the most primitive and shameless anti-unionism, it gave a quick answer with no excess reasoning: "This is no *rassemblement*, no gathering

---

[8]*Le Droit*, Ottawa, October 2, 1956.
[9]*Le Temps*, Québec, October 24, 1956.
[10]*Nouvelles et Potins*: "News and gossip." Tr.

of minds, but a pack of good-for-nothings that can inspire no confidence among the upstanding people of Quebec."[11]

But a few unexpected comments reflected the development I mentioned at the start of this chapter. For example, the review *Relations* which, six years earlier, had given *Cité libre* such a cool welcome, had kinder words now for the *Rassemblement*:

> If this movement should fail in its campaign for a better-informed and healthier political climate, the task to be accomplished is so urgent and important that others would have to rise up to carry on the work and bring it to completion.[12]

And the Toronto *Globe and Mail* summed up what it knew of the movement:

> The *Rassemblement* has not yet completed or announced its working plans, but at least its constitution clearly establishes the movement's philosophy. It is not a political party, and is not and will not be affiliated to any party. . . .
>
> The movement will work toward the establishing of a political climate in which it will become possible for politicians not only to discuss public affairs with honesty but also, perhaps, with intelligence.[13]

Perhaps we should have been suspicious of this approbation from conservative sources, the first that the Quebec left had ever received. Why were conservatives—intelligent and honest in this case, but conservative just the same—suddenly interested in supporting our initiative? On the other hand, why had we created the *Rassemblement* if not to attract *all* democrats, including honest conservatives?

---

[11]*Nouvelles et Potins*, Montreal, October 22, 1956.
[12]*Relations*, November 1956.
[13]Robert Dufy, *The Globe and Mail*, Toronto, November 18, 1956.

We were to learn very shortly that it is easier to gather people under a single banner than to make them live there together peacefully! From the first months of its existence the *Rassemblement* encountered this difficulty.

As was to be expected, the political parties had their axe to grind. While the Union Nationale declared war on us, other parties showed their democratic credentials in order to join a movement that contained hundreds of uncommitted—and eminently recruitable—enthusiasts. Four months after the founding of the *Rassemblement*, its leaders were obliged to make the following points, in a public statement:

> Recruiting has created a certain number of problems for your executive, not because it was going badly, but, in a way, because it was going too well. In fact the executive has from the start been obliged to take a position on membership requests from people who are more or less active in the political parties.
>
> We must remember that the *Rassemblement* was created because in their present state, and for reasons that vary from one party to another, none of the existing political parties seemed capable of successfully undertaking the task of civic education and democratic action so urgently needed in Quebec.
>
> Of course not everyone is obliged to agree with this diagnosis. There may be very honest men who believe a civilized democratic conscience can be created in Quebec through the actions of the existing parties. But their place is not in the *Rassemblement*. By definition, its members believe that only a new movement, absolutely independent of the existing parties, of the anti-democratic practices that characterize them, and of the prejudices that encumber them—only such a movement can help the majority of Quebecers to complete their personal apprenticeship in democracy.

The members and leaders of the Liberal and Social

Democratic parties had different ideas. They accused the *Rassemblement* of a lack of realism, and of preaching a democracy with no flesh and blood. How dared we turn convinced democrats away from the parties? What kind of democracy could one found on principles alone? The flesh and blood of any parliamentary democracy was the struggle among parties. The rest was an intellectual's dream.

This argument went on as long as the *Rassemblement* existed, and was never settled, because the party people's thesis had some plausibility. It might even seem today that the movement was only an alibi for men attracted by politics but as yet unable to take the decisive leap. No doubt there would be some truth in this, too. But the real explanation is more complicated.

I said above that the purpose was to gather together the scattered forces of a non-partisan opposition. Perhaps that opposition was wrong to shun the parties, but the fact is that it mistrusted them like the plague. And I am referring not only to union militants, whose reservations I have already explained, nor to intellectuals with cold feet. Everyone who, at that time, was involved in any kind of social action considered the political parties as a threat to the integrity of honest citizens. The traditional parties had earned this reputation. The practice of electoral banditry, of fraud and corruption, surrounded them with an unsavoury legend. Everyone remembered the Liberal candidate in the thirties who, on an election night, was asked to explain why there were more ballots in the box than voters on the list. He gave the following historic answer: "I don't know, I suppose it's the enthusiasm...." As for the Union Nationale, its leader repeated, gloating, a saying of his own invention: "You don't win elections with prayers!"

Worse still, the new parties such as *Action liberale nationale* (ALN) in the thirties and the *Bloc populaire* in the forties had presented the citizens of Quebec with a sorry spectacle. The ALN had crumbled before our eyes, almost all its elected members having succumbed in turn to the charms of Mr. Duplessis. (The singer–comedian Jacques Normand in his cabaret *Les Trois-Castors* once greeted the entry of Mr. Paul Gouin, ex-leader of the ALN, with these words: "Ladies and gentlemen, let me introduce the man who was premier of Quebec for twenty minutes—until Mr. Duplessis found out about it.") And no one had forgotten the founding of the *Bloc populaire* in 1942: the movement had broken into two rival groups before it had even properly existed.

Going a little farther afield, one found a strange dichotomy in what was taught about our political parties. On the one hand, our teachers—mostly nationalists—denounced as traitors to our race (that was the vocabulary of the time[14]) all the old parties that had come to power, whether in Ottawa or Quebec, since the beginning of the century. On the other hand, nothing flattered them more than to point to former pupils who had become politicians in one of those same parties. In Nicolet, for example, as soon as Rodolphe Lemieux or Hector La Ferté appeared on the horizon the priests in the seminary would roll out the red carpet! I remember how their respectful bowing and scraping seemed to me hard to reconcile with their condemnations of all politicians—all of them ready to crawl at the behest of the old parties, according to our teachers. I was certainly not the only adolescent to wonder at this phenomenon.

The *Rassemblement* spoke to all those who refused not only the regime but also the political mores of the time. It had to take into account this double rejection. Its sponsors knew very well that the road to change led to action through political parties, but many of its members were not ready to admit the fact, and congratulated themselves on this refusal. No doubt this is why the movement's first written declarations unwittingly display some of the virtuosity of the tight-rope walker. For example:

---

[14]Revived by the Saint Jean-Baptiste Society in 1981–82.

[The] *Rassemblement* is *more than a mere collection of study groups*. By thus defining itself as an activist movement, it was trying to dispel another perennial illusion among us, which consists of believing that the intellectual conception of ideal models is all that is needed to bring about a better society.

This is a common error among intellectuals; but it is also current among certain unionists, members of cooperative movements, farmers, merchants and others who feel they have done their civic duty when their associations have submitted an annual brief to governments which is quickly put on the shelf.

Some maintain that politics are too dirty...but what they lack—apart, occasionally, from courage—is the understanding that in a democracy it is not enough to depend on others...because, under a democratic constitution, the "others" are still and always ourselves.

The *Rassemblement*, then, was an effort to create a tool for education and democratic action that could in no way be compared with a party. "Election fever," we read in the same declaration, "is an ailment that has killed at an early age most of the movements in our society which wanted to regenerate political life."

We were not going to concern ourselves with elections. With what, then? As I re-read the *Rassemblement's* statement, I discover an outline for educating the populace which is not without its interesting points. As of the winter of 1957, some sections began to be organized throughout the province, and the leaders of the movement made available to them an initial working tool in the form of a questionnaire. It was designed to gather certain basic data in each riding: its area, its total population, the number of members. The survey, carried out by members, was to discover how the voters' lists had been drawn up for the last election and how the polling stations had been chosen and distributed. The next step was to establish a profile of the

elected MLA and analyze and publicize his speeches in
Parliament, his actions in the riding and the composition of
his team within his party. Then the section was to proceed
with the same kind of analysis of the concrete realities of
each municipal government and school board. When one
thinks of the state of indifference to which the authoritarianism of the Union Nationale had reduced the citizenry, it
is easier to realize that such an inventory, properly taken,
might have troubled the complacency of the men in power.

This fundamental work was supplemented by specific
attempts to enlighten public opinion. The *Rassemblement*
was one of the first organizations in Quebec to realize the
usefulness of the media. Governments were not the only
ones that could make use of this "public address system."
Any organized and alert group now had access to radio and
television, provided it demonstrated a minimum of intelligence. The Canadian Broadcasting Corporation (one cannot say as much for the private stations) was then
scheduling many public forum programs where all shades
of opinion could be aired. The Corporation's public affairs
programming was developing, and the printed press, stimulated by this competition, fell into step. Papers like *La
Presse* and *Le Devoir*, who had never opened their columns
to readers' letters, were obliged to do so, or to provide
space for independent articles where opinions could at last
be expressed. Reporters began to cover, not only the official meetings and ceremonies of the establishment, but also
the demonstrations of different groups interested in public
affairs.

When historians begin to investigate seriously the decline
and fall of the Union Nationale, I am willing to wager that
they will find this coverage to have been one of the principal causes. Astute and cunning as a brace of monkeys, Mr.
Duplessis was none the less out of phase with his time. He
failed to see the approach of danger. Not only did he
systematically avoid appearing on television himself, he
prohibited his ministers from doing so. Daniel Johnson

admitted as much to me one day. Having refused to take part in a televised debate of which I was the moderator, he told me, "It's a mistake, I know. But the *Chef* doesn't agree. He thinks that if we accept we're contributing to building the reputations of guys like you and your friends. And that, of course . . . ."

But this showed a lack of comprehension of a phenomenon that was plain for all to see. I don't know if Mr. Duplessis believed he was strong enough to successfully boycott television, but the obvious result of his attempt to do so was that his own team was kept out of the limelight. At the end of the fifties only a few ministers (I think of Daniel Johnson himself and Paul Sauvé) managed to cross the barrier at last. But it was too late. The star of the election campaign in 1960 was René Lévesque. Because of television.

Well before the creation of the *Rassemblement*, specific plans had been made to generate public debate. The first one I remember goes back to 1953. Four people were involved in its origin, three of whom became sponsors of the *Rassemblement* in 1956: Arthur Tremblay, Jean Marchand and myself.

The *plot* was hatched in an incongruous location: the now defunct Reform Club on Sherbrooke Street, the sanctuary of the Liberal party of the day. It was the first time I had set foot in the place, and neither Tremblay nor Marchand frequented it. It was our fourth *accomplice*, Paul Gérin-Lajoie, who had invited us there.

We had barely sat down at our table in a small basement room when Arthur Tremblay asked the question: "Do you all agree with me that in the next general election education should be one of the issues?" To imagine the audacity of such a proposal, we must remember that education was then a forbidden subject. With few exceptions, it was not discussed in public, either in the newspapers or on the air, and still less at political meetings. This was the private hunting-ground of the episcopate, and poachers were exposed to the fury of the clergy.[15] The very idea of making it an election issue verged on sacrilege. But Arthur Tremblay, then director of the School of Pedagogy at Laval University, was already obsessed by the grand design that was to occupy his lifetime: educational reform. And his reflections had led him to conclude that such a reform would either be democratic or nothing at all, and that what was necessary above all was to break down the wall of silence, resolutely invade the boundaries of the private hunting ground and force the government to take on the responsibilities which it all-too-gladly left to the clerical monopoly.

Arthur Tremblay knew that the operation would not be easy to carry out, and foresaw a lengthy preparation period. In the fall of 1953 there were three years to go before the next provincial election. This barely left time enough for the purpose. For the plan to succeed, the Liberal party would have to be led into debating this most taboo of subjects, thus forcing the Union Nationale into discussion. Gérin-Lajoie was to bring his persuasion to bear on the Liberal circles of which he was a member. But as things stood, he had little chance of success. The Liberal elders, not without reason, would see this project as a suicide mission: the Union Nationale already accused their party of crypto-communism, hostility to the Church and other heresies. They would have to be persuaded that such a debate responded to a profound wish of the people of Quebec. The problem had to be submitted to public opinion. Whence the presence of Jean Marchand and myself at this improvised encounter.

I don't intend to talk in detail about the operation that followed. My memory is rather vague, even about the part of the scenario in which I was personally involved: a series of mass meetings throughout Quebec, on the subject of educational problems. I know that I spoke with conviction, because my own children, in a suburb near Montreal,

---

[15] See Roger Rolland, *Matériaux pour servir à une enquête sur le cléricalisme*, *Cité libre* no. 7, May 1953, pp. 38–43.

could get only limited schooling for lack of
adequate quarters. As this situation was gene
I had great success with the following tirade

> How is this possible in a civilized country: .
> did not make our children in secret, it was not an illeg
> activity! And we immediately declared each birth. The
> government, therefore, and the school boards knew
> perfectly well, five years in advance, what to expect.
> But they weren't able to build the schools we needed in
> time. Not only do they refuse today to let our kids into
> school before they are seven, but thousands of little
> Quebecers, seven years old as the rule says they must
> be, are allowed only half a helping of education!

In these meetings, in the debates we organized, and in the
reports and commentaries dealing with them (the movement quickly snowballed) all the aspects of the question
were examined: school attendance, quality of teaching,
free schooling, access to secondary and university levels,
teachers' pay, etc.

In any case, in the summer of 1956, for the first time in
living memory, the question of education was raised a
number of times in the course of a hectic campaign. The
result? Hard to measure. But one had to be satisfied with
modest gains in those days. To stimulate some awareness,
involve a major political party in a cause until then prohibited, open another door to the future, even if only a crack—
this was enough to put us in the mood for a new effort at
the first opportunity. And the *Rassemblement* was to be a
permanent, urgent, institutionalized opportunity.

When I re-read the writings of the *Rassemblement*, I can
feel the whole political atmosphere of that time come to
life, and I marvel at it, astonished.

What were the themes of the second convention, in
December 1957? Freedom of association, academic freedom, and political freedom. But these themes did not

ander off in theoretical essays: all three alluded to very precise problems. One resolution mentioned the strike of the metalworkers in Murdochville and the situation on the Gaspé "where industrialization is achieved under conditions that are unjust and needlessly hard," where "The Gaspé Copper Company deprives its workers of that absolute right of every citizen: the right of association." Another debate dealt with the fact that Montrealers had no leverage with the school authorities of their city, deprived as they had been for nearly a century of the right to elect them. As for political freedom, attention was monopolized by the scandals of the law on the electoral ridings, recalling that at that time the numerical weight of the metropolis was simply conjured away in favour of rural areas by means of an electoral map so outmoded it was absurd. Montreal, with more than 40 percent of the population of Quebec, elected barely 16 percent of its provincial MLAs. In 1956, for example, the Montreal riding of Laval had 135,000 voters, while the riding of the Magdalen Islands had barely 5,000. And as the population of Montreal was increasingly immune to the charms of the Union Nationale, Mr. Duplessis was not about to correct this situation, grotesque as it might be, as long as it was to his advantage. The same went for the law that then regulated the electoral process. As full of holes as a sieve, it was an invitation to the most blatant malpractice, and almost guaranteed immunity to political tricksters.

Still more striking was the off-handedness of the regime in violating the rules of democracy day after day on the slightest pretext. In December 1957, the *Rassemblement* had formed an information committee on current events. A few weeks later it published its first release, with this eloquent preamble:

> The *Rassemblement* notifies the people of Quebec that as of the first month of 1958 its elected representatives have restricted its democratic rights at two different levels.

1.—The municipal council of Montreal adopted a resolution requesting the Legislature to change the percentage of votes needed to validate certain major decisions of the said Council.

...In this way the [provincial] legislators would retroactively give a meaning to the Montreal election of October 1957 which it did not have [at the time of the vote].

2.—The Quebec legislature has passed a bill under whose terms legal proceedings contesting the municipal and school board elections are to be heard by magistrate's court rather than the Superior Court, with no possibility of appeal.

...Such a piece of legislation is even less acceptable in view of the fact that this same government, during the Caron inquiry into municipal corruption in Montreal, modified the provincial law expressly to give a right of appeal to those the inquiry might find guilty.

Not a bad harvest for our committee[16] after only two months of existence, Christmas holidays included.

Those would have been heady times for a protest movement, if the word had existed. But "protest" did not yet have the meaning it acquired during the 1960s, and, above all, the protesters were few. Public opinion barely reacted to our complaints in the beginning. But the climate began to change, slowly at first, then with increasing rapidity as the abuses became more frequent.

That, of course, is the nature of authoritarian governments: blinded by their own rejection of criticism, they fail to see the dangers threatening them and literally run to their own perdition, accelerating rather than slowing down.

The *Rassemblement*, however, was undermined by the ambiguity that had plagued it from the beginning. In 1958,

---

[16] The information committee on current events was made up of Pierre Elliott Trudeau, Jacques Hébert, Paul King, Guy Lamarche and Gérard Pelletier.

its president, René Tremblay, noted in a message to members that they had to make a choice between the two tendencies within the movement: those who held out for a continued non-partisan action, and those who were eyeing the political parties and thinking of the next election.

The second tendency won out.

It was to be only two years until the official Quiet Revolution. But that revolution, as we have seen, had been initiated long before. The cracks in the wall became more noticeable every day and militants of all shades grew more impatient. We understood at last (and the *Rassemblement* helped us to do so) that the regime could only be defeated in an electoral struggle. Above all, we felt that the 1960 election would be decisive, and that it must not, this time, turn into another opportunity lost. How could one bear to think of a fresh mandate for the Union Nationale—four more years of stagnation for Quebec—when our historical lag was already taking on disastrous proportions?

From this point of view, non-partisan action seemed like an academic exercise which aroused no enthusiasm. We had to deal with the immediate, and that meant the provincial election of 1960.

It should not be concluded that the extra-parliamentary opposition thought it was jumping on a winner's bandwagon: that still seemed highly problematical. The regime was shaken but not condemned. There were scandals at the hatching stage, but nothing open. Mr. Duplessis's clerical support was under attack, but he continued to enjoy its benefits. Employers were uneasy about the growing discredit that hung over the Union Nationale, but they were even more uneasy at the thought of a political change that they suspected might turn into a greater upheaval after sixteen years of repressive politics. We could take nothing for granted. Far from it.

Confronted by a still cock-sure Duplessism, the parliamentary opposition remained uncertain and divided. Jean Lesage, attracted to Quebec by Jean-Louis Gagnon and

Maurice Lamontagne, had just taken the destiny of
Liberal party in hand, but his still shaky hold on the
leadership did not allow him to bring the party's platform
up to date in any spectacular way. (In fact, when he tried to
do so two years later, the results turned out to be very
modest.) And the new leader did not even have a seat in the
Assembly, where the Liberals were the sole opposition
party. An alliance with Social Credit in the 1956 election
had put not a single disciple of Réal Caouette in the
Assembly. Caouette remained a real force to be reckoned
with, but his impact at the provincial level was hard to
measure.

Another unknown in the political equation at the time
was Jean Drapeau. Since the Mayor of Montreal has confined himself strictly to municipal politics since 1960, we
have all had time to forget that he often, and to many
people, appeared as a possible recourse against Duplessis in
the fifties. The Caron inquiry into municipal corruption in
Montreal, carried out against the will of and despite ob-
struction by the *Chef* and his friends, Drapeau's election as
mayor in 1954 and the spirit of independence he showed
toward the Quebec government during his first term were
quite enough to make him a plausible candidate, and a
more likely one, it seemed to some, than Jean Lesage, who
was still rather underestimated. Lesage had at his disposal
an organized party, but this was his weakness as well as his
strength. We must remember the liabilities of the Liberal
party of Quebec. It was an old party, as people said then,
and even after sixteen years in opposition had not lived
down the scandals that caused its fall in 1936, nor the
practices that had tarnished its reputation.

Drapeau, on the contrary, had the look of a new man.
His Civic Action League was based only in Montreal, but
was already pushing out feelers toward the regions. The
ex-mayor himself (he had been defeated in 1957) seemed
open to such a venture. No doubt he gave it some consider-
ation, but how seriously I never knew.

ng in that period he invited Trudeau, Jean-
nd myself for a drink at his home, in the
ere we had a lively discussion in the base-
ad known Drapeau for a long time. As a
the war he had campaigned with him in
ainst General La Flèche, against whom Dra-
battle that was lost before it started, identify-
ing   the conscripts' candidate. But Trudeau and
Drapeau had seen little of each other since then, and their
respective political philosophies had little in common. Our
host made remarks about democracy that raised Trudeau's
hackles, and Trudeau invoked principles that were very
disturbing to the practical mind of Drapeau, who still bore
the scars of a bitter defeat (the only one in his career) in the
municipal election of 1957. In short, the conversation
revealed no sign of an elective affinity between the two
men.

But, as already noted, in the circumstances no one could
afford to turn up his nose at a possible ally. Drapeau had
cleaned up the city's administration between 1954 and
1957, thanks to the work of Pierre DesMarais and Pax
Plante, and he saw as clearly as we did the catastrophes
toward which Duplessis was leading us. Drapeau may not
have been an enthusiast for democracy, but at least he
supported it. He would certainly have subscribed to
Churchill's aphorism that democracy is the worst system of
government, except for all the others.

But Trudeau was already thinking about a new plan. He
realized that the *Rassemblement* no longer satisfied the
needs of the situation in Quebec. We had to get directly
plugged in to the electoral forces that could unseat the
Duplessis regime. There had to be immediate action, with a
possible later return to a non-partisan stance if necessary.
The *Rassemblement* had wanted to enlist *individuals* in the
promotion of democratic values, but now we had to gather
opposition *parties* in a kind of committee of public safety
with a minimal platform—sparing Quebec the reelection of

the Union Nationale for another term.

This was the *Union des forces démocratiques*, of which Trudeau wrote the manifesto. The task was to bring all the opposition groups together and come to an electoral understanding that would allow them to work in unison, despite their divergencies, at putting an end to the Duplessis regime. I cannot give an account of this final episode, since for reasons which I cannot recall, I was little involved in it. I only remember the drafting of the manifesto and the discussions that took place in the process. And I heard the accounts of stormy meetings held in the old Cercle Universitaire on Sherbrooke Street near Berri. Among others present, Jean-Marie Nadeau represented the Liberal party, and Jacques Hébert the Civic Action League. The Social Democratic party (today's NDP) hesitated to commit its non-existent troops to such an impure undertaking.

I also cannot say whether this attempt at union had any influence whatever on the tumble taken by the Union Nationale two years later. What I do know, however, is that it put an end to the *Rassemblement* adventure. Now all energies and hopes were turned toward 1960. There was no more talk of non-partisan action. Then events took over: the death of Maurice Duplessis at the end of the summer of 1959; the sudden demise of his successor Paul Sauvé in early 1960; and the succession of Antonio Barrette as leader of the Union Nationale just a few months before the June election.

Another thing I know about for certain is the invaluable experience gained by Trudeau in both these undertakings. Until then he had remained, like the rest of us, remote from all parties except the NDP. The *Rassemblement* and the *Union des forces démocratiques* put him in direct working contact with some policy-makers. He ceased to be an observer, a philosopher and an adviser, and became a man of action, however modest his role still was. Pierre Trudeau's political career did not start in 1965, the date of his first election to Parliament, but in 1956, and the whole sequence of his relationships with political reality was to be strongly marked by the action that got under way with the *Rassemblement*.

As for Jean Marchand, the *Rassemblement* probably taught him nothing that he didn't already know. Heavy union responsibilities (he had become president of the CTCC in 1959) were absorbing all his energy. The parties were beginning to be interested in him, but he had no time to listen to their siren songs. He had sworn to complete the modernization of his Federation, which was no small undertaking.

Nor did René Lévesque have any political projects. His television program, *Point de mire*, had imperceptibly turned from international affairs to internal problems in the late fifties, and his concerns had come closer to our own. "[We][17] were disgusted by the excesses of the *Union nationale*," he wrote in *My Quebec*, "and opposed to the present, endless regime."

But to lead him from disgust to action, it took another event which in Quebec marked the end of the decade, and will, in the same way, mark the end of this book.

[17][We]: "Four of us, Jean Marchand, Gérard Pelletier, Pierre Elliott Trudeau (who was the least well-known) and I...." René Lévesque, *My Quebec* (Toronto: Methuen), p. 9.

CHAPTER 7

A Kind of Cultural Revolution

*Today, as always, the well-spring of
culture is in the people. Montaigne and
Rabelais knew it, and Pascal and Péguy,
who were not communists for all that.*
EMMANUEL MOUNIER

Culture is not inherited, it is won.
ANDRÉ MALRAUX

In the fall of 1952 a cultural event of prime importance
took place in Quebec. For the first time in our history a
great patron of the arts spoke to all those who could write or
speak, saying: "Express yourselves! Here are the means for
doing so. But faster! We have no time to wait. We need
novels, commentaries, plays, analysis, stories, debates—
whatever you can imagine and all you can produce. But
there's not much time. Get to work!"

Need I say that this was a true, an authentic revolution?
Our culture, our ideology, our economic situation—all three
of them—had tended from time immemorial to restrain and
repress expression, whether spoken or written, rather than
helping them develop.

Our education, based on a monkish authoritarianism,
favoured silence. It mistrusted speech. To describe an insub-
ordinate pupil, the teachers in our schools said, "He's a child
that talks back." The expression showed little taste for

dialogue. We were also told that wisdom consisted in "turning your tongue around seven times in your mouth before you speak," which did not make for sprightly conversation. And if one made it past these two road-blocks, a third loomed up at once: the poor quality of our spoken language, on which our educators hailed a constant storm of complaints, recriminations and condemnations. Before we had ever felt an emotion, acquired a conviction or conceived a thought, we knew that we would express it badly. The walls of our classrooms were covered with posters that denounced our flabby mouths, our poor elocution and our talent for using the wrong word. I must credit our pedagogues with their good intentions. But it's a miracle that we didn't all end up with paralyzed tongues and vocal cords from the campaigns we suffered in favour of speaking properly (and against speaking as we had always done).

If, after this obstacle course, we still kept some desire and ability for self-expression, our troubles were only starting. We then had to find subjects that were not taboo or dangerous or deadly boring. Within the minor orthodoxy that reigned in Quebec at the time, this was not an easy quest.

So far as religion was concerned, it was explained to us promptly that, while laymen should certainly have some knowledge of it, only the clergy had the right to speak of it. As this was the subject that occupied by far the greater part of our studies, the restriction was a far-reaching one. And by an extrapolation that was common in those days, the rule of silence applied not only to theology as such, but to all the areas of life in which the clergy had a hand. Respect for what was sacred protected the doctrine of the Church; respect for authority made sacred anything that had to do with the clergy. But the clergy had to do with everything, so that it was almost impossible to touch on any subject without risking an interdict.

Of course we could talk about literature, but within the limits of the Index—or the *Novels to Read and Not to Read* by Father Bethléem. Nothing prevented us from tackling labour problems or economic questions—as long as we didn't transgress the Church's social doctrine. If psychology interested you, you were allowed to talk about it, as long as you ignored Freud, of course, who had scoffed at Christian morality. You could break out of this virtuous circle only at the risk of various punishments ranging from the gentle or subtle threat (paralyzing just the same) to public condemnation and the loss of your job.

To these doctrinal fetters was added the secular hobble of ideology: nationalism, "a certain idea" of Quebec and French Canada, which was barely less restrictive. A freedom that is limited is like a shrunken garment: it pinches at the armholes. Who would have dared in the early fifties to say out loud in our community that our traditional nationalism had led us astray? Just a few on the lunatic fringe. No one wanted to appear to be a traitor or to be denounced as a heretic.

The ideology did not limit itself to domestic politics, either. One was supposed, for example, to hold in high esteem the sinister make-believe of Portuguese corporatism. Even after the war Franco himself was seen as the saviour of the Church and protector of the faith. Democracy was certainly tolerable, but it was not the ideal regime. One had to keep one's distance.

All things considered, was it not better to be silent than to risk the fatal stumble at every sentence? And even if one decided to brave all these perils, there was the problem of finding the opportunity and the medium for speaking out.

Education? It remained largely the private preserve of the clergy and the orders. In the primary schools, lay teachers were beginning the invasion that would soon put them in charge of that whole sector, but at the secondary and university levels the clergy still held almost all the key positions. One had to show a stainless record to compete for them.

Journalism was freer—of clerical influence, that is, but certainly not of the prevailing conservatism. For one daily like *Le Devoir*, where there was great freedom, how many others held their editorial staff in a reign of mitigated, stifling terror! At *La Presse* it was taboo to mention the Senate or its members because the chairman of the board was a senator. At *La Patrie* there was the same atmosphere of suffocating mediocrity. (An old editor from this paper, whom I met by chance in a students' boarding-house just after my arrival in Montreal, explained to me one evening: "Yes, I'm a journalist. But don't try to recognize my name. You've never seen it. I have never signed an article. At our paper the editorial writers aren't employees, they're part of the furniture.") And at the *Action catholique* in Quebec City, a secular pawn, hardening the line rather than mitigating it, interpreted the orders of his bishop, who was the legal and functional master of this clerical daily. *Le Soleil* and *L'Evénement* of those days were pale carbons of their Montreal counterparts, but just as lacking in courage, imagination and conscience.

What about the magazines? They were also divided between the two main tendencies; they were either clerical or nationalist, and in both cases were losing money. I should mention some notable exceptions, however. Because of its editor, André Laurendeau, *l'Action nationale* was not narrowly nationalist. And thanks to the religious order that published it, the *Revue dominicaine* was in no way arch-conservative. But the spectrum of opinion still remained very narrow. Before 1950 hardly any magazine except *La Relève* and *Amérique française* escaped the prevailing polarization. From time to time a new publication would appear, like *L'Ordre* and *Renaissance* put out by Olivar Asselin, and a fresh wind would blow for a moment. But it never lasted. It also happened that a party organ, *Le Canada*, suddenly decided to broaden its horizons and give pluralism a try. But it died in the attempt. Freedom of expression existed legally, but it was not embedded in our customs.

It was quite possible, of course, to publish books, if one could find a publisher. But the publisher, as a rule, was caught on one or the other horn of our dilemma. And the writers of the period had to have an ascetic streak. Print runs were minuscule, and the critics kept a vigilant eye out for any departures from established principles. At best, one received from the publication of a book (unless it was a school text) an evanescent fame accompanied by a pittance in royalties.[1] Speaking and writing were starvation trades.

Then came television.

In a few months television was to turn everything topsy-turvy. Not only were we summoned to say something (anything at all, said our detractors), and not only was the work paid for at a decent rate, but—surprise—hundreds of thousands, and before long millions, of people would be the attentive audience of this wave of communication.

After radio, with its austere budgets and its blind and inattentive audience, TV seemed like a millionaire benefactor. But above all, the CBC had a monopoly, and as it entered the world of images it completed its post-war mutation.

Let me explain what I mean. The Canadian Radio Broadcasting Commission, from its creation in the early thirties, had reacted strongly—too strongly—to the commercial clutter of private radio, which until then had ruled the airwaves. No doubt this was due to the high aspirations of this new State radio, as well as to the BBC model which somewhat obsessed it. The American style had to be avoided, and the French style was almost unknown, so the British manner became the order of the day. This resulted, to be sure, in many fine programs, but at the price of a stiff and starchy manner which André Laurendeau once described with the following words, at the end of a critical broadcast: "Midnight. An announcer identifies the station to mark the end of the day's broadcasting. He speaks with a warm voice in an icy tone, and this is the trademark of the CBC."

Laurendeau had no real fault to find with this particular style. But the war had left him some painful memories. The

---

[1]Novels like Roy's *The Tin Flute*, Lemelin's *The Town Below* and Ringuet's *Thirty Acres* are exceptions that prove the rule.

pages he wrote on the brutal boycott of the "No" campaign
by the Crown Corporation during the 1942 referendum on
conscription are worth reading.[2] This arbitrary refusal to
give a hearing to one side in a supposedly democratic
plebiscite was merely the high point of an attitude which the
CBC took a long time to shake off. In front of its micro-
phones in the early years, one was obliged not only to affect
a certain grave rigidity, it was also necessary to choose one's
words and opinions carefully, to remain noncommittal. The
tone always remained cool, though it was always less hostile
to official occasions than to the noisy confusion of everyday
life. In short, our public radio in the thirties and during the
war years imposed on itself a voluntary censorship that
turned it into an ice-palace, a passive supporter of everything conservative.

After the war, the CBC underwent a slow thaw. Long
before our large newspapers did so, it began to welcome a
diversity of voices and opinions, a variety of commentaries,
and some discussions. Its public affairs programming grew
less stilted. Humour was allowed. (How I remember *Carte
blanche*, in which Fernand Séguin, Gérard Berthiaume and
André Roche performed wonders poking fun at their most
prominent contemporaries!)

Thus the groundwork was done in preparation for the
explosion that came with television. It would be a serious
error to think that the federal authorities had foreseen the
phenomenon. They were the first to be astonished, as I
realized one evening as I interviewed the prime minister,
Louis Saint-Laurent. It was just a few months after the
inauguration of the TV transmitters, and in the complete
euphoria of this beginning audiences were delighted with the
first programs, and the producers were delighted with themselves. Questioned as to the impression made on him by this
obvious success, Mr. Saint-Laurent shrugged one shoulder,
then the other, smiled through his white moustache, and

[2]André Laurendeau, *La crise de la conscription* (Montreal: Editions du Jour,
1962).

finally replied: "I must admit, I am astonished. I hesitated for a long time before allowing the CBC to go into television. It is such an expensive invention! We had to spend tens of millions of dollars. I was afraid of the reaction on the eve of an election. I was certain we would be accused of squandering money. I got ready to refute these objections. But, no. On the contrary, people are congratulating us. They are thanking me. I was afraid television would be a millstone around my neck, and it has turned into a halo around my head."

Apparently no one in government had given a thought to the cultural, psychological or social impact of this very "expensive invention." But then, who did dream of it in those days?

The launching of the system was carried out in an atmosphere of enthusiasm and happy improvisation. During the summer that preceded the start of broadcasting, I took part in a number of trial reporting expeditions. Those who saw it will, I think, never forget the first Saint Jean-Baptiste parade to be telecast and viewed in the "strange lighted windows" of our brand-new sets. Not because of my commentaries, to be sure: they were anything but unforgettable. But that year the traditional allegorical floats so dear to our national Society, which organized the parade, were missing. They had been burned during the night when an unfortunate fire had devastated the sheds where they were stored. But the costume department had escaped the flames, so we saw, filing by in period dress, several hundred extras borne by whatever vehicle could be drummed up on a moment's notice. Louis XIV was perched on the seat of a jeep and Jeanne Le Ber (or was it Jeanne Mance?) looked down unhappily at the crowd from the dusty back of a truck. One thought of a modern version of the Terror: motorized Ford tumbrils carrying a shipment of Robespierre's victims to the guillotine before the stupefied gaze of Montreal's curious public packed along Sherbrooke Street.

While we journalists had our first timid try at televised

reporting and commentary, the actors, singers and directors found themselves confronted cold by brand-new cameras operated by apprentices. There was no one who knew this new trade. Everyone improvised the best he could. As American television had not yet crossed our border, we were not inhibited by any existing model. For once there was no question of imitating foreigners, because we didn't know what they were doing. We had to invent. We also did not have to fear their critical gaze: we would be judged only by one public, our own: viewers as new and lacking in prejudices as we were in experience.

At a time when the arts and even criticism in Canada suffered from chronic mimesis and a debilitating mania for referring to foreign standards, our inexperience in TV turned out to be invigorating. No one could throw Racine or Balzac at us, as happened too often in the case of a young writer's first play or a novelist's first book. In this new kingdom of television there were no classics. Even the most masochistic of authors could have searched in vain for pejorative comparisons or masterpieces likely to discourage their efforts and justify their inaction. At that particular moment of our cultural development this was a healthy state of affairs, at least for a time. We needed above all to acquire confidence in ourselves and forget for a while the search for an undying masterpiece. And I don't think there are any such masterpieces to be found in the archives of our early television. What will be found there is the record of an extraordinary collective liberation, a time of creation (and recreation) such as we have seldom experienced.

Television in 1952 had no choice but to fill without delay several hours of programming a day. Thus it was necessary to mobilize a whole team of producers, actors, set designers, commentators, authors and technicians. Of course this could not be done without creating a certain chaos and making some hasty judgments. There was no time to apply to this selection the traditional criteria of Quebec society. Suddenly it was less important to be orthodox. What was needed was daring, energy and inventiveness, not to mention effrontery.

Our society had never favoured those particular qualities, especially in the intellectual field. Thus, most of our academic and stamped-and-approved elite kept its distance for a while. It watched the train pull out but never jumped aboard, which perhaps explains why it later ostracized the "CBC types"—a term that remained for some a perjorative all through the fifties. The important thing, however, was that all those "types," most of them not yet thirty, went to work with no complexes. They had to appear in public when they could barely walk? Very well, they would run!

If, for example, a producer had to put together a TV drama in a few weeks with actors who had never performed for film or television cameras, and set designers who were rank beginners, do you think the novice producer would prudently choose a curtain-raiser or a sure-fire success? Not at all. He would at once tackle Sophocles, Shakespeare, Claudel, Molière or Diderot. For a variety show they would build a nightclub from top to bottom, with its stage, dance floor, accessories, customers and waitresses. We had no puppet shows because our stage tradition had never included them? Never mind. For its children's series television would conjure up from nowhere the puppets, puppeteers and voices. While children's TV in Europe and the U.S. hesitated, falling back on old films and serving their young audience in driblets, a complete schedule of children's programming took shape in Montreal. Not all its programs were masterpieces, but they had the great virtue of existing.

Our hungry society was discovering unexpected riches. From the Film Board, from youth movements, recreational services, theatre groups and from radio came teams of creative people (including many women) to take up the tools offered them by the new medium. Most of them had until then worked in ill-paid obscurity, with no security, unsung and doubting their own usefulness. Now they were needed.

They were even called to come to the rescue of this new undertaking.

The importance of this sudden change was not to appear until much later. At the time, the job to be done held everyone's attention. Those who were faced with the challenge thought little about the implications of their adventure. They were too busy producing. And the rest, the professional critics, had little grasp of this new phenomenon. With some reason, our master-thinkers were concerned about the horrendous appetite of the tube. Unable to foresee its stimulating effects, they perceived only its overweening demands. They feared, for example, that our rare writers would exhaust their talent in writing weekly drama series and that our composers would write nothing but background music. For our professors they dreaded an intellectual scatter-effect: if they were dragged continually from their classroom or study to take part in public consultations or improvised debates under the studio lights, they would have no time left for profound thought.

Our intellectuals worried even more about the audience. Their anxiety showed during the first rush to buy TV sets. How could people afford such an expensive item without unduly denting the family budget? And it was the common people, as they called them in Outremont, the manual labourers and clerical help who rushed to the stores to buy receivers on credit, on the instalment plan or with the help of loans at exorbitant interest from the finance companies. The well-to-do looked on with disapproval, as did the intellectuals. During the months that followed the first TV broadcasts it was fashionable for them not to have a set at home. Among the working classes it was just the opposite. You had to have seen all the programs, because each one was the subject of endless conversation and passionate discussion in factories and offices.

As a permanent union employee, my job gave me a front-seat view of the phenomenon. To realize its importance one must remember that the workers of that time had little schooling: four or five years on the average, for adults. They did little or no reading outside the newspaper and saw movies perhaps once a week, mainly B-category American and French films. The other films were shown only in the well-to-do neighbourhoods of large cities. They saw little or no theatre and made no visits to the few museums we had. The urban scene exhibited few works of art. There were concerts, but only a tiny minority of people had access to them.

The workers' diet in ideas was just as meager. There were sermons from the pulpit and tirades from the platforms during election time, but the content of these orations was generally as slim as it was predictable. There was seldom a collision of ideas within our finicky orthodoxies.

Imagine, in this context, the impact of our new television, which had not yet settled down to routine and which dumped in our homes pell-mell, but in an accessible form, tons of images, each one more stimulating than the last. What I found wonderful was the direct, spontaneous reaction of the popular audience to works whose existence it had never suspected.

As there was only one French network at the beginning, everyone saw its productions. There could be no question of providing two different menus, one for the people and one for the elite. And the people found that just fine. For them a comedy by Molière or a Diderot play were not classics: they were shows they'd seen yesterday on TV. They accepted them as they accepted plays by Guy Dufresne, André Giroux, Roger Lemelin or Germaine Guèvremont. It was the content that got through to them, the feelings and ideas on which they passed judgment. I have just been reading, in an account of the twenties in Moscow,[3] a description of a similar attitude. The author tells about an evening at the theatre in the first days of the revolution in the U.S.S.R.

---

[3]Lotte Schwarz, *Je veux vivre jusqu'à ma mort* (Paris: Editions du Seuil, 1979), pp. 90–91.

During the intermission, [she writes] there were animated discussions. "If I was in Yuri's place I'd never have let them push me around. He should have watched his step!" "Think of the problems that girl had. Between love and patriotism...." "Well! That Pyotr Maximovitch really believed in his little father the Czar, didn't he! You can tell, he never knew life in the street, he'd never seen real life." No one criticizes the actors or the author or the set. No one puts himself outside of or above the play and its problems. It is the real questions that touch these playgoers, naive perhaps, but how alive! They will go on for a long time discussing whether you can love your country while despising the people, whether there are several kinds of sincerity, whether love excuses everything. What a difference from Berlin or Paris, where everyone considers himself the supreme judge of a performance and often misses the real content.

It was much the same in Montreal in the beginnings of television. Some critics and a certain elite turned up their noses at the quality of productions which the audience, in the flush of discovery, swallowed greedily, not stopping to see if the packaging was neat.

In the domain of ideas the revolution was even more visible. I already mentioned the change in the CBC just after the war, its more relaxed style and the gradual erosion of the self-censorship it had imposed on itself for so long. It was the arrival of television that gave the final push in this direction. The need to produce was so urgent that one had no time to wonder for days on end how some sector of the population or the establishment would react to a particular and daring program.

Oh, we all had our difficulties with "top management" about this or that program. I remember the lengthy debates I had on returning from Algeria, about a report on the war between the French army and the militants of the FLN. Certain producers who committed audacities of another type saw their shows cut because of language that was too free or breasts that were too exposed. But generally speaking the "ideological corridor" was suddenly widened, and a distinction was made between modesty and false modesty. Some who remember those days may remind me of the great scandal about *La Belle de Céans*, a TV drama whose author had made a few timid incursions into the sentimental life of Marguerite d'Youville, the founder of the Grey Nuns, who was up for canonization. There was, indeed, quite a fuss, and the indignation was all the more general because the play, as I recall, was not a masterpiece. But the scandal took place *after* the broadcast of a text which, a few years earlier, would never have had a hope of reaching the public.

In the social and political areas the liberalization was even more striking. It began, I believe, with the appearance of televised debates, which soon became very popular. And as this kind of programming was inexpensive there were soon a number of them, on the most varied topics.

Politicians of every shade were invited to appear before the cameras. The invitation amounted to a summons, as public opinion would have interpreted their refusal as an evasion. The same went for employers and the whole class of notables, powerful but secretive, who had never before been asked to justify their decisions in public: hospital administrators, chairmen of school boards, officials from the universities, etc. At first there was the predictable reluctance. Accustomed to their privacy, some of the highly-placed disliked the bright lights of the studio. They had to be coaxed, some for a long time. But eventually they realized that if they refused to speak and open up in public, they would simply be forgotten. They had to reckon with a public opinion that was more and more aware. The TV debates were a democratic tribune from which one could not stay away with impunity.

For the moment, everybody was having fun. For the TV debate was not only an intellectual exercise. Above all it was a show which did not always owe its success to the collision of ideas.

The series *Prise de becs*[4] arranged every Sunday evening for a battle royal at close quarters among the most disparate of adversaries on the most oddly assorted subjects. The program lived up to its title. The participants went at each other (verbally) hammer and tongs, and sometimes unkindly. I remember a discussion among playwrights, actors and theatre critics which ended very pleasantly. One of the protagonists, choking with indignation, decided to leave the set in mid-program because of a real or fancied insult. But she was far from slim: she was, in fact, corpulent, and as the decor was closed like a Roman arena, and the program was live, one saw an enormous backside bouncing around on the screen for interminable seconds, searching for an exit that was not there, accompanied by a terrified goggling sound. Finally, the lady had to sit down again amid her stunned colleagues, and stick it out until the program ended. The CBC's dignity took a sore beating that night.

I have another memory, one with a political flavour this time, starring the journalist René Lévesque, already feared by public figures. The program was called *Conférence de presse*, and every week a cabinet member had to submit to questioning by four correspondents. I was one of the team that day, and we were in Ottawa to quiz a member of the Diefenbaker government whom chance had seated at my side. René was at the other end of the table. We began our interview. The minister replied to our first questions with such impressive self-assurance and olympian calm that we feared the program would fall flat. It threatened to put us and the audience to sleep. Then came René's turn to intervene. He had barely finished his first phrase when we were aware of a strange noise pervading the studio, like a chattering of teeth. The farther René advanced in his preamble and the closer he got to his question, the louder grew the noise. The floor manager looked anxious and the cameramen checked their machines. Then the noise stopped as suddenly

---

[4]["Bickering Session." Tr.]

as it had begun. The minister had just grabbed his right knee in both hands to keep it from beating out the frantic rhythm of his nervous state on the partition in the set which stood by his chair. He never once let go of it until the program ended.

Jean Marchand also showed himself to be a redoubtable participant in TV debates. Réal Caouette must have remembered to the last day of his life the drubbing he took from Jean in 1962, during a memorable jousting session. Caouette at the time was the terror of the airwaves. With disconcerting virtuosity he wielded everyday speech, popular imagery and the disarming comparison. His political adversaries, especially when they were brilliant lawyers, feared him like the plague. They envied him his immediate contact with the audience and were apprehensive about his trick of showing up his opponent to be an abstract or pretentious intellectual. The moment he heard them pronounce a word with three syllables or more, Réal Caouette would explode in pretended indignation, in a tone of profound sincerity: "My dear sir, would you please stop stuffing our heads? Do we look like suitcases? Talk so that everybody can understand you! People like you have been hiding their intentions for too long behind fine phrases. The people have had enough!" It was not easy to break that kind of hold in the Caouette variety of judo.

But even Caouette occasionally underrated his opponents. When he decided to concentrate his fire on the trade unions in the early sixties, he knew, no doubt, that he would eventually run afoul of Jean Marchand, as indeed he did. Exasperated by the constant accusations of the Social Credit party and still more by its infiltration of the CSN, Marchand finally succeeded in challenging the great Réal to a televised duel. It was a massacre.

For once Caouette was confronted by an antagonist whose language rang as clear to the "uneducated" ear as the harangues of the *créditistes*. Marchand never went in for simplistic demagogery, but he was as familiar as Caouette with the expectations of the small wage earner, his hopes and difficulties. He knew how to choose words that evoked a picture. He also knew how to lay a snare. That night Réal caught his finger in one, and despite all his wiles and impertinence he never succeeded in freeing himself.

Caouette had made some allusion to the money supply in the Canadian economy. Marchand innocently asked him if he would supply the figure. Without hesitation, Réal quoted a sum so far from the right one that his honour as a *créditiste* was immediately at stake. The mistake would have been less serious if another man had made it, but the audience knew Caouette's dogged insistence on basing *all* policy on economic data. And the money supply always had pride of place among those data. But now it appeared, for the first time, and in front of millions of viewers, that the supreme pontiff of Social Credit, Réal himself, had a grossly inaccurate notion of that basic figure. The Pope of the *créditiste* church, in short, could not count the persons of his own Trinity.

In vain he thundered, protesting loudly that his figure was correct, disputing the one quoted by Marchand, accusing Jean of ignorance, indignant that he should dare "without knowing what he was talking about, question the competence of an old militant like myself." Nothing doing. Réal Caouette's infallibility crumbled on the spot, except in the eyes of his unwavering supporters. But even they had to yield to the facts on reading the next morning's paper. Their leader had quoted a figure that had nothing to do with reality. From that day on, no one took Réal Caouette very seriously when he quoted figures. The demagogue survived, but the prophet–economist had faded away during that debate. (What few suspected, and what remains to this day a well-kept secret, was the effect of that broadcast on the political career of Jean Marchand. If he had not publicly roughed up the Social Credit leader that evening, he would doubtless have been a provincial MLA a few weeks later, and then a minister in Jean Lesage's cabinet. But that is another story, and belongs in the chronicle of the sixties.)

Though Réal Caouette experienced on television one of the most stinging humiliations in his life, he nonetheless owed the medium some remarkable electoral successes.[5] No party understood the importance of the media as his did. No other party used them with more consistency and skill, or at such a low cost. In every regional town, every week for years on end, the great helmsman of the Social Credit movement preached the good word to his faithful. The recipe was simple: he had to find a commercial sponsor.

As a rule it would be a prosperous merchant, a party member, who would buy time on a local station for him, at the same time attracting party members as customers. But the main ingredient, unique and irreplaceable, was Réal Caouette with his verve, his ironic humour and his truculence, along with his intense desire to convince his audience. His populist instincts, his profound knowledge of the feelings and frustrations of the lower middle class worked wonders. The Social Credit leader did not share Duplessis's illusions. He knew that no political manoeuvring, no prohibition or boycott would diminish the power of TV. On the contrary, he believed—and proved that he was right—that an astute use of the "picture box" could delay the erosion of his political party. It was doomed, but he prolonged its life by many years.

And what did Pierre Trudeau think of television in the mid-fifties? Nothing very complimentary. He considered the time spent watching or being watched as largely wasted. But then, he barely read the daily papers. Newspaper articles, including those he wrote himself, never appeared to him as serious writing. He skimmed over them, simply to know

---

[5] An article by Hélène Pilotte (*Magazine Maclean*, September 1962) suggests that Réal Caouette owed much to TV for his first big electoral success in June 1962. She writes: "Immediately [after founding the Ralliement des créditistes du Québec in June 1958] he tries to think of a way to reach the masses. He thinks of television. He buys quarter-hour periods for 8 weeks, at his own expense, at $110 a week. Then he asks the viewers to subscribe money for the following programs. They do, every week for four years. Soon he covers the regions of Jonquière, Sherbrooke, Trois Rivières, Rimouski and New Carlisle."

what was going on in the world, but hastily and not every day. He was not one to flatter my journalistic vanity. If he ever mentioned a piece with my byline in a daily, I always asked at once: "Who told you about it?" "I think it was so-and-so," he would reply with no hesitation or embarrassment. It was understood between us that friendship had its limits. Ours did not oblige him to read my articles any more than it obliged me to attend his law courses. It is true that for a few months he was a regular contributor to *Vrai*, Jacques Hébert's weekly, but that was in the darkest of the dark ages when every means had to be used to combat the oppressive official ideology. And who could resist the cajolery of Jacques, who published his weekly by sheer will-power, with no other support than his determination and no reward except his sense of having done his duty?

Trudeau had to be coaxed into a television studio. He always had something else to do that was more urgent or more important. But when he finally gave in, his appearances were noticed. He had a presence on the screen and an intellectual solidity and agility that were typical of his later career.

He did not despise journalism, nor underestimate the power of television. These media interested him, but mainly as sociocultural phenomena. He never felt the itch to become involved with them himself, except as a critic of society. For that matter, none of the forces active in contemporary society left him indifferent.

Toward the mid-fifties we got to know Albert Béguin, the successor to Emmanuel Mounier on the review *Esprit*. Béguin was not merely a "noteworthy mind," as de Gaulle was to say of Sartre, but also, and above all, a conscience, a man of impressive culture and a marvellous partner in conversation. There was nothing of the haughty intellectual about him, or the pretentious man of letters. I mentioned earlier that we had met Mounier himself in France just after the war, and had been reading his writings since the forties. But Mounier impressed us so strongly that friendship with him was impossible. We considered him a mentor.

With Béguin our relationship was quite different. It was he who came to us. (Mounier died without ever having crossed the Atlantic.) His stay in Canada left him more leisure than he would have had in Paris and during the few weeks he spent in Montreal we saw a great deal of him. Our discussions often went on until the small hours of the morning, and when we heard of his illness after his return to France, and of his death a short time later, we wondered if we had taken advantage of his good nature.

In the boarding-school atmosphere that then prevailed in Quebec, Béguin's visit was like a breath of fresh air. He came from abroad bringing the fruits of his reflections pursued on every continent. His remarks on India, where he had just passed some time, come back to me after twenty-five years with a clarity that speaks for their worth. We needed this view of the world, not in order to escape from our own reality, but to compare it with others so as to see Quebec in a more accurate perspective.

We were not passive listeners. I remember a veritable attack we made on Béguin on the subject of television. It seemed to us that French intellectuals in general, and those of *Esprit* in particular, were neglecting this phenomenon. No doubt they had a good excuse: the development of TV in Europe was lagging far behind the astounding growth of electronics in North America. But, we said to Béguin, that's the whole point: we count on the acute sense of the future you have always shown. And now is the time to think about this question, before the structures of the new media settle immutably into place. All cultures are going to be attacked, shaken and upset by the arrival of electronics.[6] This is a frightening challenge. And who are we, in Quebec, of all French-speaking countries, to absorb alone the first shock of the attack? A few million francophones the great majority of

---

[6]I would like to believe that we were already aware of the computer revolution and anxious to predict its effects, but unfortunately I cannot confirm this, at least as far as I myself am concerned.

whom are barely emerging from illiteracy! If you, the intellectuals of France, fail to take the trouble to *think* what television should be, is not the whole francophone community in the world likely to suffer the results? You will find yourself carried away by Anglo-Saxon pragmatism, in this field as in so many others. And us along with you, of course.

At first Béguin was not convinced. I am not sure that he even understood our concern. But Pierre Trudeau took a lively interest in this aspect of the media. He foresaw the transformations television would bring about in our political life, even if we were still far from the TV duels of Nixon and Kennedy and the cameras had not yet found their place in electioneering. Television was already emptying the movie theatres and altering our whole way of life. Associations and movements, including the unions, had trouble getting their members out to meetings. Glued to their sets, they no longer answered the call. Were we coming to a collective life where all messages and communications would have to pass via hertzian waves? Was access to the cameras about to become a precondition to any effective social action? We were beginning to think so, and, of course, we were not far from the truth.

We had other basic questions about the proper use of the media. Did they mean the end of the written press? And the theatre? And in the long term what changes in our civilization would come from these still-jerky pictures which were already rivals to print and seemed even to threaten direct contact among humans? It was true that TV did away with physical distance. Was it by the same token about to create new distances of another type? Isolate the individual? Atomize the community?

Our European friends were a little astounded by all these questions, as they were not yet familiar with television as a mass phenomenon. It is not by chance that Marshall McLuhan emerged from Toronto, rather than London or Paris. Albert Béguin finally, with touching modesty, revised his position. He listened until the morning hours, and joined us in our self-interrogation. If he had lived longer, no doubt we could read today his responses to our questions at that time. But he had no time to formulate them. In the spring following his second visit to Montreal he died of a heart attack in a hospital in Rome.

There never was a special number of *Esprit* devoted to television. The only echo of our nocturnal discussions with Béguin was in a special number of *Cité libre*. On re-reading this meagre collection of articles today one would never guess the intensity of the debates that inspired them. But one does find an obscure awareness of the revolution that was under way. We were not the only ones in Quebec to realize the importance of the phenomenon. The media were jostling too many old habits, opening too many doors on the future, to leave cold any observer of their irruption into our community life. True to our North American temperament, our first reaction was action itself. Instinctively we rushed toward the audiovisual experience and thought about it later, if at all. But our instinct was sound. The awakening of Quebec, the Quiet Revolution, the process of catching up that took place in the following twenty years—all that, I believe, could not have happened so rapidly without the help of the media. And God knows, we needed to hurry after twenty years of stagnation under the reactionary Duplessis regime.

The coming of television, which spread like an epidemic across North America, took the form of a slow contagion in Europe. Even nowadays most European intellectuals talk of the media as a marginal phenomenon despite the immense place they now occupy. We must remember that in the mid-fifties French television was still in diapers and the intelligentsia had more pressing things to think about: the Algerian war, General de Gaulle's coming to power, and the crisis of conscience which was to last almost a decade and absorb the best efforts of militants and thinkers.

(Twenty-five years later it is interesting to note the lead we still enjoy in Canada in the use and development of the audiovisual. Every year young people from Montreal, Trois Rivières, Quebec City or Rimouski arrive in Paris to complete their studies and improve their knowledge in this field. But the French, ordinarily not so prompt to confess a weakness, are astonished to see them in France. "It's in Canada," they say, "that the state of the art is most advanced. You're the leaders in this area.")

Every time I hear such remarks, I wonder again at the accidents of History. Just after the war it was essential that France should liquidate its colonial empire. It had no choice. But what an interminable crisis it was to pass through before making up its mind and carrying out the needed amputation! And how long that country was absent from the world, turned in upon itself, for how many years busied only with examining its own entrails while the post-war world set its course for the year 2000! The flagship of French culture lay moored in Algerian waters while we, francophone communities of the diaspora, took to the sea in scattered order in more modest vessels. Forgive the extended metaphor, but it is a way of understanding the intellectual solitude we lived through for those years.

French-speaking Canadians, like their counterparts in Belgium and Switzerland, have never looked for political leadership from France. As I mentioned earlier, we were never in the slightest inclined to support French colonialism in the Algerian conflict. We were all the more inclined to condemn it because we too, at another level and in another way, were its victims. It is impossible to measure exactly the cultural importance to us of the very fact that France exists—a country of fifty-five million people who live in French. But when France withdraws from the world, a long blackout is created that is not easy to live through. This happened twice in my generation.

It was in 1940, at the age of twenty, that the men of my age understood what the eclipse of France meant to us. Until then we had rarely thought about cultural solidarity. We lived with it as a fact, without thinking about it. Books, magazines, textbooks, dictionaries, records and films in our language all came from the "old country." Our native production was very small in literature and music, and non-existent in films. We took for granted this daily bread that was baked for us abroad, six thousand kilometres from our shores, without which we could not survive. We paid for it in gratitude, admiration and rhetoric. Oh, the sentimental eloquence of those days, on the theme of the mother country, France, our wet-nurse, our spiritual ancestor. There was also an ambiguity to our relationship with this community overseas, which had *betrayed* some of our most sacred *values*. But we had to accept our nourishment from her or starve.

Before 1940 it never occurred to us that the cultural supply-line might one day be broken. This was why the shock was so great when the German occupation cut us off from France, from one day to the next. Suddenly we were left to our own devices, alone in the vast Anglo-Saxon world. We had the choice between accepting the challenge and improvising a kind of instant cultural autonomy, starting from scratch, or resigning ourselves to total dependence on the prevailing anglophone culture and getting along until the return of France to its former place in the world.

Of course we chose the first, the most difficult and the least realistic solution, true to ourselves and in keeping with our history. And we were right to do so.

Fortunately we didn't clearly see the tremendous obstacles that stood in our way. With a fine nonchalance, one would plunge into publishing, another into theatre, another into symphonic music or the popular *chanson*. I think of Félix Leclerc as an exemplary case. In 1943 the Leclerc family was sharing a house with us, a great barn of a place in Outremont that was the home of the Compagnons de Saint-Laurent.[7] Félix was then writing for radio, as his great interest at the time was in literature. But often in the evening, when my wife and I left our quarters on the ground

[7]Theatrical company founded by Father Emile Legault.

floor and went up for a drink with Félix, we would find him sitting on the floor, his guitar in his lap, singing songs of his own making. We never suspected that "*Notre sentier*," "*Le petit bonheur*" or "*Bozo*" would make their way around the world. No more did Félix, if we can judge from his long-drawn-out refusal to give his songs to the public. Only a few of his friends were acquainted in those days with his rough-hewn poetry. Yet he was already in the process of launching Canada's contribution to the contemporary French *chanson*.

In the following year, with the help of some emigrant French film-makers, there were some pathetic experiments in feature films. All these activities went on in some disorder, with a push-me-pull-you quality about it; but our optimism and ambition were equalled only by our cultural poverty. And it was that poverty that the eclipse of France allowed us to measure for the first time. Of course, it had been much talked about. At the turn of the century it was one of the favourite themes of our more thoughtful journalism. The existence or non-existence of a French-Canadian literature, for example, had been the subject of long polemics in the days of the *Nationaliste* under Olivar Asselin and Jules Fournier.[8]

But in 1940 there was no time for polemics: we had to act, to do something. During those war years we learned that our cultural debt to France was enormous, and we found out the extent to which we were dependent on France. From that time we can date our fierce resolve, not to break with French sources, which would have been absurd, but to break with our own passivity and become productive ourselves. We realized that France was "keeping" us. And we decided, only half consciously, that when peace came we would be in a position to cooperate with France, that is, to give as well as to receive. We wanted to become adult partners within a common culture.

Our second experience of the same kind came fifteen

[8]Jules Fournier, *Mon encrier* (Montreal: Fides (Nénuphar), 1970).

years later, in 1955. This time France was not occupied by a foreign power, but merely too preoccupied with herself to be interested in others, or in anything but her problems of the moment. For more than five years the French were not absent but *absent-minded* about everything except the Algerian conflict. Once again we felt the lack of a certain basis of comparison with our own and American reactions: we lacked the French interpretation of the world, their analysis of phenomena that were then making themselves felt, their reflections about the computer world, for example, or on the Twenty-second Congress of the Soviet Communist Party. I don't mean that Paris was silent about all these events. But the commentaries suffered from the fact that commentators seemed to be thinking of other things.

I don't want to imply that in normal times we accepted as oracular everything said by the French intellectuals. On the contrary: we needed them to test our own mettle as much as for our nourishment. But there was a time when we had little critical sense, and accorded exaggerated respect and admiration to everything French, the mediocre as well as the sublime. Any Frenchman who got off the boat in Quebec City or Montreal became the object of indiscriminate adulation. Even if he had written the most insignificant books or painted the most hideous academic daubs, he received the dazzled admiration of our New World provincials. Before the war even our own homecoming travellers, members of our tribe who had spent some time overseas, had the benefit of this credulity.

Were we foolish? Perhaps a little bit. But our excessive homage came more from ignorance than anything else. Because we had never been in France we had to imagine it. And the orphan's imagination is always generous when he dreams of lost parents. Since they must be re-created, why not imagine them as perfect? After the war we came in contact with the reality and saw the everyday France, not an invented dream. French society certainly did not embody all the perfections our naiveté had attributed to it. But it offered a striking contrast with the cultural fragility of our own society. It was not culturally threatened, not a minority, not deprived or hesitant. Above all, our contact taught us the things that make up the greatness and dynamism of a cultural community: the extreme diversity of the tendencies it brings to light, and within each tendency the high intellectual quality of its best representatives.

There were communists in Canada, but no Marxist thinker of any stature. There were Christians, but our theology was anaemic. ("If there were any real theologians in our universities, we would know about it!" exclaimed Jean Le Moyne during a public debate in Montreal.) We had surrealists, pale copies of Breton, sub-disciples of Philippe Soupault. And so on in almost all the disciplines. This was why our ideological discussions were at such a low level. In France we learned that pluralism allows the inter-fertilization of different streams of thought on the condition that each one is expressed at its peak of excellence. We also learned that the mind is sharpened not by protecting it from outside influences but exposing it to them; and that the monolithic ideology of Quebec was a form of paralysis. Thirty years later, in Paris in 1977, I was to hear the following dialogue between the Secretary-General of the Quai d'Orsay and a Quebec cabinet minister:

"You know, Mr. Secretary-General, we can say that the Quebec intelligentsia is unanimously behind our government's plans for sovereignty."

"Unfortunate man! Your intelligentsia is unanimous and you are pleased about the fact?"

In short, we were learning how to cultivate a critical attitude which we were later to apply to France itself and its cultural influence on our community. We were also discovering how precious the French presence was to us if we wanted to create valid works that could add up to the creation of a modern and original society in North America.

I say "original" because that has been our ambition for centuries. It would be easier to give in to the influence of the United States and come up with a perfect imitation of American civilization. The French presence in the world would have little meaning for such a project. But we have a project of our own, utopian as it may seem. We have for too long performed variations on negative themes: rejection of American trends, resistance to French influence which was considered harmful, isolation imposed by History or freely chosen in order to protect ourselves, defend ourselves, a suicidal withdrawal into our own borders.

Yet it seems that despite certain appearances our efforts in the last twenty years have taken a more positive turn. We are ready to accept the cultural contributions that are offered to us; and without straining when they come from the United States, which simply by its proximity and power exerts great and constant pressure on us. And nowadays we consider ourselves less and less to be exiles from Europe, and more like North Americans.

Our relations with France call for greater effort. The historic break that affected them, the actual distance diminished very recently by progress in communications, and still other factors make our exchanges more uneasy than we would like. Yet they are developing, and will continue to do so.

One major achievement of our cultural revolution is that we now want to perceive and make the choices that concern us. We have won back the right to speak first on the future of our collective life.

It may be hard to believe that in the early fifties we still left to others the task of airing our problems and condemning our weaknesses, though we, of course, denounced these condemnations as intolerable interference in our internal affairs.

I remember an incident in which I was involved in early 1950 or late 1949. A reporter in Toronto had published in a Queen City daily some devastating articles on the protection of children in Quebec. In them she dealt with the fate of orphans and "illegitimate" children as wards of the State in our province's institutions. If I remember correctly she also denounced a certain illicit trade in babies by which a few unscrupulous obstetricians and their confederates were making money from rich buyers across the border.

The ensuing scandal provoked an intense defensive reaction in our press. Disinclined to look at the facts and test the reporter's accuracy, our papers leapt spontaneously to the defence of *our* crèches, *our* orphanages, *our* religious orders and *our* government. (I believe they conveniently forgot to mention *our* dealers in human flesh, but I may be wrong.) It was the reporter who took the beating. What business was it of this *foreigner*? No one had asked for her opinion. Weren't we free to do as we liked with *our* children? In short, all they saw in this investigation was one more manifestation of the well-known Toronto contempt for all Catholic and French-Canadian institutions.

As a young reporter on *Le Devoir*, assigned to social problems and a page for the young, I had the immediate and no doubt presumptuous feeling that somebody had invaded my territory. What bothered me most was to see so many defenders at work and so few critics. With the agreement of my publisher, Gérard Filion, I also launched an investigation on the subject which was to keep me busy for several months and plunge me into a nightmare that I find painful to recall even today.

The situation I uncovered, guided by my psychologist friend Claude Mailhot, a specialist in the area, was enough to shake the most hardened reporter. My Toronto colleague had seen only the tip of the iceberg. I spent long weeks visiting thousands of children living in dozens of institutions that were almost all alike, cooped up in a system that implacably transformed all of them into more or less deranged urchins, ill-adapted to the outside world, pathetic wrecks unfit for adoption into a normal family.

Then there were the extreme cases, unbearable to see. In a

Montreal establishment, after a long argument with the authorities, I saw the cage for those with dementia praecox. Half-naked boys climbed the bars like young monkeys, while the normal children, boarders in the infirmary on which the cage looked out, had to put up all day long with the animal cries and haunting wails of these small patients. In those days there were no specialized institutions for dementia praecox cases. The government was *talking* about establishing one.

Upstairs in another orphanage, adolescents slept in an attic dormitory where I saw large rats run under the beds. In a reform school I heard the admission that the boarders, boys in the age of growth, did not get enough to eat. The government subsidy was insufficient. It did not ensure that they were reasonably well fed.

If I told of all the horrors I discovered, I would never finish. When I went home at night I was ashamed of the comfort—modest enough—in which my own children lived.

But the saddest part of the story is that the educators responsible for these houses, men and women, religious and lay instructors, were as unhappy and powerless as their pupils, prisoners like them of an outmoded system, bound by tradition and the niggardliness of the State. And yet there already existed a solution a thousand times more humane—foster homes—which almost all of North America had been applying for some years. But because no one raised a voice, because people chose to defend the system rather than reform it, why should the government raise a finger?

When I finished my investigation, I published "A Story of Sad Children," first in *Le Devoir* and then in pamphlet form. I can no longer find a single copy of it. But if I had it before me, I am still not certain I would recognize the situation I described (though I have certainly not forgotten it), because I had been obliged to restrain my indignation in order to avoid shocking the touchy readers of the papers. Just the same, the facts must have come out without too much camouflage, as my publisher was summoned to answer for them to the religious authorities of Montreal. On his return from the Archbishop's offices he told me what had been said. I recall part of this edifying dialogue, somewhat as follows:

"Your reporter has been telling things, Mr. Filion."

"Did he tell the truth, your Grace? That's the big question."

"Perhaps. But he does not take into account either the circumstances or the context. After all, you cannot expect people in these establishments to maintain the standards of the YMCA."

"No?" said Filion, astonished. "I really fail to see why we should be satisfied with inferior standards. You are responsible, you have the authority. Demand that the government stop saving its money in this shameful way at the expense of unfortunate children."

                              *   *   *

As the decade wore on, the breakthroughs of the critical attitude grew more frequent. One of the most spectacular and highly symbolic was doubtless the stormy arrival of Frère Untel on the ideological scene toward the end of the fifties.

To understand its importance one must realize in what low esteem the occupation of teaching brother was then held in clerical circles. The Brothers were the proletariat in the Church and in the intelligentsia of the time. They were assigned to the most humble drudgery of the mind, confined to primary education and forbidden to go beyond it except via the side-track of the upper primary, one of the most marvellous dead ends ever invented. The supreme symbol of their inferiority was a ban on teaching a word of Latin in any of their schools. Latin, however, was the key to secondary education and access to the humanities, and thus to university.

People often made fun of the teaching brothers, and they, conscious of their status, were generally content to bow their heads and suffer in silence. Some of them, particularly after the war, pursued more advanced studies. Others, like the botanist Marie-Victorin and the writer Clément Lockwell, had forced the doors of the university. They were pioneers, to be sure, but they were also great exceptions to the rule. The tradition that surrounded the brothers as well as certain clothing regulations which insisted on their wearing funny hats and having their hair grotesquely cut made them an easy butt for jokes. No one gave them credit for having an interesting intellectual life, still less a sense of humour.

But one fine morning *Le Devoir*, in its letters to the editor, published a brief text signed Frère Untel. In a few paragraphs he showed himself to be a writer.

He affected the modesty of the teaching brother, his heavy shoes, his simplicity and his innocence. He talked about his school, his classroom, his pupils. But under his humility one sensed the sharp claw of a highly gifted writer, that of the humorist and satirist. What he was up to, with a smile and without seeming even to touch on the subject, was a thoroughgoing criticism of our educational system, its disastrous results and, by extension, of our whole society.

He returned to the charge during the following weeks, encouraged by André Laurendeau, who took care to publish his letters in a conspicuous place. I remember, for example, one that hit home. The brother had read the words of "O Canada" aloud as dictation, and one of his pupils had transformed the third line "Ton histoire est une épopée" into "Ton histoire est une des pas pires."[9]

But Untel was not content with making people laugh. His good-natured irony with every phrase called in question the "best educational system in the world" and its "improved French." He taught us to laugh at ourselves and others, without spite but also without pity.

Who was Frère Untel?[10]

---

[9] [A phonetic joke, the two quotes translating literally as follows: "Thy history is an epic," and "Thy history is one that's not so worse." Tr.]
[10] ["Brother So-and-so." Tr.]

No one knew but André Laurendeau, who jealously guarded the secret of his identity. No one ever suspected that he was a real teaching brother. People speculated. For a whole winter this became the society game. We convinced ourselves that the pseudonym concealed a well-known writer. We admired the way this hoaxer was able so easily to counterfeit the personality of an "ignoramus," lend the latter his wit, feign the brother's innocence, and hide his own arrows in Untel's quiver.

I hope that Jacques Hébert will find time one day to tell how and by what subtle devices he managed to track down Jean-Paul Desbiens, in religion the Marist Pierre-Jérôme, persuading him to sign a publisher's contract, storming all the barriers put in his way by the writer's hierarchical superiors, and finally bringing out *Les Insolences du Frère Untel*.

In a few months the book became the all-time best-seller of Quebec publishing, selling over 100,000 copies. This extraordinary success was revealing. It showed clearly that a critical attitude and desire for reform were no longer confined to a small, isolated group of a few union "piano-players" or middle-class intellectuals. Frère Untel's genius lay in placing his critical writings at a previously unexplored level of humour and common sense. He also had the gift of finding the unexpected phrase and giving a special flavour to certain words. The term "joual," for example, used to designate our urban working-class slang, may well have been invented by Laurendeau. But without Desbiens it would never have come into such general use. And without him, all the different reformers and dissidents would not have learned until much later what an impressive army they constituted. The *Insolences* was a gadfly to our official culture, reviving in Quebec the verbal irreverence we had almost lost.

Thus, our cultural revolution was the by-product of two wars and the coming of the electronic media. All the forces that came together to trigger it are still at work, and it is still going on. Future chroniclers will record its coming episodes. Whatever else they say about it, when their turn comes, I'm willing to wager that in their remarks, as in mine, there will be the thread of our relationships with France, the continuation of our dialogue with the media, and the eruption into our lives from time to time of clear-sighted jesters who can make us laugh at our own expense.

CHAPTER 8

Confrontations

But it was not because he was humble
that a man was not a man. Nor because
he was proud.
ELIO VITTORINI

Time, as is well known, waits for no man. It also has no respect for the meanings of words, or their content or their emotional impact on those who hear them.

The word "strike" is no exception to the rule. For most people it now calls up painful and distressing images: hospital services paralyzed, subway trains immobilized in twenty-below temperatures, schools and colleges closed in mid-year, sabotage on construction sites...

Every time the population has felt itself trapped or penalized, the innocent victim of a group of striking workers or civil servants, the reputation of the union movement has been tarnished. Worse still, certain worker's organizations have fallen into the hands of known criminals. We know that the underworld has used it as a favourite tool. And why should organized crime not operate under this cover, after aping the captains of industry for nearly a century? The mafia knows how to adapt.

In the course of writing this book, each time the words "strike" or "union" turned up, I was aware of facing a challenge. Could I succeed in substituting the fervent image of a working-class movement just new-born, still fragile and vulnerable, for that of a workers' institution fully established, recognized, and still indispensable, but fatally bureaucratic and exposed to the abuses that come with any kind of power?

The unionism I am talking about here was never on the winning side. A growing force, but still threatened, it lived in the state of grace of all great ventures in their early days. And my story would give a truncated impression of our 1950s if the workers' struggles did not have pride of place, because they were at the very heart of the fight for progress and freedom.

As a permanent employee of a federation of unions, I was involved, closely or not so closely, but mostly the former, in most of the decade's union struggles.

From those days I can still evoke certain scenes that were singularly impressive, in vivid colours and with undiminished emotional impact. Louiseville, for example, triggers violent memories.

*   *   *

On a chill December morning in 1952, I see the outside staircase leading up to the local of the striking weavers, right in the centre of the little town. A group of workers is climbing the steps after a demonstration, to go to the daily union meeting. Suddenly shots ring out behind them. It was the police who fired. A worker collapses, a bullet through his neck. The group scatters in panic and disappears as if by enchantment. A few comrades remain outside to help the wounded man, who will be taken to hospital. Immediately the provincial police intervene in large numbers and set up a cordon around the town. After months of patience on the workers' part, marked only by rare incidents, the forces of order have finally carried out their plan: block the dispute in the dead end of violence and settle it by police action.

It was sheer luck that the wounded man was not killed. But he was not the intended victim. The actual target, Raymond Gagnon, who was leading the strike, later showed us his felt hat with a bullet-hole through it.

The atmosphere this day at Louiseville recalls the atmosphere in Asbestos on May 6, 1949. The citizens are holed up in their houses. Provincial Police patrols are seen in the streets, guns in hand. The police have closed their snare on a group of outside unionists who have come to demonstrate their solidarity with their comrades in the striking textile workers' union. The visitors, if caught by the police, will be taken to court. The scenario is ready-made. They will be denounced as foreign elements, agitators who have come to create violent incidents here, while the honest, peaceful Louiseville workers want nothing better than to go back to work without any of the advantages they were striking for. The court will pronounce the sentences. Contempt of court, the judge will decide, because the prudent employer has taken out an injunction ordering the workers to take no action against the strike-breakers—the scabs—to prevent them from going to work in place of the strikers.

Three years earlier, Mr. Duplessis had condemned the Asbestos strike as illegal. But the Louiseville strike is legal, beyond all suspicion. The workers complied with all the quirks of the law, which did not change the behaviour of the Quebec government one iota. Our comrades, just because they staged a march waving signs, will acquire a criminal record and perhaps get a few months in jail. We know all that. We have been through it all a few times since Asbestos.

This is why there must be no delay in evacuating our visitors, first digging them out of the homes of Louiseville strikers who had put them up, then arranging for the more or less clandestine transport that will get them around the roadblocks or bluff a way through them. "Down along the shore," an old militant assures us, "I can guide a group to Pointe-du-Lac without being seen. And I pity anybody that tries to follow us. You know, Raymond, you skirt along the marsh where we used to catch frogs for the Dupuis strike. Remember?" Raymond remembers, and so do I, the tree-frogs strewn along the lingerie counter during the strike against the east Montreal department store. The frogs turned out to be a better deterrent to customers than any elaborate demonstration.

After much palaver I am assigned to smuggle two or three visitors through under the noses of the police. My car has a Montreal number, but I'm a reporter, which means that I have a legitimate reason for being in Louiseville today without risking trouble. The Provincial Police have arrested me only once on the job. And regretted doing so. Public opinion does tolerate Mr. Duplessis's underhand tactics against the freedom of the press. They are quite willing to pretend not to know, as long as an effort is made to save appearances. But arrest is too blatant, even for those who approve of the iron hand. Tonight, after dark, I will turn up at the roadblock on Highway 2, my car filled with a whole crew of supposed journalists who never set foot in a news-room, and we'll be on our way to Montreal with no trouble, as soon as a suspicious officer has taken a hard look at each of my passengers. I am astonished to experience again on the shores of Lac Saint-Pierre the same emotions I felt five years earlier in Austria and Hungary under Soviet occupation.

*   *   *

It is important to recall the union struggles of the fifties because they are among the most significant and decisive events of the decade. Whether at the Vickers shipyards in Montreal or Alcan's aluminum works at Arvida, there was the same fight for the union's right to organize, which was still disputed or only half accepted by the employers and the government of Quebec. This struggle, begun in the twenties and thirties (one thinks of the tough conflicts at Sorel, Drummondville and Montmorency during the Depression), and taken up again after the war by the Asbestos strike, was not really won until the end of the fifties. Up till then, every strike was an explosive situation and each one signalled a particular forward step. A Belgian specialist, Professor Urbain, noted that labour relations in Quebec in the fifties still developed in a conflictual structure. The first structures based on cooperation appeared with the Quiet Revolution in the sixties.

In Shawinigan in 1952 it was the grievance procedure that triggered the strike at the local Alcan aluminum plant. The workers had realized that the best agreement in the world wouldn't help them if the employer remained free to interpret its application as he wished.

Three years later in the Saguenay, still in the same industry, it was the definition and evaluation of jobs that caused the problem. Alcan at first tried to exclude the union from any participation in this process, whose consequences for the daily life and the income of workers were of the first importance. Then, in a second phase, the employer conceded that the employees should play a part in it, but only *after* the strike, i.e., when the workers' militantism was weakened and their vigilance lulled. Then the employers could with impunity postpone the signing of an agreement indefinitely.

In another case, in Murdochville, the metalworkers of the *Fédération des travailleurs du Québec* were in dispute with an employer who hadn't yet given up trying to get rid of their union, and had concentrated his fire on a few leading workers who were more exposed than the rest. I could cite dozens of other examples. Each one would help to make clear how the workers had been obliged to conquer step by step the territory they occupy today. And a few cases of wildcat strikes, set off by chance and without preparation (I'm thinking of the work stoppages of 1955 in the paper mills at Shawinigan and Grand-Mère) would show with what disastrous setbacks the wage-earners had to pay for their slightest blunders.

I must also say that labour struggles then took on a significance that went far beyond the field of industrial relations. For example, when the strike at Arvida turned the spotlight of public opinion on the exorbitant privileges enjoyed by Alcan, the whole of Quebec became aware of the concessions which governments had made in the past to the exploiters (in both senses) of our national resources. The government of Quebec had neither rented out nor loaned the hydraulic resources of the region: according to the word of the *Chef*, quoted earlier in this volume, it had given them away. After God, the employer was master of the waterfalls and of the dams with which they were harnessed. Arvida had originally been a company town where Alcan's word was law, where the company owned everything including the housing, the stores and even the police forces.

The institution of the "company town" was an expression of the attitude of those times. Essentially, it consisted in ceding to industrial companies complete municipal power over the populations of those towns. The workers were thus deprived of all their democratic rights so far as local government was concerned. They were handed over to the whims of the companies, which were the legal Municipal Councils and which exercised their authority as they pleased. The citizens had no say in police matters, the regulation of businesses or any of the municipal services. These excessive concessions had passed almost unnoticed when the government made them. But when strikes brought them to light, they appeared in all their incongruity.

In the same way, at Baie Comeau and Hauterive it took a labour conflict to draw attention to these distant, isolated regions, where industrial magnates were the undisputed bosses who treated whole populations like minors deprived of elementary democratic rights.

In 1950, Clarke City was a model of its kind, a sort of quintessence of the sinister. I had no sooner started working for the CTCC than I was sent to look into the situation in this little North Shore town I had never heard of before. Jean Marchand explained to me that there was a pulp mill there, a few hundred workers and an embryonic union making uncertain progress. All we knew was that the employer had lodged a complaint about several of its leaders for "union activity on company property," thus blocking all negotiation. My task was to go and have a look, reestablish contact and perhaps even publish an article about the place. "The situation seems rather special to me," said Marchand. "I want you to look into it. You have a good week's work ahead of you."

Thus began for me the most extraordinary and unpredictable of excursions into the heart of *nineteenth*-century capitalism.

First, I had to get there. Clarke City was then a small, straggling village of twelve or thirteen hundred souls neighbouring Sept-Iles, which itself had a population of less than three thousand. A road ran between the two villages, through the northern forest. Apart from this road and the Iron Ore Company's railway, which led off into the landscape toward New Québec, there were no land communications at all with the rest of the world. One had to go there by boat, aboard old tubs belonging to the Clarke Steamships company which then had a monopoly over passenger traffic between Quebec City, the Magdalen Islands and all the little ports along the shore: Baie-Comeau, Franquelin, Pentecôte and so on. You boarded the ship at dusk in the port of Quebec, and next morning awoke in the middle of the Gulf, stopping at each of the coastal ports, to arrive in mid-afternoon at the roadstead of Clarke City.

Gilles Vigneault had not yet sung of Natashquan or the Mingan River. This was a brand-new world for me, as exotic as Alaska or Greenland. Under a June sun, I discovered a splendid region where the majesty of the shore is allied to that of the sea. For hours we sailed past a series of small coves and great bays, rocky capes, rivers and streams whose blue ribbons led far back into the land from their mouths. And the dimensions of the scene made the Montreal landscape look Lilliputian. The words "wide-open spaces" here took on a meaning they did not have in the

South. It was breathtaking. All this was part of our country and we knew nothing about it? I felt that I had been robbed, dispossessed by my ignorance of geography. How on earth had I been able to live this long believing that Tadoussac and the Gaspé marked the north-east limits of Quebec? And when I had looked at maps, how could I have believed that all this northern space was a waste land of tundra and foul weather?

What was gliding by in the sunlight was a pleasant coastline in lively colours, with white villages as milestones. At every port of call, children and fishermen came down to meet us, chatting and showing off their catch. Women came to claim their mail in the middle of the uproar caused by our arrival and by the noisy chore of parcels being unloaded or hoisted aboard, with a great deal of joyous shouting and profanity. At one of the villages our coaster tied up just as a newlywed couple, the bride in white, came out of the church.

But Clarke City was another story. It gave neither the grandiose impression of the approach to Sept-Iles, where the tall, black rocks rise out of the dark water, nor the happy air of the other villages along the coast. The incredible ugliness and unrelieved industrial gloom that England exported throughout the world in the nineteenth century had invaded this place over fifty years ago—a hideous plant, identical workers' houses planted in rows, a few public buildings, each one more wretched and misshapen than the next. It seemed like a nightmare: a Liverpool or Southampton slum that had drifted this far across the Atlantic, a bit of urban hell set down in a natural paradise. The long jetty of grey wood looked sinister in spite of the bright sunlight, and showed no sign of life, unlike the other little ports with their joyous animation.

This Britannic greyness was not accidental. In fact, it was a London company with a noble Lord, said to be an intimate of Winston Churchill, as president, that exploited the surrounding forest to produce wood-pulp (not paper, only pulp, which was delivered unprocessed to the United Kingdom).

Could Clarke City be a part of Canada and Quebec? There seemed to be room for doubt. It was impossible, in fact, to get accommodation there unless you were on Company business, for it owned all the buildings, down to the last shed. As it was out of the question for union organizers to ask the employers for hospitality, the technical adviser who was accompanying me had brought along his car aboard the ship. We stayed at the hotel in Sept-Iles and drove back and forth, morning and evening, on the thirty kilometres of gravel road that led to Clarke City. On the day we arrived we made contact with the local leaders in a hall where the Company authorized them to meet.

Even after thirty years I can see again, with feelings as fresh as on that day, the extraordinary faces of those comrades. Above all, I can hear their voices, the Magdalen Islands accent with which almost all of them spoke, the slightly childish way they pronounced certain words, the particular melody of their intonations, the dental sounds articulated in the Acadian way, very softly. Most of them were short, but sturdy, broad-backed, with a healthy colour and eyes that were porcelain blue, and a glance that expressed as much confidence as timidity. We were fellow members of the union, therefore friends and allies.

"Ever since our union was founded—" began the president in reply to my first question, but I stopped him. What I wanted to know was how this little group, dispossessed, disarmed, deprived of everything including elementary schooling, isolated between the North Pole and the Atlantic, had managed to form a union under the very nose of a hostile, all-powerful employer. What extremity of poverty or injustice had led them to take such a risk? I wanted to hear the whole story, right from the start. Two of them, then six, finally a dozen of them were talking.

Like all episodes in labour history, this one sprang from a feeling of collective despair, out of which, in the late forties, grew a sense of solidarity among the few hundred employees who worked the mill. "We said, it's no good, it can't go on. We have to do something." What couldn't go on was not only the starvation wages, the long hours and the heavy work. They played a role as well, but first and foremost came the humiliating, unbearable living conditions and the impression of being bound hand and foot, despised and powerless. "You should come here in the winter if you want to see. Did you look at our houses? From outside, like that, they don't look too bad. But when it gets cold, they're terrible. You can't heat those shacks. The walls aren't insulated. They're dripping with damp. You have to cover them on the inside with blankets. Our kids are sick all the time."

While the union president was telling his story the others nodded in agreement. And when he stopped another comrade carried on, after asking, "Do we tell them about the widows?" The president nodded. "We have nothing to hide from them."

The other went on: "We know we're not the only ones on low wages and living in rotten, freezing houses. But the guys in other places can always hope to get away. Here in a company town, don't count on it! We can't buy or build anything, not even a backhouse. Everything belongs to the bosses, the lots, the houses, the streets, the sidewalks, stores, everything. Take the houses: we all pay rent. But we haven't got a lease. Just as long as you're working, that's all. You get the house with the job. If you die working, your wife and kids have to leave town. No more room for them here. Out with 'em!"

"Where do they go?"

"Where do you think? If you take a Clarke boat to Quebec City or Montreal it's almost as much as a passage to the old country in Europe. So they move to Sept-Iles. Take a look on the edge of town. There's two streets they call the widows' quarter. That's what's left for our families when we disappear."

This statement was followed by an embarrassed silence.

We were to learn for a fact what we now guessed: this widows' quarter bore a strange resemblance to the prostitutes' area in large cities. There was little else at the time that Sept-Iles could offer in the way of employment for women.

"And have you seen the stores?" a third militant went on. "They're all we've got and all we'll ever have. You can't start a business in Clarke City. It's not allowed. A person can't even sell door to door, not even a shoelace. Last month a Sept-Iles baker tried it. He was selling bread five cents cheaper. He was here one day, and the next day the company sent their police to block the road where you come into town."

"There's no other police but the company police?"

"No. The bosses can have us arrested any time they like, at work or outside the factory."

"Now I understand," said my companion, who had not said a word until now. "The complaint they've lodged against you for union activity on company property—"

"That's right," said the president. "You've got it. I was on the church steps after mass, lining up people to go to our meeting. But the church belongs to the boss as well, and the church steps too, that's clear. We're guilty, Mr. Bergeron. There's no doubt we broke the law."

In any other union the last sentences would have been said with derision or bitter irony. Here they had a tone of hopelessness or despair. These men *felt* guilty, despite the absurdity of the situation. How on earth had they managed to form their union in these circumstances? I asked. Tacitly the reply was left to the oldest among them, who took off his cap, ran his fingers through his grey hair and began:

"It wasn't easy, Mister. It wasn't easy."

The "Mister" jarred in this union setting. I was thirty years old. Anywhere else a man of sixty would have called me by my first name without thinking about it.

Not here.

"For a start, we got up a petition. That took months. You can imagine the guys weren't keen to sign. At first they wouldn't do it. Then a few made up their minds but nobody wanted to be the first to sign. The man at the top of the list would have got the boot the next day. Out! Kicked out of his house and on the way to Sept-Iles. So it took a while. We were getting nowhere. We'd have given up if we hadn't been treated like dogs. Finally one night I got the idea that nobody would sign first—we'd put the signatures in a circle to protect everybody."

I couldn't believe my ears. This was the second time I had heard of a "circle" petition. The other time was in a book, a history of the labour movement that recounted the workers' coalitions in France in the mid-nineteenth century. A hundred years earlier the same causes, the same oppression had had the same result. And Quebec workers in 1950 were inventing the same procedure as the silk workers of provincial France or the Parisian bookbinders before 1850.

"But somebody had to present the petition to the boss?"

"That gave us some trouble, too. We could have slipped it under his door. We thought of doing that. But we said, he'll only throw it in the wastebasket and we'll never hear any more about it. So finally he's the one who went and delivered it."

As he said this the senior member pointed to a crippled man whom I had noticed as the meeting began, a man around forty, deformed, almost a hunchback.

"We thought, the shape he's in, they couldn't take it out on him. And what's more he's deaf and dumb. And they couldn't demote him; he's a sweeper, it's all he's fit to do."

*   *   *

Late in the northern night, on the way back to Sept-Iles, I discovered a further detail on the helplessness of these men. The technical adviser told me of the difficulties of the union treasurer, who had opened an account in a Sept-Iles bank in the name of the union. Later, he had written cheques, but without ever going back to the bank to have his pass-book brought up to date. Now the bank had notified him that the union was out of funds. He didn't understand: there were still two thousand dollars in the pass-book.

I have never been back to Clarke City. I imagine that the workers I met there in 1951 have been freed from their slavery by the extraordinary development that took place in New Quebec and the North Shore. For me, they stick in my memory as a moving example of courage, and as witnesses to an era of unspeakable cruelty to marginal workers in an industry making millions. I learned from seeing them the price in suffering and poverty paid by the working class to ensure the development of resources that later profited everyone.

I also remember Clarke City as an extreme case of historical lag. It was the opening scene in my personal chronicle of the fifties, which will end with a conflict of quite a different kind and of a different colour: the producers' strike at Radio-Canada.

The North Shore workers lived far away, on the fringe of the community: isolated, neglected, forgotten by the powers that be and by their fellow citizens. The television producers worked in the heart of the metropolis, in the full glare of publicity. Everyone knew their work. Their programs were seen every day by millions of viewers. Wages in Clarke City were barely above subsistence level; the Montreal producers had comfortable salaries. But oddly enough, it was the very principle of unionism—the basic right of association—that was at stake in both cases.

For the North Shore workers in 1951 the problem was presented in primitive terms: the employer made life hard for the union by all the means at his disposal, and the union, simply in order to survive, had to carry on an exhausting and unremitting struggle. But eight years later the situation had changed a great deal. In the vast majority of cases employers no longer denied the unions their right to exist. Factory workers had set up powerful organizations. Unionism had entered the services sector, invaded that of information, and even, though still timidly, touched the Civil Service and some of the liberal professions.

In Radio-Canada, for example, all non-management employees, both blue- and white-collar, were already organized. When the producers were setting up their association in the fall of 1958, they were raising the problem of management personnel for the first time in Quebec and perhaps even in Canada. In fact, the producers were not wage-earners like the others. They exercised authority, delegated to them by a supervisor to be sure, but they exercised it just the same. Once the decision was taken at a higher level to launch a production, they became largely responsible for it, first in the rehearsal hall and then in the studio. A producer was thus at the same time boss and employee, which is the very definition of junior or middle management in a modern company.

Did management have the right to organize? Obviously the CSN's answer was yes. We pointed to the European experience of the last few decades. We saw the unionization of junior management as a natural development and a necessary extension of the union movement to this new group of wage-earners. They were responsible neither for hiring nor firing within Radio-Canada. They hired actors, musicians, hosts and script-writers, but for a fee and for one program at a time. If they felt the need to unite and negotiate collectively on their working conditions and pay, what legal objection could be made to their exercise of this right?[1]

We knew the employer's answer to this question in advance: the producers' right of association would be refused in the name of other rights of which much was being made at the time—management rights.

Jostled by the marked progress of unionism in the fifties, resigned to giving it a place in company life, sure that a reactionary Duplessism had no future, Quebec employers nonetheless tried to make an orderly retreat. They wanted above all to draw a firm line behind which to fortify their positions. The name of the line became "management

---

[1]Canadian law did not oblige the CBC to negotiate collectively with its management personnel; neither did it forbid it.

rights." They drew the line at management unions, and the Radio-Canada strike marked the beginning of a long struggle to define where that line should lie.

If the reason for a strike often remains obscure or confused, this was not a case in point. Three times since the start of television seven years earlier, the producers had tried to associate for purposes of collective bargaining. Each time the Corporation or the Canadian Labour Relations Council had aborted the project. And each time Radio-Canada had put forward the same reasons for rejecting the request, stating that "the Corporation was in no way opposed to the producers forming an association *within management*, but that union affiliation and the right to collective bargaining were incompatible with the producers' role in management."[2]

What solution did the employer propose as a substitute for union membership? A generous paternalism from which the producers had certainly profited individually, but which turned out to be incapable of resolving certain conflicts of authority in the Corporation and which tended to grow more arbitrary as television developed. Paternalism, as is well known, can be quite effective in a small business, but it is intolerable in a large undertaking. What father can know all his children if he has several thousand of them?

Like all first strikes called by a budding union, the work stoppage was rather abrupt, in the midst of great enthusiasm and the inevitable confusion typical of all fresh starts. In his remarkable study of this labour conflict, Jean-Louis Roux writes of a "great outburst of feeling as irrational as it was cordial."[3]

It is not my intention to go into the details of the ten-week strike, nor to try to measure its impact on the union movement at the time. What interests me is the coming together, within this event, of René Lévesque, Jean Marchand, André

---

[2]Jean-Louis Roux, *En grève* (Montreal: Editions du jour, 1963), p. 191. My italics.
[3]Roux, *En grève*, p. 191.

Laurendeau and a few others. Each of these men was to go through the experience in his own way. Each drew his own conclusions from it. I will try to explain why these conclusions were so different, sometimes even contradictory, and heavy with consequences for the years ahead.

At the start, on the evening of December 23, 1958, when the few dozen assembled producers authorized by an almost unanimous (96 percent) secret vote the calling of a strike "at an opportune moment," none of the people mentioned above was present. They came on the scene one by one, at intervals that were more or less widely spaced.

That evening it was Jean-Paul Geoffroy, legal adviser, who represented the CSN. If I also was at the meeting, it's because there is always a reporter, as the saying goes, and also because Jean-Paul and I had been working as a team for the last ten years, ever since the Asbestos strike. To this nervous group, irritable and exasperated by the employer's behaviour in the last few weeks, Geoffroy did not mince his words of warning.

As usual, he told the whole truth: yes, the producers had made the right choice. Only a union could solve their difficulties and rationalize their relations with Radio-Canada management. No, they could not renounce collective bargaining. Yes, the dispute justified a work stoppage, as all other measures had failed. But you don't call a strike lightly, and this will be a difficult one. Unionized management doesn't exist here. We are trying to create a precedent. The resistance will be fierce. Radio-Canada will be backed not only by the government which sets the Corporation's budget, but by all employers, unanimously. A breakthrough like this is always extremely difficult, and the producers are a small group. If the other workers respect the picket line there will certainly be a lot of pressure brought to bear. But think about it: you're asking some 3,000 employees to walk out, that is, to sacrifice their income for an indefinite period, just to support a strike by seventy producers who are better-paid than they are.

Someone in the back of the hall shouts, "It won't last long. They need us." He gets a salvo of applause. But Jean-Paul is not carried away by this easy enthusiasm which can be so deceptive. "Listen, you guys!" he replies quietly, "I've seen too many strikes not to warn you. If you start a fight, it may be a long one. First of all, the stakes are high. And in any strike, without exception, the day you go back to work is unpredictable until the last minute. Don't fool yourselves: there's a serious risk, you have to face up to it."

But that night the producers had reached the point of no return. I left the meeting with the clear impression that nothing could stop them but the opening of serious negotiations.

In the days that followed I was one of those who tried in vain to convince the Corporation of this fact. Like others who made the same attempt, I ran up against, not a stone wall, but a tangle of confusion and disarray. Trying to find a responsible spokesman in the Corporation was like fishing for eels. It was not that top management of the CBC's French Network were refusing to talk, however; despite the Christmas season they agreed to the meetings we proposed, sometimes at odd hours.

I will never forget my visit to Gérard Lamarche, then manager of the French Network. If it was not the day before Christmas, it was Christmas day or Boxing Day—dates more propitious for rejoicing than for union negotiations. Gérard lived in a duplex which I think was near the western end of Boulevard Saint-Joseph. As I went up the interior staircase to his apartment I felt a surge of hope. For the first time in ten years of union activity I would be dealing with a man I had known well, and for a long time. Gérard Lamarche had been the creator of Radio-Collège when we were students. He was a friend, a cultured man that you could talk to. I was sure that we could come to an understanding and find a way to avoid a senseless conflict.

But I had forgotten the bureaucratic structures in which Lamarche was prisoner. (He was soon to find freedom as manager of the Place des Arts.) Despite generous servings of whiskey—it was bitterly cold outside—the discussion did not get far. The French Network's autonomy stopped on the threshold of the union question. No one in Montreal had enough authority to commit the Corporation to real negotiation. This was the source of a current joke:

"What do you think of CBC management?" says one employee to another as they sit in the Café de la Régence.[4]

"That'd be a good idea," the other replies.

It would have been a good idea, indeed.

Between December 23 and 29, 1958, an opportunity was lost because no management spokesman could or would take the risk of speaking in the Corporation's name. They passed the buck, right to the top of local management, and from that peak to the President of the CBC, Mr. Alphonse Ouimet, who happened to be vacationing abroad.

When I hear Mr. Ouimet repeat today, as he will no doubt do in his memoirs, that the Radio-Canada strike was quite unnecessary and not at all inevitable, I am in profound agreement with his words, but not necessarily with the meaning he gives them. A word from him by telex from the wilds of Jamaica, assuring the producers that he agreed to negotiate with their association, and the Trojan war would never have been fought. But in order to hear those words there had to be a ten-week wait on the picket lines in Arctic cold. We had to lay siege to the Diefenbaker government in Ottawa and carry on a fruitless dialogue for whole nights at a time with many different interlocutors from Radio-Canada who seemed to have been chosen for their remarkable inability to understand what was at stake.

Failing the slightest sign of life from the employer, the producers had actually gone on strike in the afternoon of December 29. With their feeling for theatricals, they had taken the decision in public, in the lobby of the main CBC building on Dorchester West, using as a speakers' platform

[4]This café on Dorchester Boulevard in the basement of a small hotel was the favourite meeting-place for producers and actors at the time.

the large stairway that occupied half the space in the lobby. Fernand Quirion, president of the Association, had announced the immediate implementation of the strike vote. Spontaneously the actors' union, via its president Jean Duceppe, declared its support, and undertook not to cross the picket lines until the producers had won their case.

The strike was on.

In a bitter cold that was to last several weeks, the association set up its picket lines that very evening. And the following morning Roger Baulu went up and down those lines serving a glass of solidarity-cognac to the shivering picketers. All through that unusual strike we were to see spontaneous gestures of this kind, warm and unexpected. The fact was that in the decade's long list of strikes this was the first one involving wage-earners who led a comfortable life. The producers were certainly not, as Mr. Duplessis put it, plutocrats cushioned by enormous incomes (the *Chef* found an opportunity during the strike to ask aloud in the Quebec Legislative Assembly "whether these people, who preach virtue and unselfishness, are not earning $40,000 or $50,000 a year").[5] But their average yearly salary of $7,500 (which they were then earning) placed them among the privileged. Inflation was not yet at work in 1959. Some picketers came to their task in luxury sports cars, and others dressed with an elegance which I had surely never seen in Asbestos or Louiseville and which they had to renounce in any case when the February temperature dropped to at least minus 21° Fahrenheit.

If I don't mention Trudeau at this point, it is because a skiing accident had confined him to his bedroom before the strike was called. He followed its ups and downs from a distance, thanks to our occasional visits of encouragement in his time of trial. I can still see myself hurrying up the stairs to his room in the house on McCullough Street. In passing I would nod to a little painting by Braque, the first canvas by a famous painter I had ever seen outside a museum. I would

[5]Roux, *En grève*, p. 245.

knock at Pierre's door and almost always find him at work, sitting in a large armchair, his right leg in an enormous cast, suspended at an angle. Some false move on a Laurentian slope had broken a bone in his foot. I'm sure it was not due to recklessness, because Pierre liked only calculated risks. He was generally thought of as a daredevil in those days, and perhaps encouraged this flattering legend. But while he enjoyed physical exploits and tried to surpass his previous performances, he was not foolhardy. Neither was René Lévesque, as we were to discover during the first weeks of this strike.

On January 2, 1959, Jean Marchand arrived in Montreal to take over the leadership of the union forces. Jean-Paul Geoffroy had begged him to come, explaining what was at stake in the conflict, not to mention the serious difficulties we already foresaw.

Jean moved into a hotel on Peel Street since the CSN secretariat was too far from the CBC building. His room was to become our headquarters for the duration of the strike. From early morning (Jean had always been an early riser) until late at night we saw a parade of the most peculiar collection of union members: seniors and greenhorns; producers, of course; but also actors and actresses, electronic journalists, properties men, clerks, administrators and announcers—in short, every category of workers that was involved in Montreal's radio and television world.

In fact, the fate of the producers did not affect them all directly, but they were all caught up in this conflict because of a picket line that gave them a very clear choice: go through the line, or respect it.

From the very first days there was little hesitation. Only members of top management came to work. The other employees, with very few exceptions, would make a gesture toward entering the building, then give in easily to the persuasion of the strikers and go home again.

We had to take into account the competitive militancy which had already begun to make itself felt in 1959 within the Quebec labour movement. Two tendencies then shared the allegiance of the workers: the *Confédération des travailleurs catholiques du Canada* (which a few months later became the *Confédération des syndicats nationaux*) and the *Fédération des travailleurs du Québec*. The rivalry between these two federations was not new. It went back a few decades and had been characteristic of the history of unionism in Quebec since the turn of the century. The FTQ stood for the American tradition of so-called "international" unions, while the CTCC represented an old tradition of strictly Canadian unions. The CTCC, which had originated in Quebec and remained staunchly Catholic until the forties, had for a long time remained a weak competitor for the Canadian branches of the American labour movement. But starting with Asbestos and all through the fifties it had become an increasingly well-defined threat to the predominance of the American unions in Quebec. And now it had to be taken seriously.

It might be useful to explain here why the CTCC at that time was making such remarkable progress. For one thing, under the impetus given by Gérard Picard, Jean Marchand and many other militants, it had just gone through the changes I described at the beginning of this book. Better armed than before, endowed with a stable team of union staff and a respectable strike fund, freed from clericalism and inspired by a well-defined plan of action, it had become one of the most effective organizations in the Canadian labour movement. Its membership was increasing. It was still much lower than the 200,000-odd members of the Quebec "internationals," but it was sufficient to provide it with means in accordance with its ambitions. It devoted a large amount of money to organization and recruiting, and it was attracting new classes of workers into its ranks, workers who had previously been neglected by the unions, such as civil servants, office workers (as opposed to manual labourers) and—now—junior management.

Moreover, the CTCC had its roots in the social compost of

Quebec, roots much deeper than those of the "international" unions, which suffered from a serious handicap because of their south-of-the-border origins. It was true that they could count on the support of enormous numerical and financial resources (millions of members and millions of dollars), but the epicentre of their movement happened to be located in Detroit, Pittsburgh or Washington, which had its disadvantages. Most of its leaders, even in Canada, knew little if any French. Their communications with the mass of Quebec workers were ineffective. We had observed this on several occasions, for example in Rouyn in 1953, when the metalworkers struck at Noranda Mine. They had had to fall back on speakers from the CTCC to boost the morale of their troops, who understood no English. The national officer from Toronto spoke no French.

The CTCC, on the contrary, had a resource indispensable to any mass movement: a thorough knowledge of its community. All its militants, from the most important to the most modest, were products of it. I can still hear the rough voice and halting accent of Rodolphe Hamel speaking to strikers in Rouyn. "Old Man Hamel," as we called him, had made his mark in Asbestos in 1949 as president of the *Fédération des travailleurs de l'industrie minière.* But in his youth he had been an underground miner in Abitibi, in Rouyn to be exact. He knew the levels of the Noranda mine by heart, at least the older ones, and he knew the miners' slang. His audience couldn't believe their ears: a militant from outside talked their language, spoke with precision about their place of work and their joys, their efforts and their frustrations labouring hundreds of feet underground, while their own union leader made a speech in a foreign language.

This example goes farther than it appears at first sight. It did not stop with a single speech made by a militant to a strike meeting. The whole CTCC knew how to speak to the great majority of Quebecers in a language—and above all a style of speech—that was immediately accessible because it was fed with their culture and their folklore. In the circumstances of that period, when the important thing was to give the labour movement a kind of public support that it still lacked, this weapon of speech was much more to be feared (because of its effectiveness) than the distant millions of American members and dollars.

The "internationals" themselves were beginning to be aware of this. They had in their ranks a large number of CBC employees. If the CTCC got one foot into the Corporation, what would become of their predominance? Yet apart from these rather crude calculations, the internationals had to think of their image as seen by the Quebec public. Could they show themselves indifferent to this first effort at unionizing management personnel? Because it affected television the strike would inevitably have strong repercussions. Could they afford to appear as shirkers on an occasion like this?

There was also the fact that the American Newspaper Guild, the International Association of Television and Stage Employees, the Building Services Employees International Union and several national unions with a Toronto allegiance and interested in the conflict, were in danger of being outflanked by the individual decisions of their members. In other words, their membership would be strongly tempted to obey the social pressure of their place of work rather than the directives of their union leaders.

This was exactly what happened, starting in the very first hours of the strike. Without asking anyone's advice, almost all the unionized employees of Radio-Canada fell in step with the producers. Their union leaders were faced with a fait accompli: some three thousand of their members had failed to show up at work, in flagrant violation of their collective agreements, to support the strike of seventy producers belonging to a rival organization, the CTCC.

If the conflict lasted only a few days it would not create serious problems. But if it went on longer? The union leaders, taken by surprise, were unsure what attitude to take.

They weren't the only ones.

René Lévesque, for example, told me of his perplexity, in the first days of 1959. I had run into him by chance, and let him know my astonishment at not having seen him on the picket line.

"What are you doing, René? It's your gang that's on strike. Whether you like it or not, you're identified with Radio-Canada because of the time you've been there. It's *your* strike, this time. After all your commentaries about other strikes, nobody's going to understand—"

"Okay, okay! I know what you're going to tell me. But I'm a freelancer, not a regular employee or union staff like you. I signed a personal contract, damn it. I have to honour my signature. You know very well what side I'm on, but it's not as simple as you seem to think."

It was indeed much simpler for me. A freelancer on television myself, but without a contract, I was first and foremost a member of the permanent staff of the CTCC. There was no question for me of hesitating for a second; and no one, not even anyone in the CBC, could question my primary allegiance to the union. René was scratching his head, and I understood his dilemma. He had only one livelihood: the CBC. But more important than the money was his deep loyalty to his work, and to the institution that was involved. Radio-Canada had made René, as he, in large part, had made Radio-Canada in the information field. Without him and Judith Jasmin and a few other reporters, television journalism might well have existed in Montreal, but at what level of professional quality? In a reverse view, it is certain that René's light would not have remained under a bushel even if there had been no publicly owned broadcasting system. He would have made his breakthrough sooner or later. But would he have developed with the same ease and in the same atmosphere of freedom?

René Lévesque had his own ideas on this score, and I knew them well. The Corporation inspired in him equal measures of respect and fidelity and furious impatience. He

saw it as an institution that was indispensable to social
progress, and as such he almost revered it. But he did not
always find it true to its mission, and this provoked his
resounding recriminations. His relationship with the CBC
was reminiscent of that of a passionate lover with a woman
who misbehaves. At that time I knew of no more resolute
apologist for public broadcasting in Canada, and no more
devastating critic.

Two memories come back to me, among hundreds of
others, concerning René's behaviour during this strike,
which for me elucidate its immediate significance and its
ultimate consequences.

The first one was at the beginning of the conflict. Was I the
one who invited René to come and discuss it with Jean Marchand, during the accidental encounter I mentioned above?
Probably. But René had no need of me to give him the idea.
He and Marchand were old friends.

In any case, he appeared one night at the hotel room, torn
by the dilemma he had described before and determined to
resolve it. I think it was the first time I saw the two men
together. The contrast was striking. Jean was the confirmed
man of action, the undisputed leader of a strong union
federation, the militant who had his supporters in every
corner of Quebec—factory workers and trade union members who maintained personal contact with him and had
absolute confidence in him, loyal almost to the point of
worship. For hundreds of miners, metalworkers, textile
workers or those in the chemical products industry, he was
"Jean" (or "Ti-Jean"—little Jean), their man.

Thanks to television, René was equally well known but in
a different way. In those days he was still *Mister* Lévesque,
TV star, united to hundreds of thousands of viewers by the
special bond the media create. The relationship has a deceptive intimacy about it. Via the TV set the viewer had invited
the star a hundred times into his living room or kitchen. The
performer had become one of the family. Yet if a member of
his public met him in the street, the erstwhile viewer would

be astonished at being face to face with a stranger.

Moreover, René Lévesque, in *Point de mire*, had the status of an intellectual. He was one of the few TV stars who appealed to the audience's understanding rather than to its emotions. He was dealing with the world and international affairs, and not, like a TV play, with the sudden passion of Whatsis for Miss So-and-so. This put him at once in a category apart. But René also possessed a very rare quality: the gift of communicating his knowledge and insights in such a way that the viewer felt *himself* to be intelligent, instead of blissfully admiring the commentator's talent. In the case of *Point de mire* the viewers were astonished not by a brilliant exposé delivered by someone else, but at the fact that they themselves suddenly understood complex questions of foreign affairs that had always seemed to them boring and indecipherable. Thus René inspired confidence and gratitude rather than admiration, which had the effect of bringing him closer to his public.

This is not to say that, on that evening in January 1959, the intellectual René Lévesque met up with the militant Jean Marchand. Neither of them lived fenced in by such categories. Marchand's militantism never excluded culture or reflection, and the intellectual in René always felt strongly attracted to action, an inclination to which he would give in a few months later. I even had the feeling that night that a transformation was taking place before my very eyes.

In a few sentences Marchand swept away Lévesque's scruples, which René asked nothing more than to be rid of. Was there a real problem at the CBC? Had the producers stopped work on a sudden impulse? Could a public corporation, without falling into disrepute, block the unionization of management personnel, be against a natural and necessary development in the relationship between employers and employees and appear as an enemy of progress? René himself was aware of the unhealthy climate that had been created in his place of work in recent years. Could he pull out of the game at the first sign of a real effort to improve it?

The rules had changed on the first day of the strike, when the CBC had publicly refused to negotiate. Before that, the producers' problem had been their own, but now a more general question had been raised involving the whole institution and affecting a fundamental democratic right. Could one refuse to take sides? What reason could justify abstention in such circumstances?

This conversation was the starting-point of a highly personal campaign which René was to carry on for two months with prodigious zeal. From that moment on, he was heart and soul behind the strike, as if he had never done anything else in his life. Sparing neither effort nor time, taking barely enough for sleep (but always late in the morning), brimming with ideas, accepting the most thankless jobs, he was always on the move, inside and outside Montreal, tired after three days but indefatigable to the end.

All through the eight weeks that followed I worked very closely with René Lévesque. Both of us, along with Jean-Louis Roux, were assigned to writing jobs: press releases, manifestos, proclamations, denials and God knows what else. We wrote like Trojans, the three of us at a single table, mostly in the middle of the night. Our editorial room was set up in premises on Stanley Street which a military club, British and hospitable, had placed at the producers' disposal for the duration of the strike. We drank too much coffee and had Homeric arguments as to what should be said and not said, and how the strikers' viewpoint should be presented.

Jean-Louis Roux and I watched with interest as René gave birth to those incisive phrases of which he held the secret. They came to life amid a flood of words, some nervous scribbling, pages noisily crumpled or torn, heart-felt curses and anguished expressions that succeeded each other on his wearied face. The birth was rapid, but painful and noisy. When he was satisfied with his text, René would gulp a final coffee, puff a final cigarette, re-read his text with an air of perplexity, then disappear into the night like a gust of wind, on his way to his next chore.

He was game for any undertaking, except in the morning. Toward noon, however, he would manage to drag himself out of bed and appear, late, at the Salle du Gésu where the union leaders took turns speaking to the strikers and sympathizers gathered there. In the afternoon you would find him on the picket lines. And in the evening, when he was not on tour in some country town, explaining to other union members the reasons for the strike, he would turn up at the *Comédie canadienne* in the show called "Temporary Difficulties" put on by actors associated with the strike.

René had made a slow start, but now he was running at the head of the team. As I watched this, I felt I was in on the birth of a man of action. From one day to the next he ceased to "repress to the maximum his faculty of impatience and indignation," as Gérard Bergeron had put it. He was now giving these faculties free rein, talking like a militant, with an ardour he no longer tried to restrain and which led him to make the second decisive gesture I want to mention here.

It took place on March 5, 1959. That evening all the union leaders involved in one way or another in the producers' strike held a press conference. The spokesman was Jean Marchand. As Jean-Louis Roux explains in his study, the object was to "bring the debate more than ever before the public, and expose the perfidy"[6] the CBC had shown in its negotiations since the beginning of the conflict. Marchand was determined to hide the facts no longer. Until then, as a skilful negotiator, he had prudently avoided cornering the Corporation. He knew all too well that an adversary, if publicly humiliated, will insist on saving his honour before making a settlement, even if this prolonged the conflict weeks or even months at the workers' expense. But by early March he calculated that the time for sparing feelings was past. The dialogue with the CBC and the federal government had been stalled for some weeks. Then it went into reverse. It was time to tell the public the whole story, so that it could base its judgment on the evidence.

---

[6]Roux, *En grève*, p. 264.

ie central revelation of the press conference was to be
Corporation's reneging on clauses agreed upon several
ys before. Despite all obstacles, negotiations had actually
iade some progress since the start of the strike. In spite of
the incredible mediocrity of the employer's negotiators,
floundering in a function about which they understood
nothing, the principle of a management union had finally
triumphed, along with the right of the producers to negotiate a collective agreement governing their working conditions. But the producers had had to give up all union
affiliations, keeping only the right to acquire by contract the
technical services of the union of their choice. The clause in
the agreement which stipulated these two symmetrical concessions, already initialled by the CBC several weeks earlier,
was suddenly denounced by the Corporation "because of the
interpretation certain journalists [sic] had given it." The
employer went back on his word and demanded more
explicit guarantees.

The CBC went into reverse gear at the very moment that
three thousand sympathizers with the producers were beginning to find the strike too long. No one needed to tell Marchand the dangers of this final manoeuvre. He knew better
than CBC management that the sympathizers were at the end
of their tether and their union leaders despairing. The
militant spirit of the "international" unions never held out
very long on a question of principle, especially in a case like
this when the principle was being defended by a rival federation. Unless there was a sudden turnaround in public opinion, support from these unions threatened to wear away in
the next few days and put an end to the producers' case. To
trigger this turnaround Marchand was counting on the
natural reaction of most citizens to an exhibition of bad
faith. This, to his mind, was the argument he would have to
develop during the press conference.

But René Lévesque did not see things that way. Had he
premeditated the very different strategy that he put in practice on this occasion? I think, rather, that he gave way

spontaneously to the impulses that had been driving him for weeks, without realizing that on that day he was about to make the first public profession of his nationalist faith. Without warning anyone, he launched into a virulent attack on the English Canadians in the Corporation's management; on Prime Minister Diefenbaker, on Mr. Nowlan, Secretary of State; and Mr. Starr, minister of Labour; on the press; and, finally, on the whole English-speaking public. His conclusion?

> Some of us, and maybe many, come out of this strike with a tired and unworthy feeling that if such a strike had happened on the English CBC it would have lasted no more than half an hour. To this day, ours has lasted 66 days. Of such signal advantages does the privilege of being French consist in this country. And even at the risk of being termed "horrid nationalists," we feel that at least once before the conflict is over we have to make plain our deep appreciation of such an enviable place in the great bilingual, bicultural and fraternal Canadian sun.[7]

Could anyone doubt, after this diatribe, that René Lévesque had resolutely taken the nationalist turn that would mark the rest of his career? One would have had to be deaf.

Some wrote it off as one of René's passing moods. But those who knew him well had no doubts, nor did those who knew how to read between the lines. André Laurendeau, for example, had asked me a week before this occasion: "Am I dreaming, or is Lévesque turning into a nationalist?"

If Laurendeau thought he was dreaming, it was because such a development was hardly foreseeable. In René's

---

[7] Roux, *En grève*, p. 265. Jean-Louis Roux's introduction to Lévesque's remarks is as follows: "René Lévesque makes in English—obviously for the benefit of *Star* and *Gazette* reporters—a virulent attack on the English Canadians in the Corporation's management, on Messrs. Diefenbaker, Nowlan and Starr, and on the anglophone press and public."

professional past as a journalist, in the commentator's visible leanings, nothing pointed to this orientation. René had always described himself as a convinced internationalist, to the exclusion of other positions. No doubt he grew indignant, like anyone else, at certain injustices toward francophones in Canada, but he never made much of them. And he certainly drew no political conclusions from them. Over the years he had shown quite a lively sympathy for certain foreign nationalisms: that of Mossadegh in Iran, of the FLN in Algeria and others. But he never, in public at least, drew any parallel between these after-effects of a dying colonialism and the situation of Canadian francophones. That was still to come, but was clearly announced by his attack of March 5, 1959.

The expression "signal advantages" prefigured the parallel he was to draw later between the fate of French-speaking Montrealers and the attitude of certain anglophones whom he baptized "white Rhodesians." The "fraternal Canadian sun" was a first sample of the bitter irony that became the standard tone of all his comments on Canadian political life. Curiously enough, he would never appeal to nationalism by name, as if he harboured a certain repugnance for the term even though he had embraced its doctrines. He almost always put the word in his adversaries' mouths as an accusation they had made against him or his party.

Laurendeau, for his part, liked the term. He had been born into a nationalist background and had been preaching, illustrating and defending this position since his adolescence. For him, the nationalist cause was nothing to be ashamed of. It constituted the highest political tradition of our community. He knew its snares and its excesses. He condemned the electoral use Maurice Duplessis had made of it for twenty years to mask his profound conservatism. Laurendeau had constantly steered his nationalism toward the left, and had little use for the reactionary reflexes that still persisted among most pure, hard-line nationalists, especially in Quebec.

Since he had left active politics on the disappearance of the *Bloc populaire* toward the end of the forties, André had watched the generation that followed his with a sharp but friendly eye. He felt strongly drawn to Marchand and, as a journalist, gave his unreserved support to the development of a militant unionism. Trudeau disconcerted him. In the days of the struggle against conscription he had thought Pierre was a nationalist, discovering only later that he questioned the legitimacy of that doctrine as a political position.

But Laurendeau was able to discover and admire the value even of those who did not think as he did. As long as they were honest and intellectually consistent (a quality he insisted on) he could maintain the friendliest of relations with them. In this connection, as he often mentioned to me, René Lévesque remained a mystery to him. He couldn't place him. There was no doubt about his talent or his honesty, but what was the real orientation of this little man with the astonishing verbal agility? Where did he belong? Laurendeau found in him none of the common traits that characterize the men and women of our community and group them in spiritual families. René almost seemed to him like an American. Not, of course, because he espoused uncritically the political attitudes of our super-power neighbour. On the contrary. But his style, his judgments, a certain pragmatism too, the admiration he seemed to feel for American achievements and dynamism—all these things combined to create an unusual personality that André found fascinating and a little shocking.

"That fellow," he told me one day, "has reactions completely different from mine. I don't take my own temperament for the cultural standard of my community. But it's odd, just the same, that I'm almost always bewildered by his actions and his judgments."

At the end of February, shortly before the press conference just mentioned, Lévesque had paid a visit to *Le Devoir* and

Laurendeau's bewilderment had ceased. During a long conversation (no doubt monopolized by René) there had been a meeting of minds. René had poured out all the frustrations he had built up since the beginning of the strike. For the first time, André told me, René was not reacting as a reporter or observer, but as a man involved. He had made the strike his own. This was his fight. And he had run into the slightly haughty indifference of our anglophone compatriots and occasionally their hostility.

After all, René protested, the right of management to organize had nothing to do with the language you spoke or the culture to which you belonged. But if you read the papers in Montreal you were led to believe the opposite: the English-language dailies all took the CBC's side against the francophone "agitators," while almost all French-speaking journalists showed their sympathy with the strikers. Worse, the Toronto producers refused to move even a little finger in support of their Montreal colleagues. Yet it was their cause at stake, too, because the two groups performed the same functions and worked for the same employer. But in the Ontario capital they were satisfied with an association that was barely recognized, without a collective agreement or the right to negotiate. In Montreal itself the majority of English-speaking actors and announcers crossed the picket lines from January 11 on. Only a handful of anglophone employees supported the producers' strike.

As for the unions, René vituperated against the "international" and national union leaders in Toronto, who encouraged their membership to go back to work, even if the producers' cause were lost in the process. "Because it's happening in Quebec, they don't give a damn. If it was a Toronto strike it'd be a different story."

On this point, Marchand's union experience led him to quite a different conclusion. One night, as we were driving back to Montreal on a snow-covered road after a tiring evening of negotiations in an Ottawa hotel, Jean broke a long silence as if he were waking from a dream: "Do you

know what I'm thinking about? About the universi
cialists in labour relations in the year 2000 trying to u
stand how this strike went on so long, how we've been
to keep three thousand people off work in support ⟨ a
handful of producers, not even a hundred of them. I can see
the experts holding a seminar on the subject. They'll have
some fun explaining it."

The paradox of this strike was that the three thousand
supporters—actors, stagehands, decorators and clerks—
were suffering far more from the work stoppage than the
producers directly involved. They were living off improvised
strike assistance and running up debts at home, because
most of them had only a modest income even in normal
times.

But René had his ready-made solution. Union solidarity
was to be taken for granted. If the American or Canadian
leaders in Toronto were fretting or hesitant, it was only
because the producers were francophones and Montrealers.
Hadn't the *Monde ouvrier*, the official organ of the FTQ, felt
impelled to defend itself in an article, in English, denying
everything in its title: "There is no racial or nationalist issue
in the Montreal CBC strike?"

As for the attitude of the federal government, Lévesque
deduced from it his best argument in support of his thesis.
He found that it was scandalous for the responsible ministers to sit on the sidelines and refuse to intervene and end the
strike. On several occasions since it began, Messrs. Diefenbaker, Nowlan and Starr had ostentatiously washed their
hands of the whole business. Though they allowed a Conservative MP, Mr. Egan Chambers, to play the mediator, it
was at his own risk. He himself admitted that he held no
mandate from his political masters.

Why this stony indifference, René wanted to know? It
was customary for the minister of Labour to become personally involved when a dispute involving a public institution
reached an impasse. But this time the government took
refuge in total inaction, which it justified by invoking the

sacred independence of the CBC from government interference.

Yet to tell the truth René Lévesque and the strikers themselves held fast to this principle, just as much as did the ministers. They would never have tolerated interference by the government in the Corporation's programming or content. But did the principle apply when there was a labour conflict that did not affect the Corporation's message or its mandate? Why the scruples? It was said, moreover, that the cabinet had not been shy about stiffening the CBC's resistance, fearing that the recognition of a single management union would have a domino effect on other groups in both the public service and the private sector.

Why the double standard? René's reply was simple, and to his mind left no room for doubt. Messrs. Diefenbaker and his consorts adopted this attitude because the strike was in the French Network of the CBC. Never, he thought, would the government have allowed an English Network strike to drag on in this way. Never! The discontent of the anglophone majority over the shutdown of its television service would have weighed so heavily in the political scales that the ministers would have rushed to the bargaining table. There would have been no lack of official mediators. Divisions within the cabinet (Minister Nowlan considered the producers' strike illegal; Léon Balcer considered it legal) would have taken on new importance, and everything would have been settled in no time—in less than half an hour. But in Canada some linguistic communities were more equal than others. francophones, said Lévesque, were always in an inferior position, like all the colonized people in the world.

André Laurendeau, who was not to live long enough, alas, to learn the answer to his question, wondered, "Is this René's Road to Damascus?"

CHAPTER 9
Epilogue

I am interrupting my story on the threshold of the sixties. I have no choice: the reader's endurance has limits which an author must not test.

Will I ever have the leisure in which to extend this tale beyond the years of impatience and tell about the following decade, one of stirring events and great responsibilities, of hard choices and important decisions, of Martin Luther King and the hippies, of the hopes and disappointments of the Quiet Revolution, of *our* terrorism and the Algerian peace? The desire to do so will not be lacking.

After having described a Quebec and a Canada immobile on their surface but moved in their depths by hidden currents of rare power, I would like to recount the emergence of the new forces that had been latent until that time. We began to live on a planetary scale. Our accelerated development, a little rushed and hectic, was in tune with the spirit of the age, even in its inner contradictions. The winds of the world blew in, and mingled with the breeze of separatism. The clergy laid off the frock by the hundreds, and a whole swarm of sects appeared in our community, but at the same time there was a revival of fervour in a Church that had lost some of its riches and power.

The men I have been writing about chose different paths. The *Cité libre* team broke up, as did Quebec society. While Pierre Vadeboncoeur, Marcel Rioux and others withdrew within Quebec with René Lévesque, Trudeau, Marchand and I left for Ottawa, and Jacques Hébert, like many others, confirmed his federalist choice.

There would be all that still to relate, without resentment or regrets, looking to the future. The play was written, as I have noted, and from that moment onward each played his chosen role. But the various performances held many surprises in store for us. No doubt they hold many more for the decade of the eighties.

And why not?

That is the price of freedom. When men acquire the right to make freely the choices that concern them, they lose the habit of straining together to turn the same millstone. Rabindranath Tagore, on returning to India in the thirties, felt ill at ease and anxious on observing the too-perfect unanimity that reigned among his countrymen. Yet that unanimity had taken form around the prophet Gandhi.

I would like also to describe the colour and flavour of that particular epoch, to speak about its theatre, painting and songs as well as its politics and journalism. I would like to tell how I arrived at *La Presse* and how I left it—each time unexpectedly, each occasion being significant and revealing in relation to the times—and how I lost my political virginity by supporting René Lévesque in his first election campaign. (For the first time I appeared on the hustings, and my task was to refute the accusations of communism that were levelled at René!) I would also recall how René phoned us from Newfoundland at Lac Ouareau to beg us, in the name of his own experience, not to join the Liberal Party in scattered order but to go in "at least three at once" as a team. That was at the end of August 1965, as Marchand, Trudeau and I were preparing to take the leap.

As I write I become aware that these lines are not really an epilogue to what went before, but rather the beginning of another book. The only real epilogue to the fifties is the chronicle of the next decade, so closely are the two periods hinged together.

If God gives me life and time...

Paris 1977–Lac Ouareau 1983

INDEX OF NAMES